Praise for *MINDFUL LOVING*

"Any couple who picks up this book is in for a treat. Not only will they will find a challenging and exciting new way to think about their relationship and how to transform it; they will also find very clear, well-organized, and effective processes and exercises to help them create a spiritual marriage. Grayson has integrated psychology, spirituality, and the new physics into concrete theory and practice that sheds light on the how couples make themselves miserable, and how, by transforming their thoughts, they can achieve mutual joy. I highly recommend it."

—Harville Hendrix, Ph.D., author of *Getting the Love You Want: A Guide for Couples*

"In this important book, Dr. Henry Grayson shows that love can flourish only when we let go of the boundaries that separate ourselves from others, when we are willing to *become* another. At a time in history when everyone is searching for greater security, the temptation is to build defenses and barriers around ourselves. This impulse is fatal to love. That is why Dr. Grayson's message is not only wise but timely as well."

—Larry Dossey, M.D., author of *Healing Beyond the Body*, *Reinventing Medicine,* and *Healing Words*

"*Mindful Loving* is filled with excellent, practical resources to guide you in developing meaningful and loving relationships and connections."

—Bernie Siegel, M.D., author of *Love, Medicine & Miracles* and *Prescriptions for Living*

"Grayson's book will help you tap into your deepest capacity to love in the soul-stretching initiation of intimate relationships. Dr. Henry Grayson is a trusted teacher with high integrity."

—Judith Orloff, M.D., author of *Intuitive Healing* and *Second Sight*

"*Mindful Loving* is a powerfully insightful book on relationships that will bring new understanding to those who face relationship problems." —Gerald G. Jampolsky, author of *Forgiveness: The Greatest Healer of All* and *Love Is Letting Go of Fear*

". . . Grayson's studies, quizzes, and techniques purport to help end harmful, ego-based relationships, replacing them instead with successful, healthy, and—most importantly—spiritually based ones."
—*Psychology Today*

Dr. Henry Grayson is a preeminent psychologist who has spent more than two decades exploring the connections between psychology, physics, and the world's spiritual traditions. The coauthor of three professional works and the bestselling *Sounds True* audio teaching series on which *Mindful Loving* is based, he founded and directed the National Institute for Psychotherapies in New York City and its Center for Spirituality and Psychotherapy. Frequently invited to speak at churches, hospitals, libraries, and professional conferences, he conducts workshops both in America and abroad. Dr. Grayson practices in New York City and Westport, Connecticut.

To Nancy,

MINDFUL LOVING

10 Practices for Creating Deeper Connections

HENRY GRAYSON, PH.D.

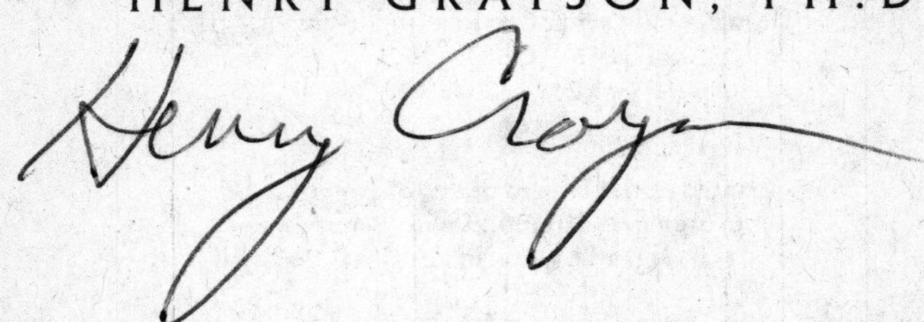

GOTHAM BOOKS
Published by Penguin Group (USA) Inc.
375 Hudson Street, New York, New York 10014, U.S.A.
Penguin Books Ltd, Registered Offices: 80 Strand, London WC2R 0RL, England
Penguin Books Australia Ltd, 250 Camberwell Road,
Camberwell, Victoria 3124, Australia
Penguin Books Canada Ltd, 10 Alcorn Avenue, Toronto, Ontario, Canada M4V 3B2
Penguin Books (NZ) Ltd, Cnr Rosedale and Airborne Roads,
Albany, Auckland 1310, New Zealand

Published by Gotham Books, a division of Penguin Group (USA) Inc.
Previously published as a Gotham Books hardcover edition.

First Gotham Books trade paperback printing, March 2004
20 19 18 17 16 15 14 13 12

THE LIBRARY OF CONGRESS HAS CATALOGED THE
GOTHAM BOOKS HARDCOVER EDITION AS FOLLOWS:

Grayson, Henry, 1935–
Mindful loving: 10 practices for creating deeper connections /
by Henry Grayson.
p. cm.
Includes bibliographical references.
ISBN 1-592-40026-4 (hc.)
ISBN 1-592-40061-2 (pb.)
1. Man-woman relationships. 2. Interpersonal relations.
3. Love—Religious aspects. 4. Intimacy (Psychology) 5. Thought and thinking.
I. Title: Thinking person's guide to love and intimacy. II. Title.
HQ801 .G683 2003
306.7—dc21 2002192708
Rev.

Printed in the United States of America
Set in Stempel Garamond with Penumbra
Designed by Sabrina Bowers

To my first teachers of unconditional Love:
my mother, my father, and my aunt Lois.

Contents

Acknowledgments

I am deeply grateful to so many people who have contributed in very different ways across many years to the evolution of this book and its concepts. As with all of us, our greatest teachers are those whom we have appointed as "special." We learn not only from their positive contributions, but also from the challenges they present to us. I have learned much from my parents, my wives, my three children, and others to whom I have attached "special" expectations. I have learned from the things that worked well and from the things which did not work, to make the relationships more loving, whether that love is coming from me or from them. I thank all of them from the bottom of my heart, for without them being all that they were and are, positive and negative, I could not have learned the lessons which helped the concepts in this book to evolve. I especially thank all my family members for giving me periods of time to write the book when I could have been spending that time with them in activities we would have enjoyed together.

I also want to thank the hundreds and perhaps thousands of people who have opened their lives and relationships to me as patients, most of whom trusted me to be their friend as well as therapist. They have taught me so much about relationships and how the principles presented here have actually worked in their lives to bring notable transformations. I even learned from those who were unable to open themselves to me or to stick with the process to a joyful conclusion. I also wish to thank those who have attended lectures, workshops, or classes, and who raised provoking questions or challenged my concepts.

They forced me to think things through more clearly, for which I am grateful.

I wish to thank my wonderful editor, Lauren Marino, who has been an enormous help, even in the midst of helping to establish the new imprint at Penguin Group, Gotham Books. She has persevered consistently in giving input to help make this the "best book possible." Thank you, Lauren, for believing in me and in what I had to offer in the book. I'm glad I traveled with you from your previous publishing house to Penguin Group.

My manuscript was originally divided into two parts: theory and practices. I vacillated for months over whether to have one or the other first, liking neither. I am very grateful to Billie Fitzpatrick who was able to take my manuscript with these two distinct parts and skillfully weave them together into a blended format which works so much better. It was a joy to work with her.

I am extremely grateful to Tammy Simon, president of Sounds True, who originally invited me to record a six-tape audio series, *The New Physics of Love: The Power of Mind and Spirit in Relationships* where I presented a lot of the same material. Preparing to record this series helped me to formulate and organize many of the ideas contained in this book. Two of her staff members, Sarah Wheeler and Randy Rourke, were of enormous help. I thank all of you. It was Tammy who introduced me to my agent, Kim Witherspoon, saying, "Why don't you meet with her? I think you will like her," which I clearly did from the first meeting. Kim is not only a skilled negotiator, but has helped and supported in so many ways the bringing of this manuscript to fruition.

I am very appreciative toward many colleagues and friends who read the manuscript at various stages of development and gave me most insightful and encouraging comments: Dr. Clemens Loew, Dr. Kenneth Frank, Dr. Kenneth Porter, Janet Ettele, Michelle Rosenthal, Dr. Barbara Blum, and Frank West, with whom I have spent many hours discussing the concepts over lunches, and who gave me permission to use examples from his personal life.

I also want to express deep thanks to two individuals who have now passed on from their bodily existence, but who had a profound influence in my awakening—therefore leading to this book. I thank physicist David Bohm for the stimulating hours spent with him which led to an epiphany—changing my way of seeing the world and my place in it. It was the beginning of my coming to understand all our interconnectedness. My thanks also go to Dr. Victor Frankl, the Austrian psychiatrist who survived the concentration camps. I thank him not only for his books, but also for the seminar hours I spent with him when he was visiting professor at Boston University. He planted the seeds for me to see the incredible importance of our thoughts and attitudes—often of life and death importance! I wonder if I would have embarked on this journey if it had not been for Dr. Frankl and Dr. Bohm.

I am also deeply grateful to other sources of great inspiration: the Bible, the teachings of the Buddha, Yogananda's Kriya Yoga program, the writings and teachings of Satya Sai Baba as well as his personal communications, the Kabbalah, Meister Eckhart, Carl Jung, Rumi, Krishnamuhrti, the St. Germain Discourses, Maharishi, and especially *A Course in Miracles*, the most comprehensive and in-depth psychospiritual work I have found. And there were many others too numerous to mention.

Most of all, I am deeply grateful to the guidance of the Spirit within, without which we can do nothing.

MINDFUL LOVING

Introduction

When most couples seek me out to help them solve their relationship problems, they usually arrive with certain expectations. They hope that as a psychologist I will help change the partner, making him or her more loving, more understanding, less angry, or less baffling. And they believe that if these changes occur, then they will be happy together.

Through the years of working closely with both individuals and couples, I have focused on helping my patients solve many of their conflicts by getting at the roots of their personal issues so that they could experience satisfying personal growth. But it wasn't until *I* experienced a very personal turning point, an epiphany to be exact, that I finally understood how I might best help my patients with their persistent, pervasive, relationship problems. Amazingly, I could finally see a path to helping them not simply alleviate the pain of conflict, disappointment, and suffering in their lives and in their relationships, but learn how to achieve lasting, indisturbable happiness and love.

The story of this epiphany and where it led me is the subject of this book. It is the story of how I discovered an amazing convergence of science and spirituality, and how I found a solution to our human suffering—in a mystical place where science and spirit meet. But before I tell you that story and share with you the theories and ten very simple practices that can help you and your partner heal your relationship, I want to give you some background on who I am and how an agnostic, perhaps atheistic, scientifically minded psychoanalyst came to write this book on spiritual practices for healing relationships.

My spiritual journey began after college, when I went to theology school at Emory University for three years in order to become a protestant minister. Strangely, I do not actually remember deciding to apply to theology school. Since it was the one profession most esteemed throughout my extended family, I suppose I applied automatically in order to gain family approval. However, it took only one semester to learn that theology school was not leading me to the truth I was seeking, and by my second year, I considered myself an agnostic, perhaps even an atheist. I was certainly not a theist, for I had stopped believing in the traditional concepts of a medieval, flat-earth "sky God," a deity that was far removed from us humans on earth. This concept of God as someone who lived in a geographical place in the sky had lost meaning for me because it felt so alienating. I was also troubled by the church's language and liturgy that portrayed us human beings as separate, little, and powerless, and as unworthy sinners. As a result, I constantly questioned such theistic precepts in all my courses, and so was greatly surprised when I was elected by the faculty as the "Outstanding Senior of the Year."

Could it be that my sincerity in questioning is what resonated with the faculty? I took it as such, and this conclusion only spurred me on as I continued to question and search for answers to what was missing in my life. Specifically, I was compelled to understand how I might be able to help relieve suffering in the world and lead people to find more peace and therefore happiness in their lives. Wasn't this, after all, the role of the minister?

But after my degree in theology, I continued my search for answers and was inspired to earn a master's degree at Boston University [S.T.M.] in psychology and pastoral counseling while serving a stint as a parish minister in Massachusetts for four years. In order to do so with integrity as an agnostic, however, I rewrote all the liturgy so that it would be more humanistic and spiritual. I did my best to convey a God that was present and everywhere and, most important, *within* us—instead of the separate and apart, judging sky God who had to be called upon and beseeched to be present, as was part of the standard liturgy. I wanted my parishioners to feel connected to God in every aspect of their lives—body and soul—and help them make this connection real, vital, and tangible so that they would feel better equipped to deal with their pain. Again, I was compelled to help them find joy, peace, and happiness.

While many parishioners were very happy with my rewritings and found new meaning and inspiration in their religious practice, some were clearly upset by such changes in ways of thinking about God and spirituality in general. Increasingly I knew that the parish ministry was not my place, especially since it had not been a conscious decision, but rather an attempt to gain love and approval from my family. I then thought that to practice psychotherapy as a psychologist would allow me to be of greater help to more people in rising from their human suffering.

I was now in the midst of a rebellion against much of my past, ready to overthrow most of my previous religious and moralistic (but not moral) teachings. I relinquished my ordination as a minister and soon enrolled in a Ph.D. program at Boston University, where I straddled two departments, clinical psychology and psychology and pastoral counseling, and took an extra year to fulfill the course requirements for the Ph.D. in each.

Although I would view it differently today, the pastoral counseling side began to seem somewhat superficial to me. And though I found clinical psychology exciting, it still left many gaps in my understanding of how to really help people in emotional or spiritual distress. So, after earning my doctorate, I concluded that if I entered training to become a certified psychoanalyst, I would then find the rest of "the real truth" about mankind and about life. Surely, I thought at the time, the depth of psychoanalysis would lead clients to greater understanding of themselves, which in turn would help lift their anxiety, depression, or despair—their emotional suffering stemming from psychological issues.

The four years of postdoctoral psychoanalytic training added significantly more knowledge and skill to my repertoire of ways to help people, and the great majority of my patients seemed to grow and resolve many of their problems. Yet soon I came upon the limitations of the Freudian psychoanalytic process, which seemed unnecessarily slow and not applicable to many problem areas, especially in the area of relationships.* In fact, all this focus on oneself, essentially an analysis of the ego, often seemed to increase a sense of narcissism, thereby increasing a person's sense of powerlessness instead of the opposite. And by and large, relationship problems persisted—conflict, anger, and disappointment seemed to reign and problems between partners seemed to be solved only temporarily.

Before long, while still in my psychoanalytic training program, I concluded that there should be a well-grounded postgraduate training institute where therapists could get advanced training in the integration of the various psychotherapeutic approaches, rather than just having to choose a system that demanded one's full allegiance. This was an era when the psychoanalysts, the behavior therapists, the Gestaltists, and others each claimed the right answers to the best way to achieve personal growth. So, I, along with four esteemed colleagues whom I invited to join with me, founded a postgraduate training institute in New York City that would train psychotherapists (psychologists, social workers, psychiatrists, and psychiatric nurses) to work in an *integrative* way, hence the title, the National Institute for the Psychotherapies.

Both personally and professionally, I had now moved out of the dogmas of both religion and Freudian psychoanalysis. My patients advanced further and faster, but few finished their personal-growth work with an ability to live in a real state of joy and inner peace most of the time. Like my patients, I felt that I had not yet realized true joy and peace in any lasting sense. I still yearned for an inner peace that could not be disturbed, a sense of empowerment that would not leave me at the effect of people or events, and a pervasive love and joy that would not be so dependent on current circumstances. And I wanted the same for my patients. What was the answer? After so many years of training and practice, I still had not found it! Sadly, it became apparent to me

*The newer forms of psychoanalysis emerging today, such as self-psychology, intersubjectivity, and the two-person model, are much more relevant and helpful for relationships.

that neither traditional religious nor traditional psychotherapeutic practices were sufficient to deal with the massive problem of human suffering or deliver its opposite—indisturbable joy and peace.

Finally, a profound turning point came when I was invited to spend a weekend in a seminar with Dr. David Bohm, one of the world's most esteemed theoretical physicists. In a weekend seminar, Dr. Bohm presented us—a group of forty psychotherapists and psychologists—with a discussion of the similarities between the recent discoveries of new physics and ancient mystical thought.

We sat together in a sequestered room in Manhattan as this captivating scientist began to unfold the true nature of the reality that we observe with our eyes. He explained that the reality that had been measured by sticks and weighed by gravity was only a tiny fraction of the universe as it really exists. Over the course of a weekend, Dr. Bohm literally showed us that there is much more to reality than what we observe or experience with the five senses. By using the principles of quantum mechanics and particle physics, he showed us that at this invisible level of reality, everything and everyone is interconnected in a most profound way. And we are not only connected to one another as human beings, we are also connected as mind, energy, and matter—to one another and to all living organisms. This interconnectedness leads directly to the idea that there is a consciousness or intelligence that underlies all that is visible and it is this consciousness that gives us humans power beyond our imagination.

These ideas were astounding to me not only because our being connected—as energy and matter—in the physical universe gave me insight into the world in which we all live, but also because it put me on a path of discovery in which science and spirituality converged.

When the first day and a half of the mind-stretching seminar was completed, I returned home elated, confused, and exhausted. The next and final day of the seminar was on a Sunday, which brought an unanticipated surprise. Upon awakening, I felt a strong urge to go to church, an urge which I had not felt for at least fifteen years, not since I had rejected the medieval theistic concept of the "flat-earth sky God out there who is separate and apart from us" that had permeated the services and practices of the churches I knew as a young man. At first I was embarassed at the thought of returning to the thought of returning to the scientific meeting and saying I had been to church. But my inner voice encouraged me to go anyway.

Another surprise followed almost immediately upon my entering the church. The service was just beginning. As I sat and listened, I found myself reinterpreting all the liturgy, the words of the hymns, the prayers, the scripture, and even the sermon, all in the light of the new physics. I reinterpreted the words of the liturgy to reflect joining rather than separation, wholeness instead of badness, total worthiness instead of unworthiness, and being One with God rather than God as separate from us and outside of our reality. I felt moved to the very core of my being. It was as if I had just discovered a brand-new world. It was indeed an epiphany as I sat through the service with tears welling in my eyes and repeatedly rolling down my face. It was truly an unexpected mystical experience that I would never before have imagined my scientific mind allowing. The very ideas I had rejected before now came alive for me for the first time. I got past the limiting, man-made, religious terms and narrow and limiting views of God and was able to go deeper, to the very root and essence of their meaning—their original source. I began to see "God" very differently, and as this happened, my concept of who and what I am began to change as well. When I returned to the seminar three hours late and told them where I had been and about the epiphany I had experienced, I was greatly surprised to learn that almost all the other attendees had felt a similar urge, Christian and Jew alike, and wished they had found a way to honor that inner urge as I had.

Finally my life made sense to me! If we are all connected in the universe, we are connected to God—not the pie-in-the-sky God, but a divine essence that is all around us, as well as inside of us. Through these theories of new physics I saw that we are all part of God and God is part of us. What a different and wonderful way to view both God and man! This was the catalyst for my turning upside down all my previous ways of viewing the world, who I am in it, and who and what all others are as well.

❧

That seminar initiated the process of my reexamining everything I thought and believed, leaving little unturned. The words often repeated by Dr. Bohm inspired me: "Perhaps there is more sense in our nonsense and more nonsense in our 'sense' than we would care to believe." Essentially I arrived at one central premise: If we as human beings are all interconnected, then there are enormous implications for understanding how relationships work—both positively and negatively. As I came to realize that how *I* design the experiments of my life actually determines what the outside reality will appear to be, I began to apply this understanding to relationships. I came to see that my participation in any relationship—even what I am thinking about myself or the other person—has a profound effect on its quality since there are no separate objective realities. This means that I possess the power to actually affect what happens in my relationships, becoming a cocreator in the quality of interaction.

The more I examined my beliefs, my thoughts, and my perceptions, and began to view myself and the world differently, the more often I felt free, more empowered, worthier, and happier, increasingly trusting that all things in the present and the future will work together for good. I began to see problems as challenges—as lessons to be learned. And I discovered that an insane world does not have to cause me suffering in my relationships, and that my power of decision, particularly with regard to how I perceive someone or a situation, can bring me joy and peace instead—even in the midst of pain. The implications for all of our relationships, especially those we deem special, are profound! We are not only connected in the universe, we are participants in this connection. This means that we create, shape, and choose our own reality, especially as it exists in our relationships.

As I learned how to change my perceptions of my marital partner, I saw that my happiness lay not in what I could *get* from her, but in my choosing more often to love her without expectations of what I might get back. I learned that when I was able to love her without strings attached, she often became more loving, sometimes with her love wrapped in very different-colored packages than I was asking for, yet these new colors were often richer than what I was requesting. I also learned that when I did not do this consistently, I would instantly create pain for myself and often for her. And of great importance, I came to understand her not so much as a separate objective reality, but often as a mirror of my own attitudes, thoughts, and perceptions. For example, if I thought critical thoughts about her, she was more likely to be critical of me. And if I thought loving thoughts of her, she seemed to be more loving toward me. I was receiving back what I was thinking inside.

Perhaps the most significant learning resulted when my wife did not respond with love, even though I thought I had been loving. Increasingly, I learned to view such times as an opportunity to be in touch with my love within by choosing to extend it to her, realizing through each experience that I could therefore never be without love.

All my years of training and practice had provided psychological understanding and knowledge, but I needed this extra spiritual piece to solve the puzzle of why so many of our relationships are caught in a quagmire of pain, misunderstanding, and a seeming lack of love. Once I had changed my view of who we all are—mainly seeing our unlimited power, love, and potential to create—I was able to dramatically alter my ability to help people. Since I no longer saw us as locked in by our genes, our body chemistry, or our early conditioning, I was able to lead my clients to a new awareness of their own power to choose joy and peace over misery and conflict—especially in their most important relationships.

In the years since my epiphany at Dr. Bohm's seminar on the new physics, I have been researching, testing, shaping, and fine tuning both the ideas and the practices that have evolved into this book. I have studied Western and Eastern philosophies and religions extensively, as well as all the major psychotherapies. I have observed with great fascination and joy as the men and women, individuals and couples, discover remarkable empowerment to affect their reality and cocreate their relationships. I have witnessed with pleasure and satisfaction the transformation of so many of their relationships from being marked by disappointment to being filled with peace, joy, and boundless love, and the capacity to remain centered in difficult situations. And now I would like to share these with you.

In this book, I will describe a number of ways this knowledge and insight has worked for me and for my clients, and how they can work for you. I am presenting a means by which we can become more awake, more conscious, and access more of that unused 90–99 percent of our brains—our god self—and own our inner capacity to create our relationships as happily as we choose. Specifically, I am presenting you with a choice: would you like a relationship—whether that be in the context of a marriage, partnership, family, parents, or professional—that is spiritually based? Would you like to be able to learn how to lift your barriers to love and, through the power of thought, free yourself from the inevitable unhappiness and conflict of relationship based on the ego?

You will discover a clear and simple—yet profound—way to heal your relationships, which is especially important for those relationships you deem "special." You will learn how to transform your marriage or partnership from an ego-based relationship, which is mired in conflict and almost always doomed to cause unhappiness, into a spiritually based relationship, which is based on unconditional love and the power of thought to create joy, peace, and fulfillment.

The book's process is designed to lead you to become aware of your divinelike essence within and access the incredible power of your thoughts to change your interactions in your relationships. Although theoretical in places, this book is highly practical—it is concerned with what actually works to heal our relationships and ourselves, giving you tools you can use in everyday life. During the course of the book, you will find ten powerful psycho-spiritual practices that will help you to uncover your True Self and heal your relationships at the same time. In healing your own mind, you are also healing the relationship, and by healing the relationship, you uncover your True Self, for the practices you use to heal one, heals the other.

In Chapter One, I will introduce you to the concept of the spiritual marriage, showing you how different it is from a relationship that is ego based, in the first of the Ten Spiritual Practices. In Chapter Two, you will learn the central aspects of our True Self and how science can help us to realize our True Self and make our relationships places where our greatest emotional and spiritual growth can occur. In Chapter Three, you will discover something about yourself you may not be aware of: that your thoughts control your feelings, behaviors, and beliefs. And that once you harness this power of thought, you can literally change the outcome not only of your experience, but the quality of your relationships.

In Chapter Four, you will begin to see how to break into the vicious cycle of interaction that takes place in ego-based relationships by learning Practice 2: the thought-monitoring exercises. In the next chapter, you will learn two more exercises, Practices 3 and 4, to help you transform your relationship from ego based to spiritual—making a perceptual shift and seeing others as mirrors.

In Chapter Six, you will see how by going further upstream into your identity, Practice 5, you can erase the effects of traumas and the negative beliefs that grew out of your painful experiences. This step further helps to break the vicious cycle of interaction, bringing you closer to your True Self, which in turn brings healing to your relationship.

In Chapters Seven and Eight, you will learn to differentiate between counterfeit "love" and Empowering Love through Practices 6 and 7. Once you are able to lift your barriers to love, your natural ability to love freely and unconditionally will flow, bringing healing and transformation to all your relationships, but especially to those that you deem special.

In Chapter Nine, you will learn further how to trust in the power of your True Self to solve your relationship problems and create happiness, peace, and joy by the freedom and release found in the power of surrendering your ego, Practice 8. In Chapter Ten, you will access an even deeper knowledge of the True Self through Diaphragmatic Breathing and Meditation, Practices 9 and 10, enabling you to have a tangible experience of the spiritual dimensions of yourself.

Finally, in Chapter Eleven, I will present a controversial idea: that some relationships, no matter how good or spiritual your intentions, cannot be healed *enough*. And in these cases, divorce may be the answer. I am neither advocating divorce nor telling you when or why to do it, which is always a personal question and decision. But I am showing you a way that you can approach divorce so that it is not only less painful, but also spiritually satisfying: this is the point of a spiritual divorce.

Intention alone doesn't mean that you or I will be perfect in our practices or successes. But each moment brings an opportunity for a creative choice that can totally turn around and heal a difficult situation, one in which a miracle can be accomplished. And we can make such choices over and over, moment by moment, resulting in a cumulative sense of an overall transformation in our relationships. This does not mean that you will necessarily stay in a relationship or leave, but whatever you do will come from a place of peace and love within.

While the content of this book may be welcomed by many with open arms and minds, others may find it unbelievable and wish to argue with me. Others may find it frightening, since it represents a very different way of looking at others, the world, one's self, and at relationships in particular. At times the ideas presented here will deviate considerably from the characteristic thinking of our tribal mind. Such a shift in our thinking is necessary, for if we continue to think in the way in which we have always thought, we will continue to be disturbed in our relationships. The only true answers will come from your own experiences of actually doing the practices presented here.

So I ask you to consider approaching the ideas presented in this book with an open mind and a willingness to examine all of your cherished beliefs. Through this process, you will come to distinguish your wishes, hopes, and illusions from your experience and therefore be able to choose between wanting a spiritually based relationship or an ego-based relationship.

So for now, I would like to pose a few questions:

In your close relationships, would you like to experience:

- Happiness and joy as boundless?
- An inner peace that cannot be disturbed by what others do or don't do?
- An inner strength and power that prevents your feeling like a victim of people, situations, or even your own genes?
- The ability to transcend fear, pain, depression, anxiety, rejection, loss, and suffering of all kinds?
- That you are never empty, but always full of love?

Wouldn't these changes fundamentally change all of your relationships? Perhaps, as Thoreau wrote, you might need to follow the beat of a different drummer—but now the drummer is inside! Will you join me in this journey?

NOTE: The identities of all the people in the case studies have been carefully protected. Not only have names been changed, but also circumstances, sexes, locations, and even central issues have been altered. Sometimes the cases are actually composites of several people in order to disguise actual identities.

CHAPTER 1

Rethinking the Purpose of Marriage

The Spiritual Relationship Versus the Ego-Based Relationship

TRUE LOVE AND ITS MYSTERIOUS WAYS

Marriage has served many different purposes throughout recorded history, ranging from procreation, companionship, convenience, status, need, and sometimes love. Yet, at the present time in America, I think we can all agree that our system of marriage has largely failed based on the simple fact that half of our marriages end in divorce and a significant percentage of those remaining together are not very happy—many being quite miserable. This fact is an unfortunate but very true testament to something not working. And if something is not working, especially to such a large degree, it seems only logical that we should examine what we are doing wrong. Is it not true that to persist in doing something that has been proven not to work while expecting a different outcome is a form of insanity? How could so many of us behave so insanely when it comes to creating relationships and choosing mates for marriage?

And even more distressing for me as a psychotherapist devoted to helping couples solve their problems and find peace and happiness in their relationships is the fact that many couples who are having difficulty and who genuinely want help are more often than not dissatisfied with the marriage counseling or couples' therapy they receive. In fact, many couples have reported that their marriages are much worse following their marriage counseling. How could that be so? What is not working in our marriages and what is not working in couples counseling?

Several studies actually show that only 30–35 percent of people in traditional marriage counseling find it helpful in the long run, in contrast to 70–85 percent of people who engage in individual therapy. Why the difference? In individual therapy, people go seeking help for themselves and are usually highly motivated to examine their own lives and psyches to identify the sources of their suffering with a desire to change and grow. On the other hand, those seeking marriage counseling most often see their partners as the cause of their unhappiness. They hope that the therapy or therapist will fix their partner, and make him or her into more of who they want *them* to be so they can be happy. And frequently, the marriage counselor will unwittingly collude in the process of getting one partner to agree to make changes for the other, which only adds to the person's sense of powerlessness to make a difference in himself or herself.

After many years working as a psychologist with men, women, and couples, I began to realize that a solution to a relationship problem that is based on getting the other person to change his or her behavior would only last a short time, and often add to the original problem. Why? Because asking or demanding one person in a couple to change usually means that the person demanding change is both shirking their part in the problems and blaming the other for their unhappiness. Again and again in my practice, I would observe how when one person would try to get the other to change, the asker was most often not seeing how he or she was contributing to the problem. And by shifting this responsibility from the self to the other person, they unwittingly reinforced an insidious cycle of blame that prevented true healing.

SIR GAWAIN AND RAGNELL—A *TRUE* LOVE STORY

I am very fond of the stories of King Arthur and his knights, and one of my favorites is about Sir Gawain, a knight of the Round Table. In this story, Sir Gawain agrees to marry Ragnell—a grotesquely ugly woman—in exchange for information that will spare King Arthur's life. Instead of any sense of celebration, his wedding day brought the town a great sense of mourning because King Arthur's handsome and gallant knight was being married to a monstrous hag.

On his wedding night, Sir Gawain waited in bed while Ragnell prepared herself for their first night together. When the door opened, Ragnell lay down beside him and said, "You have kept your promise and much more. You have never shown me pity nor revulsion. All I will ask of you is one kiss."

Gawain immediately leaned over and kissed her, closing his eyes. When he opened them, he discovered he was lying beside a beautiful woman. Startled, he leapt from bed and asked, "Who are you? And where is my wife? Is this some kind of sorcery?"

"Gawain, I am your wife, Ragnell. It is time to tell you my story."

And so she began her tale about how her stepbrother, Sir Gromer, had hated her because of her beauty and because she did not fear him or follow his commands. In his jealousy and resentment, Gromer went to his mother—an evil sorceress—who turned Ragnell into one of the ugliest women ever.

Ragnell then paused and said to Gawain, "There is a second part of the curse I must share with you. Since you have treated me with love and not resentment or pity, I am allowed to give you a choice. I can be a beautiful woman by day, so that all may admire me and consider you a lucky man, but I would become once more the ugly Ragnell by night, when we lie with each other. Or else I could be the ugly Ragnell by day, only to once again become the beautiful woman you see before you at night. Which would you prefer?"

Without hesitation, Gawain answered her. "This should not be my choice but yours. You must choose for yourself. I will accept either decision as long as it is your will."

With his response the rest of the curse was lifted, and Ragnell could now be beautiful both day and night. Sir Gawain's love was not concerned with his personal needs; he saw beyond them and was concerned only with his partner's happiness and well-being. His desire to empower her is what healed each of them and brought them both real joy.

This story captures the essence of what I call Empowering Love, the ability to love unconditionally, which forms the basis of the spiritual marriage or relationship. But we often lose sight of this way of viewing love, and believe that love is not inside of us, but outside of us, separate. This is much like we think of God—that flat-earth medieval sky God who is far removed from our lives here on Earth. When we think of love (or "God" as the word for pure love) as separate from us, we create a never-ceasing need to seek love outside of ourselves. This is indeed what we are all searching for—we wish to know we are loved, approved of—and yet we so often deny it, reject it, push love away—which ironically keeps us in a state of seeking love. Is this not the main motivation for our relationships? A quest to find love, secure it, and thereby ensure our happiness? But how do we avoid the temptations of the ego and instead create a relationship based on unconditional, empowering love? Some of our problems begin when we "fall in love."

THE FALLING-IN-LOVE SYNDROME

The kind of love that characterizes what we feel when we fall in love is not Empowering Love; it's not unconditional; indeed, it is based failingly on need and powerlessness. Just think of the familiar colloquial phrases to describe this feeling of falling in love: "Falling head over heels"; "being swept away"; "I'm crazy about you." All of them indicate a state of ungroundedness, as if a force has taken us away from our sanity. And a marriage that begins with our need for the other person's love is doomed to fail so long as it stays on that track.

It seems that much of this "love" is what Eric Fromm, in his classic work *The Art of Loving*, called immature love. Immature love says, "I love you because I need you," while mature love says: "I need you because I love you." He goes further and gives a more detailed definition of this kind of mature love: "Mature love is a state of productiveness which implies care, respect, responsibility, and knowledge. . . . It is an active striving for the growth and happiness of the loved person, rooted in one's own capacity to love." His definition says nothing about barter, conditions, seeking, or expectations, but focuses solely on caring for the other person.

When need is dominant, we are ultimately weakened—we see ourselves as dependent on other people as the source of love we need, and anytime others do not meet our needs in the time, place, or manner we desire, we are set up for disappointment and suffering. At this point we often try to seduce, cajole, manipulate, control, attack, or even kill that person. Hence the murders in families and between lovers.

A marriage that is based on the belief that love is a commodity that can be given and received cannot make people happy. By believing that love exists outside of ourselves, we think that other people hold the power of giving and withholding the love we need, and thus we experience ourselves as at their mercy. And when one relationship after another proves unsatisfactory, we still believe that the only solution is to fall in love with someone else. And our suffering continues.

Sarah, for example, was unhappy in her marriage, and it was quite clear to her that her husband, David, was the cause. She told me that he did not listen to her, that he did not communicate with her, that he was frequently critical, and that they had not made love in over two years. In addition to his hour's commute to his job in New Jersey, he worked late into the night at home. Often their only contact would be a little hello kiss when he walked through the door on his way upstairs to his home office. Sarah craved nurturing and complained that she'd married a man who was just not a nurturing person. Not only did she feel depressed and in fear that her marriage might not work out, but she was also plagued with a plethora of physical symptoms that were very debilitating.

Sarah, like many of us, believed that the cause of her unhappiness was that she had married the wrong person, someone who could not meet her needs. It probably comes as no surprise that David held an almost identical perspective. Each was certain their unhappiness (and possible happiness) depended upon the behavior of the other person, and each was convinced that the other was at fault! If only David became more attentive and less critical of her, Sarah would be happy and the marriage could be saved. David felt similarly: If only Sarah weren't so needy and became more independent, then he wouldn't feel so suffocated and might want to spend more time together as a couple. They were in a vicious cycle, each reacting to the other's behavior as well as their own thoughts about the other person.

Does this situation seem familiar to you? Do you believe that your happiness always seems contingent upon someone else's behavior, thinking that if only they would do what we expected of them, then we would be happy? The person we blame for causing our unhappiness could be our mate, parent, or child. But it could also be a boss, an employee, an obnoxious store clerk, or even a rude and thoughtless driver—in fact, our happiness most often seems dependent on everyone we interact with on any given day. "If only my husband would listen to me . . .", "If only my wife were more loving . . .", "If only my boss was more helpful . . .", "If only my kids would do what I ask them to do . . .", "If only my friend wouldn't make promises that she can't keep, then I would be happy."

When we're unhappy, we usually see others as either doing something hurtful to us or withholding something desirable from us. In essence, we experience ourselves as at the effect of others, not in charge of our own reactions and moods; and we also tend to blame others for our unhappiness. But people rarely do what we expect them to do; in fact, their complaint is often the same of us—if only we did what they expected us to do, then they could be happy, and then they would make us happy as well. And so when we decide that our partner will never wise up, we often exchange that person for another, and the cycle repeats. Why does it seem so impossible to have happy relationships?

THE PROBLEM OF SPECIALNESS

The need for the other person's love grows out of the problem of specialness. When we appoint someone as "special," which we tend to think of as a good or positive notion or action, we set into motion a chain of potential outcomes that create unrealistic expectations and inevitable disappointments. Consider a familiar sequence in romantic relationships. We fall in love and are ecstatic about the perfect mate who is so special and who will now "light up my life," as in the theme of so many popular songs. We may believe that it is the marriage made in heaven, and will remain so forever. Yet, after the brain chemical phenylethylamine fades, which usually takes six months to two years, we often feel disillusioned and betrayed: the other person has not lived up to the template we superimposed upon him or her of what we expect the other person to be. Most relationships either break up at this time, or they enter into a struggle to try to reform the other person. Many people fall into resentment and anger because their partner will not change, while only a small percentage of couples will use this opportunity to give love without expectations or judgments. However, the great majority of us never free up our love; one reason for the high divorce rates—about one half of us within five years of marriage or commitment walk away from our relationships in disappointment or anger, having begun to view our partners as enemies or deprivers.

Ironically, as soon as we think of someone as special and try to convince that person of their specialness, we begin to think we have a right to demand things from them. We feel we have a right to be angry when they do not fulfill our projections or expectations. In doing so, friendship ceases, and the in-love couple become far less than friends—they now become enemies, sources of danger, and it is even not uncommon to wish the other person dead. This enemy state may exist even if the couple remains together—in fact, many couples stay together, addicted to the various forms of hatred and battle that ensue from specialness.

Once we have appointed someone to be in the special role, the seeds for trouble have been planted. In the moment that we appoint someone as special we instantly connect to a childhood yearning or an unfulfilled desire. Or we expect that person to complete us or heal our illusion of separation. The special person, therefore, becomes for us the person who will finally love us enough, care for us enough, listen to us enough, and be our soul mate. We forget that everyone is our soul mate. Not only do we idealize the other person, but we also become disappointed and angry when the person doesn't live up to our expectations. To others, our expectations are usually unreasonable, but to ourselves they seem quite reasonable and justifiable. But in either case, disappointment and suffering follow. We love them because of what we want from them, so when they turn out to be different from what we want them to be, we punish them and withhold our love from them in return.

When two people say they are in love, they usually mean that they are more than just friends. But why do these same people begin to treat each other like much less than friends once they declare each other as special and begin a relationship? Why do they not extend the same kind of acceptance, kindness, and forgiveness that they extend to their friends?

Therefore, the falling in love experience is often actually an attempt to keep ourselves from really getting to know the other person, contrary to our consciously stated goal. In the falling-in-love syndrome, it is not the real person we relate to, but rather a projection of what we wish that person to be. And furthermore, we present our idealized self to the other person as well so that we do not ever really meet each other at all. Two idealized fantasies are relating to each other, while the real persons are hidden behind walls carefully constructed to hide them.

In addition to being attracted to our projected image of our inner yearnings, we are also attracted to that which is familiar, even if it was not what we would consciously claim to be looking for. For example, if we grew up in a family in which one or both parents were distant and emotionally cruel, we might unconsciously pick a partner who would behave toward us in a similar manner. We may also use the familiar relationship to reenter into the struggle to try to get love from such a person in hopes that this time, we will succeed in getting the love and attention we think we deserve. Just as unconsciously, other familiar negative characteristics might be repeated, including coldness, unavailability, volatility, criticism, and lack of affection or real communication.

Janice had grown up with a father who had been very judgmental and volatile, as well as being a workaholic who was therefore absent frequently and for long periods of time. As a result, Janice always yearned for his acceptance and attention, trying very hard to be a good girl, responsible, and charming. But no matter how hard she tried, she would either be ignored or criticized by her father.

When she married Mark, she was hopeful that this would be a wonderful relationship. He was handsome and successful, but not a workaholic like her father. Mark showered her with romantic attention during their courtship and Janice felt they were madly in love. In her perception, these qualities overshadowed the fact that Mark was a perfectionist, and when things would not go perfectly, he would become angry, impatient, and critical. Soon after they were married, Janice was actually surprised when Mark became more distant, judgmental, and volatile. All his romantic attention, it seemed to Janice, had been just that—an attempt to *win* her love. She had not allowed herself to see that he was never very interested in her feelings, needs, or interests.

When she came to see me, and we discussed the connections between Mark and her father and their shared qualities, Janice began to see how she was unconsciously drawn to those same qualities in Mark that her father possessed. Why? Because now in her marriage, her ego voice was telling her, she had a chance to try and make it better, to find the love that had been missing in her early life. The human ego, as we shall see, likes to take past hurts and turn them into lifelong struggles, and the end result of this struggling is always the same: the destruction of joy and happiness in the present.

It is not uncommon to be aware of—or even to deny—the presence of these characteristics during courtship, only to later discover them as core issues in our partners and accuse them of hiding them from us during the early stages of the relationship. Yet secretly, or on an unconscious level, we have known all along that they were there. Our hope to fix the other person so that he or she will be able to love us the way we desire is really a masked attempt to heal our old wounds. This is what Freud referred to as a repetition compulsion. But instead of fixing the situation, we take the pains of the past, bring them into the present situation, and project them onto our partners, resulting in a perpetuation of our false sense of self and our suffering.

Psychiatrist Wilhelm Reich, one of Sigmund Freud's contemporaries, referred to the falling-in-love syndrome as a period of temporary psychosis, for he saw it as a socially acceptable form of hallucination. As such, Freud insisted that his clients take a break from their psychoanalysis until after their present love affair was finished or at least had gotten past the initial infatuation stage because he knew that their idealized state would prevent them from successfully exploring themselves or their situation. In this way, the falling-in-love syndrome can actually be viewed as a condition in which real love is impossible. Often I see this state as one from which we must recover before we can have a real loving relationship.

The cause of the falling-in-love syndrome (or infatuation) is that we look to a mate or partner to make us feel complete, whole, and happy. It's for this reason that we appoint other people as special. From this sense of incompleteness, we take our past experiences of deprivation, hurt, and rejection, and project them onto our relationship (or on our partner) in hopes of finally healing our neediness. By then creating an illusion that the other person can actually fill our sense of separateness and deprivation, we now feel that it is absolutely essential to get, win, or possess the other person and his or her love. But our illusion always bursts, and we will inevitably be disappointed, perceiving a betrayal by the other person for not living up to our fantasies. This is the point at which most relationships break up. And what are we left with? Our little self, who still feels powerless, incomplete, and in desperate need of love.

Consider this couple who came to see me. Robert was powerfully drawn to Sheila. She shared so many of his interests—a desire to have a family, a love of the outdoors, and an enjoyment of arts and cultural events—but also seemed to have what it would take to make him feel whole. She was vivacious, while he was more reserved. She was friendly and outgoing, while he was shy. She had spiritual interests, while he had never opened himself to spiritual awareness. Sheila also saw Robert as one who would complete her. He was organized, while her life could easily fall into disarray. He was a successful lawyer, while she had never developed her talents for career. They quickly fell in love and were desperate to get the other person.

Sheila and Robert believed that by coming together, they would not only heal their sense of incompleteness, but would finally find happiness. But in reality, another person cannot make us feel complete, whole, or joined. Nor can we learn to own those qualities possessed by our partner if we ourselves have already (unconsciously) disowned them as being unacceptable. Hence, as soon as the love chemicals begin to fade, the qualities in each person that the other was attracted to become suddenly problematic. And they both begin to reject or criticize the other, just as they had rejected these qualities in themselves. The illusion that the other would complete them and make them happy is now gone, and they have now fallen out of love.

There is no way a relationship can survive in happiness and love when it is based on such illusions as falling in love. Further, when these relationships continue, they are often most often marked by the cycle of blame that I described earlier: one or both people in the couple blames the other for his or her unhappiness.

To have happy and loving relationships is one of our deepest yearnings, and yet relationships are one of our greatest psychological and spiritual challenges. And in our culture, we tend to place great emphasis on marriage as the ultimate deliverer of happiness. Both women and men are tied into the belief that once they find the right person and get married, their happiness will be assured. Yet sadly, I have heard numerous people say that they do not know even one happily married couple! Is there really much to celebrate about a couple just having been married for sixty, forty, or even ten years? Do we value relationships for their duration or their ability to provide love, joy, and happiness?

THERE IS A CHOICE

Over the years of trying to help couples break out of the cycle of blame and powerlessness, I finally began to see that there are essentially two forms of relationship: one is based on (or mired in) a limited view of human potential, in which we believe that joy and peace are rare if not impossible, especially in the midst of troubles, and the other is based on a belief that we as humans are indeed spiritual beings and as such are quite limitless in our potential to be happy. Essentially, in my practice, working with hundreds and hundreds of women and men, I have observed that it has been those people who see themselves more as spiritual beings—those who see themselves as empowered and able to love without expectations—who have been able to achieve lasting joy and happiness in their diverse relationships.

If you are a spiritually minded person, then you believe in love, you believe in giving it unconditionally without strings attached. You believe that the state of happiness is natural and right. You try not to judge or blame or criticize. You assume responsibility for your part in the world and your effect on it. You have a sense of your interconnectedness with the divine essence of All That Is.

The opposite of a spiritually minded person is one who lives from the ego, which wants us to believe that we are powerless, separate from all others, and victims of circumstance. In relationships, the ego-based perspective manipulates, blames, and attacks the other person instead of assuming responsibility. The ego-based perspective makes us feel guilty when we're happy or feel powerful. The ego does not believe in unconditional love, but instead teaches that love is transitory, weakening, and dangerous. As you can see, it is the ego mind's perspective that limits our potential for happiness in relationships.

The ego has a long history in human existence. It contains aspects of the myth of Sisyphus, who repeatedly struggles to push a rock up a steep hill, only to have it slip from his grasp at the last moment, rolling back to the bottom of the hill. The ego would like us to believe life is a perpetual struggle that we will always lose. In the ego's system we may feel that only doing those things that involve struggle or sacrifice will bring us joy or peace.

In Greek mythology, the Trojan Horse first appears to be a valuable gift, but is actually filled with enemy soldiers who will destroy the entire city. Or it is the sailor who is captivated by the voice of the beautiful maiden whom he hears calling to him in the wind. The other sailors must tie him to the mast so that he will not sail the ship onto the rocks in pursuit of his illusion. Therefore, the ego and its answers are not what they appear to be at first, but are wolves in sheep's clothing, arriving like thieves in the night. As such, it is the great deceiver. How often do we find ourselves chasing illusory promises, not recognizing them as wolves in sheep's clothing, or engaging in the perpetual struggle to make the impossible real?

The ego also uses certain metaphors that have become incorporated into our religious thinking, such as a desire for a land of flowing milk and honey, or our longing for a messiah to come (or return) to us who will make everything all right. We may believe we'll only be happy when we get married, or when we get divorced, or when we have children, or when the children have left home, or when we get a better job, or when we retire, or when we die and enter into heaven, where our suffering and our good deeds will be rewarded. All of these are somewhere elsewhere than where we are right now, and we exist in a prolonged state of inadequacy, like a mule following a carrot we can never quite reach. We cannot remain very long in the now without future-time illusions and projections intruding. Sometimes instead of yearning for these illusions to fulfill us, we decide that we need to ostracize, judge, or sometimes even kill the "infidels" or the "evildoers" who look or think differently from us, until only the people who think and look like us are left alive or have power. Some people actually believe that this is what God wants from us, not seeing that it is just another deception from the human ego.

If we were to look for an image from more recent folklore, the ego is also like the Wicked Witch of the West, who evokes fear and terror, only to be revealed through something as simple as a bucket of water essentially to be an emptiness without any real power than the power that we give it—as she shrivels away into nothingness.

In this book, I present to you a way that you can access this spiritual dimension of yourself, and by so doing create healing and happiness in your relationships, especially those that are most intimate. You will learn how to leave the ego-based perspective behind and feel empowered to live happily, especially in your relationships.

The process for healing and transformation is both spiritual and very practical. You will find ten spiritual exercises that literally give you the power to change the nature of your relationships, transforming them from ego-based (and destined for conflict and disappointment) to spiritual-based (opened to the possibility and probability of very real happiness). Over the past seventeen years, I have had the enormous pleasure and satisfaction of observing many couples heal their relationships using these practices, making the ideal of a spiritual marriage into a reality. I am not offering a quick-fix remedy to relationship problems, but rather a profound path to healing that will turn your life upside down. All that I ask is that you entertain one other question: Would you rather live a life in which you and your partner feel trapped by your supposed limitations, in which disappointment feels inevitable and frustration and suffering dominate? Or would you like instead to choose a life—whether you're now single or in a relationship—in which love, peace, and joy prevail?

THE SPIRITUAL MARRIAGE OR PARTNERSHIP

Essentially, from a spiritual perspective, the central purpose of all our relationships is to help us uncover our essential Divine Nature, and to help others do the same. This means that we are to transcend our limited way of loving, and recognize that we are part of the Divine. Most spiritual systems and religions agree that the way to God is through loving your fellow human being. This perspective is characterized in the Bible by the phrase: "He who loves, knows God; but he who does not love, knows not God . . ." that is, (s)he does not know his or her god Self.

When we are able to connect to this core essence of love, we instantaneously and effortlessly transform our relationships from ego-based to spiritually based. The spiritual marriage is a meaningful and happy relationship that is not dominated by the ego telling us that we need love, but rather focused on *giving* love with no expectations in return. Ideally, both partners enter into the covenant of a marriage to accomplish this purpose: to offer unconditional love. But even when one partner has difficulty accepting this premise, the other partner can often make a huge difference, not only for him or herself, but also for the entire family, by choosing to use the relationship as a vehicle for spiritual growth.

Marriage can be a place for the greatest psychological and spiritual

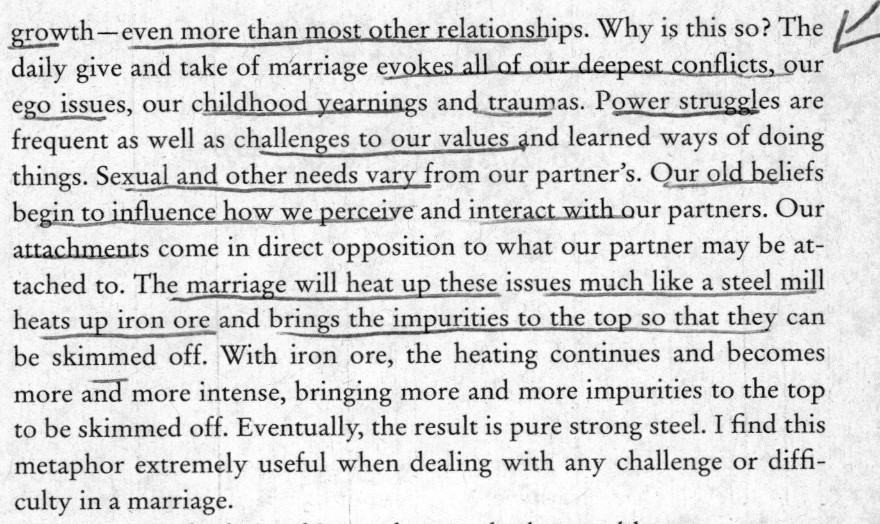

growth—even more than most other relationships. Why is this so? The daily give and take of marriage evokes all of our deepest conflicts, our ego issues, our childhood yearnings and traumas. Power struggles are frequent as well as challenges to our values and learned ways of doing things. Sexual and other needs vary from our partner's. Our old beliefs begin to influence how we perceive and interact with our partners. Our attachments come in direct opposition to what our partner may be attached to. The marriage will heat up these issues much like a steel mill heats up iron ore and brings the impurities to the top so that they can be skimmed off. With iron ore, the heating continues and becomes more and more intense, bringing more and more impurities to the top to be skimmed off. Eventually, the result is pure strong steel. I find this metaphor extremely useful when dealing with any challenge or difficulty in a marriage.

In a spiritual relationship, we learn to look at problems as opportunities to learn about ourselves—especially our barriers to love—both past and present, instead of getting stuck in conflict and struggling to resolve issues. We learn to access our god self essence (love) and naturally become more centered, more at peace, and more loving. In this way, we are more able to see the preciousness of our partner with deep appreciation, for that partner is necessary for our discovery of our essential nature as spirit. We reach heaven on earth in the marriage by going through the often difficult challenges the human ego presents to us, and then learning to transcend this limited ego perspective.

Sometimes our partners will be healed along with us as we heal our own minds. Other times, only seeds may be planted that may or may not sprout in this lifetime for us to see. But even if our partner is unable or unwilling to give or respond to love, we can still find increased inner peace, happiness, and love within ourselves more and more of the time, whether or not we choose to stay married to that person. (Later in the book, we will discuss what comprises spiritual divorce versus the ego version of divorce, which is the most common by far.)

PRACTICE 1:

The Spiritual Relationship Versus the Ego-Based Relationship

Before going any further into the theories behind how we are part of the universal divine spirit, let's see where you are in your relationship right now. The following Practice 1 will help to delineate the basic differences between a spiritual marriage and an ego-based marriage. Place a check (✓) beside each statement that you feel is characteristic of you in your marriage or other special relationship, present or past, or even as you envision yourself in a relationship for the future.

Since we are all living in bodies, which is the home of the human ego, you will undoubtedly have checks in both columns, and most in the ego column. Do not use this practice to judge yourself or to feel badly about yourself whenever you have checks in the "ego column." And above all, *do not use the exercise to judge or rate your partner*, for that will simply be the ego voice trying to get you not to look at yourself with an open mind and heart. If you judge yourself or another, you have succumbed to the ego's ploy to derail you from an opportunity to learn about yourself and heal your relationship. And please keep in mind that transforming your relationship from ego-based to spiritual may not happen in an instant. Rather, like any demanding process, it may happen gradually, over time. Use the two lists below as reminders of where you are moving from and where you hope to be heading. Like a beacon, the characteristics of the spiritual marriage should be a guiding light, encouraging you, giving you hope, and affirming your belief in all that is possible—if you wish it to be so.

SPIRITUAL MARRIAGE (Centeredness, peace, and joy)	EGO-BASED MARRIAGE (Disappointment and pain)
☐ Sees purpose of marriage as a place for spiritual and emotional growth—a place to practice unconditional love.	☐ Sees marriage as a place to get . . .
☐ Looks for ways to contribute to partner's growth and happiness.	☐ Looks for ways to get satisfaction from partner.
☐ Accepts partner.	☐ Tries to change partner.
☐ Views love as more important than passion.	☐ Views passion as more important than love.
☐ Content with no expectations.	☐ Discontent with disappointments over unmet expectations.
☐ Sees source of happiness as from God (Love) within.	☐ Sees partner as source of happiness or cause of unhappiness.
☐ Sees self as empowered to have a major effect in creating outcome of the marriage.	☐ Sees self as one to whom things happen in the marriage (victim).
☐ Wants peace above all else.	☐ Creates conflict over wants and "needs."
☐ Operates out of Love.	☐ Operates out of fear.
☐ Sees any behavior that is not loving as an occasion to extend love.	☐ Sees unloving behavior as an occasion to go into fight or flight.
☐ Extends forgiveness, knowing it is for oneself as well as partner.	☐ Holds grudges and complaints; keeps fears and resentments alive.
☐ Consciously creates positive and joyful attitude.	☐ Consciously or unconsciously creates negative, deprived, or other unhappy state of mind.
☐ Accepts, respects, and enjoys differences.	☐ Judges differences and tries to change partner to be like oneself.

SPIRITUAL MARRIAGE (Centeredness, peace, and joy)	EGO-BASED MARRIAGE (Disappointment and pain)
☐ Is respectful and listens to partner with genuine interest.	☐ Is disrespectful, interrupts, is not interested, and does not listen to partner.
☐ Knows when and how much to talk; doesn't need partner to listen.	☐ Talks incessantly and overwhelms partner, without stopping to listen.
☐ Is kind in words and actions.	☐ Is unkind in words or actions.
☐ Is generous in all ways, knowing as part of God you have abundance to give.	☐ Is withholding in various ways: love, affection, forgiveness, sex, material things, understanding.
☐ Primary devotion is to God and the Kingdom of Heaven. (Love, peace, joy, service, forgiveness.)	☐ Primary devotion is to getting gratification, pleasure, security, stimulation.
☐ Views sex as a communication of love.	☐ Emphasizes sexual relationship for getting pleasure, stimulation, love, security, and personal gratification.
☐ Supports spiritual growth of partner and self. Wants to give and give and give.	☐ Places personal needs and desires above partner's and one's own spiritual growth.
☐ Listens to and considers partner's criticisms and tries to change oneself.	☐ Rejects and defends against partner's criticisms.
☐ Thoughtful.	☐ Thoughtless.
☐ Keeps word with partner.	☐ Makes empty promises and commitments.
☐ Strives to help partner feel emotionally and physically safe.	☐ Strives to be right, whether or not partner feels safe.
☐ Trusts the voice of spirit inside as the guide for all actions and decisions.	☐ Relies on the ego voice as guide.
☐ Views self as for giving and forgiving (overlooks errors).	☐ Views self as incomplete and needy; does not forgive (overlook errors).

SPIRITUAL MARRIAGE (Centeredness, peace, and joy)	EGO-BASED MARRIAGE (Disappointment and pain)
☐ Is open to love—to extend it or to receive it—recognizes it and lets it in.	☐ Is closed to love; difficulty in recognizing, extending, or receiving love.
☐ Is mostly in the "now" moment with regard to the relationship.	☐ Lives in past or future much of the time regarding the relationship.
☐ Gives love without expectations of anything in return: gives, gives, and gives some more and is energized!	☐ Gives with expectations, demands, manipulations, and is exhausted and resentful.
☐ Refrains from judging, knowing it injures oneself as well as partner.	☐ Judges, believing it will bring safety and love.
☐ Is patient.	☐ Is impatient.
☐ Admits mistakes and is quick to apologize.	☐ Reluctant to admit mistakes or to apologize.
☐ Grants freedom to self and to partner.	☐ Is possessive and controlling.
☐ Sees every difficulty as a lesson, and is open to learn it.	☐ Feels victimized by what happens.
☐ Deals directly with partner, framed in love.	☐ Uses distractions to keep from dealing directly: alcohol, computer, drugs, TV, work, avoiding talking.
☐ Is fully committed.	☐ Has one foot out the door.
☐ Is not attached to particular issues, things, or choices—only to God (love).	☐ Very attached to issues, things, and choices, so tries to control partner and marriage.
☐ Thinks "I AM the divine love presence here and now in this relationship."	☐ My partner must be the love presence in this relationship, or I feel deprived of love.
☐ Gives proactively.	☐ Gives reactive love only.

SPIRITUAL MARRIAGE (Centeredness, peace, and joy)	EGO-BASED MARRIAGE (Disappointment and pain)
☐ Knows that giving and receiving are the same.	☐ Thinks that giving depletes and then becomes depleted.
☐ Is centered—not at the effect of outside happenings or partner.	☐ Affected easily by everyone and everything—especially one's partner.
☐ Thinks: "I actively choose to create heaven and peace in my marriage."	☐ Thinks: "I feel like heaven and peace come to me if I'm lucky or my partner brings it."
☐ Takes time to give to partner in order to help heal old emotional wounds, knowing both will benefit.	☐ Feels unfairly burdened at the thought of having to help partner heal old emotional wounds.
☐ Knows: "My safety lies in my defenselessness"	☐ Believes safety lies in defending or counterattacking.
☐ Feels connected with partner by loving.	☐ Feels connected with partner by fighting.

Remember: *When you have checks (✓) in the ego-based marriage column, do not judge yourself or become discouraged, for this is what the ego part of your mind would like in order to keep you suffering. It will not help you to learn and grow! Instead, identify the areas from the ego-based list and use those as a guide for where you need to focus. Then use the practices presented in this book with greater focus and frequency, and rejoice that you have another way available to you!* We will not be perfect in any of these spiritual characteristics, since we all have an ego voice living in our human body. Instead, this list will help us to further distinguish the ego voice from the voice of truth particularly in our marriages. We need to see ourselves on a continuing path, not as having arrived or not arrived at a destination. The spiritual relationship is a path, not a destination, for it asks us to make the decision each and every moment—throughout our lives.

CHOOSING THE SPIRITUAL MARRIAGE—IT'S UP TO YOU

A spiritual marriage is not only possible; it is your right. It is a way to get past your barriers to love, and come to know yourself as Love itself, and then extend it to your partner. Mostly, marriage is a place to give service—indeed the root word for "family" originally meant "service." Jesus once said insightfully, "He who would be greatest, let him be servant." And since women tend to be more intuitive, feeling, serving, and spiritual by nature than men, men may therefore want to consider being more like women!

We are just beginning to recover from two decades of a "me-me" culture, when we have overly stressed individual needs and desires. It even invaded much of psychotherapy. This cultural tendency has greatly reduced our ability to serve and to love unconditionally. Greed has run rampant. The me-me approach has therefore destroyed the joy and happiness in many a relationship. On the other hand, as we surrender our separate self in the spiritual marriage, we actually surrender to a much, much greater Self, to which both partners have committed themselves to awaken together.

Each of us has the capacity to love unconditionally. The challenge is learning how to tap into this inherent power. And when we are able to tap into this vast reservoir of loving energy, we can then know the power to heal our troubled relationships—from our marriages, to our family relationships, to those with our coworkers and bosses. And the most direct and effective route to this healing is by learning how to recognize and embrace the Divine within us.

In the next chapter, I will show you how to identify this cause of all your relationship problems and access your own source of empowering love. You will begin to transform your relationship by knocking down the infrastructure of the ego. You will begin to destroy the ego's illusions, including the falling-in-love syndrome, no longer remaining attached to who you want your partner to be, but seeing that partner for who she or he truly is. And you treat yourself the same way.

You will begin to know—or awaken to—that True Self that has always existed inside of you. This True Self is your connection to the Divine. Once you reconnect with your real, True Self, you will begin on the path to profound change in your relationship. You will have found the foundation of a spiritual marriage.

CHAPTER 2

The New Physics of Love:

A Spiritual Approach to Relationships

THE UNEXPECTED CAUSE OF OUR RELATIONSHIP PROBLEMS

The central problem in our relationships—the one that underlies all others, including the falling-in-love syndrome, is that we suffer from confusion about our true identity. The problem is that our basic understanding of who and what we are is in error, leading us to conclude that we are far less in every way than we are at the core of our being. This misunderstanding causes us to view love as a commodity outside of ourselves and then to look for the love we want from others, rather than understanding that we already are, in essence, the love we are searching for. Since we believe that other people hold the power of giving and withholding the love we want, we experience ourselves as at their mercy.

However, once we uncover our true identity, we can see that the lack of love we experience in our relationships is actually an illusion. The idea that we as human beings lose touch with this True Self is an ancient one, described by many peoples in many different cultures. One of my favorites appears in the story of the Golden Buddha.

Once, while traveling in the Far East many years ago, I visited the statue of the Golden Buddha in Thailand and heard its incredible story. Back in the 1950s, the monks from a monastery in Bangkok were asked to move their large clay Buddha to make way for a new highway. Since the statue weighed almost three tons, a giant crane was used to lift the statue. As they began to lift it off of its pedestal, a crack appeared in the clay statue and they immediately set it back down. And then, to make matters worse, it began to rain. The monks decided to delay the move until the rain stopped, and they covered the statue with a large tarpaulin to protect it from the rain.

During the night, one of the monks decided to check on the statue, to make certain that it was not being damaged by the storm. He looked under the covering and shined his flashlight around. When he came to the crack in the statue, he saw a bright gleam deep inside the crack. He began to scratch away some of the clay with his fingernail and found more of the shiny substance reflecting back at him from underneath. Picking up a stick he scraped away more of the clay, and then suddenly ran back into the monastery. He found a hammer and chisel and began chipping away, and continued throughout the night until he'd uncovered an almost three-ton solid gold statue of the Buddha.

Apparently, several hundred years ago, when the Burmese army (Burma is now Myanmar) was invading Siam (now Thailand), the soldiers were ransacking the land and confiscating anything of value. So the Siamese monks covered their precious statue with clay, making it appear to be a worthless clay statue, which would be of no interest to the Burmese armies. When the army arrived at the monastery, the soldiers left the clay Buddha alone, and slaughtered all of the monks who knew about the disguising of the Golden Buddha. And so the secret was kept intact for centuries—until one monk peered into the crack with his flashlight.

We are all like the clay Buddha of Bangkok. Our body is our clay covering, and our essence is very much like a Golden Buddha. It is our physical body and mental constructs (such as our ego mind) that make us appear to feel powerless and weak, and at the mercy of those around us. These bodies actually hide from us the beauty, richness, strength, and magnificence of our True Self within. It is this golden essence—whether we call it our Higher Self, our Buddha nature, our Christ consciousness, or something else—that is our True Self, which has no limits except those we impose upon it. What is this True Self? Let's take another step toward accessing this magnificent power within.

THE COUNTERFEIT SELF VERSUS THE TRUE SELF

First in order to know what is true, we must distinguish it from what is false. The Dimensions of Self diagram below illustrates the limited view we usually have about ourselves and others.

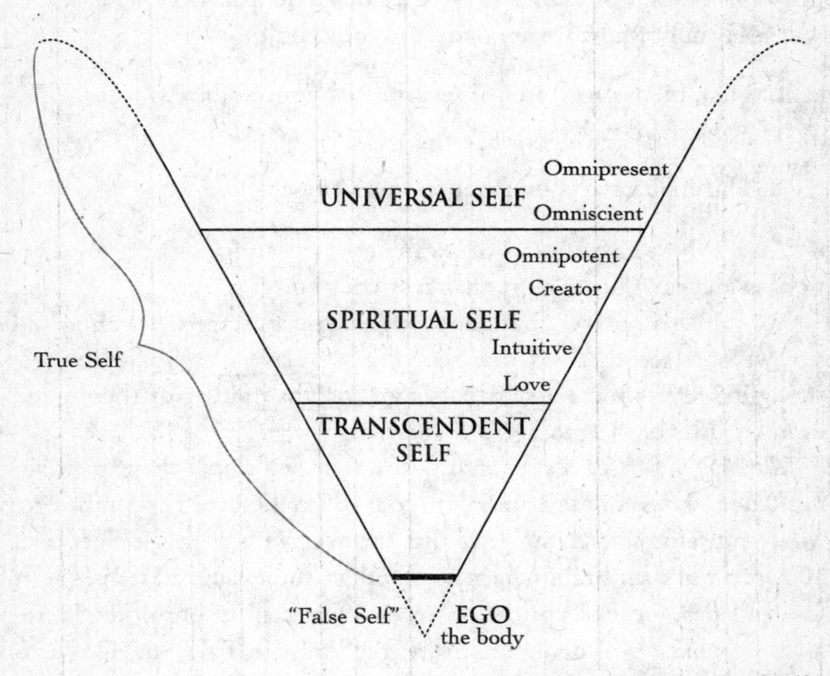

FIGURE 1: Dimensions of Self

The "counterfeit self" (or ego, as I call it) is designated in the diagram with a dotted line in the tiny, lower part of the upside-down triangle because of its insubstantial and unreal nature. As you have begun to see, in reality the ego is essentially nothing but an illusion. But the ego is so crafty that it is here where our identity confusion begins: for the great majority of people believe this to be their actual and entire self. Yet this self is as insubstantial as the dotted line suggests!

The ego is represented by the body. Yet modern science tells us that even these bodies of ours are 99.999 percent empty space, comprised of molecules popping into and out of existence, and can hardly be thought of as substantial or unchanging. Don't they simply get sick, grow old, and die?

We tend to refer to our bodies possessively—"my body," or "my arm," or "my leg." These expressions imply we are actually more than just our bodies. For example, if I ask you to do a simple exercise, you will see proof of how we are more than our bodies.

1. First, focus on an area of sensation of your body; (pause).
2. Second, observe your breath; (pause).
3. Third, observe yourself observing yourself.

Aren't these three levels of awareness (sensation, breath, observation) evidence of being more than just your body?

We can also observe that our thoughts are constantly changing and yet we still see them as our thoughts. Are we our bodies or our thoughts? Or is there a self that is greater than either of these—and even includes both of these? The answer is yes.

The upper part of the triangle is the True Self. Note the expansiveness and richness of the True Self in contrast to the smallness of the ego. Modern brain research suggests that the average person uses less than 10 percent of their brain capacity, and other studies suggest it may be as low as 1 percent. Perhaps the other 90–99 percent of our potential resides in what I will be describing as the limitless True Self. Unfortunately, it is in the confused ego state of mind where most of us live out much of our lives, reflecting this diminished concept of ourselves, and setting us up for a sense of powerlessness and unhappiness in our relationships. While living in this state, we are rarely aware of the power and love of the True Self, either in ourselves or others, except for occasional glimpses that are easy to dismiss.

If you look once more at Figure 1, you will notice how, when we're operating from the "false self," we are effectively blocked from seeing the unlimited potentialities of what we truly are. This barrier is depicted by the bold line separating the "false self" from the True Self, hiding its immense wealth that lies above. If the True Self remains invisible to us, it feels to us as if it does not even exist. And unless the ego part of our mind is disempowered and the barriers to love lifted, the veil of our True Self, as well as its limitless potential for joy and happiness, will remain hidden and our relationships will continue to be mired in conflict, anger, and unhappiness. In essence, we will be stuck in an ego-based relationship.

The inevitability of human suffering is a result of the ego's illusion that we—as human beings—are separate from one another. This illusion is exacerbated by the very realness of our own physical bodies. Even Freud stated that the "ego is first and foremost the body." The ego would have us believe that we are *just* bodies, and as such, limited, powerless, and quite isolated (in physical space) from one another. In this way, we might well conclude that the body is a primary symbol of the separation, for in our physical separation from one another, it becomes even more difficult seeing the oneness of mind and spirit we all share.

The belief that we are separate is what leads us to make comparisons, thinking we are either more or less than someone else, thereby creating the basis for all greed, envy, and jealousy—hallmarks of the ego mind. In such a state, we expend our energies endlessly seeking outside of ourselves for whom or what we believe will complete us. But if we think the permanent source of love is in someone else or anything external, we will be looking for it where it can never be found. Thus, our suffering is inevitable.

For example, one of my clients, Jack, always had to have the newest cars, the fanciest houses, and the most impressive boats. Meanwhile, his marriage was falling apart, and his relationship with his children was distant and strained. He was suffering constant anxiety and panic attacks, and he had a dangerous precancerous condition.

Another client of mine, Esther, spent most of her time at work where she felt successful and respected, and rarely had energy or time for her husband or children, who began to have serious behavioral and learning problems in school.

Tom believed that he would be happy if only he found the right woman. However, in each new relationship his early euphoria would be quickly replaced by disappointment and he would move on, looking for the right person to fall in love with. As he got older and the pattern of disappointment seemed inescapable, his loneliness and despair increased, even when he was in a relationship.

To Susan, it was urgent that she decorate her house perfectly, and she spent countless hours going from store to store and decorator to decorator in order to find the perfect pieces for each room. Meanwhile, the disturbance and estrangement in her marriage deepened every day.

What all these clients share in common (and with the rest of us) is the belief that we are incomplete as human beings and separate from the rest of humankind. Trapped inside this faulty self-concept, we believe that we are far less in every way than we are at the core of our being. When we are trapped inside the ego of the counterfeit self, we believe love is a commodity that we do not have, and so we search for it outside of ourselves. We believe other people hold the power of giving and withholding the love we need and thus we experience ourselves as at their mercy. We all enter into a search to fill that emptiness with something we believe to be *outside* of ourselves as if we are separate and not interconnected.

This mirage of separateness is a widely believed cultural delusion, an hallucination as real to us as is the hallucination of a schizophrenic, but we do not see it as such. Living in this insanity, we believe that what we think (and even sometimes what we say or do) has little or no effect on others or on the physical world. But as long as we hold on to such a false concept, we can only suffer as "individuals," as a culture, and as a planet. And we will especially suffer in our relationships.

In this nightmarish illusion that we are separate individual selves, isolated in bodies, we can only ultimately feel isolated, lonely, always in danger of being victimized by others and circumstances. In addition, we will come to believe that our pain can be relieved only by someone else or by possessing something, both of which we believe exist separate and apart from us.

Even the classical physics of Sir Isaac Newton, which have become the foundation of our Western scientific understanding of the mechanical universe, is anchored in the concept of separation. For Newton, re-

EDUCATIONAL SYSTEMS
FEDERAL CREDIT UNION
P.O. BOX 179
GREENBELT
MD 20768-0179

ACCT: *****1332
NANCY C SHAFFER

ACCOUNT-SF	AMOUNT	SEQ
TO CHECKING ACCOUNT		
*****1332-S6	155.00	108
BALANCE:	348.11	
PREVIOUS:	193.11	
AVAILABLE:	348.11	

CHECKS:	75.00
CASH:	80.00

4120568 05 MAY 10 11:36AM
BR 6 TLR 619

EDUCATIONAL SYSTEMS
FEDERAL CREDIT UNION
P. O. BOX 179
GREENBELT
MD 20768-0179

ACCT: ******1822
NANCY C SHAFFER

ACCOUNT-SF AMOUNT SEQ
TO CHECKING ACCOUNT
1332-S6 155.00 108
BALANCE: 348.11
PREVIOUS: 193.11
AVAILABLE: 348.11

CHECKS: 75.00
CASH: 80.00

4120568 05 MAY 10 11:36AM
BR 0 TLR 019

ality consisted of only what was quantifiable and measurable—what we consider objective reality. Newton's scientific method of objective experimentation had, he thought, eliminated any contamination by the observer, or subjective reality. He believed in an objective reality composed of discrete objects that interacted with—but were essentially separate from—each other. Even contemporary psychology encourages this illusion of separateness as it stresses the need for us to develop our individual selves—as if once we addressed our individual issues, all of our problems with others would be resolved—automatically.

WE ARE *NOT* SEPARATE BEINGS

There has always been an awareness that this idea of separation is a delusion. Mystics from the major religions and traditions, as well as Native Americans, Australian Aborigines, and shamans of many indigenous tribes, have recognized for centuries that not only are we far more than our bodies, but that we are not separate from any part of creation. Even studies in our hardest sciences, such as quantum physics, have come to a similar conclusion. David Bohm, one of the more prominent theoretical physicists of our time, expressed this understanding of our interconnectedness in his book *Wholeness and the Implicate Order*:

> *It will be ultimately misleading, and indeed wrong, to suppose . . . that each human being is an independent actuality who interacts with other human beings and with nature. Rather, all these are projections of a single totality.*

Similarly, the Nobel Prize–winning physicist Erwin Schrödinger, in *Mind and Matter*, spoke of there being not millions of separate minds, but just one mind in the universe:

> *Consciousness is never experienced in the plural, only in the singular. Not only has none of us ever experienced more than one consciousness, but there is no trace of circumstantial*

> *evidence of this ever happening anywhere in the world. . . . Mind is by its very nature a singulare tantum. . . . The overall number of minds is just one.*

David Bohm recognized the error in the way we typically view the world and ourselves in it when he said, "Perhaps there is more sense in our non-sense, and more nonsense in our sense than we would dare to believe." We might therefore conclude that our tribe's commonly accepted concept of separateness is actually part of the "non-sense," in what we usually call sense. (We will go into more depth about the relevance of new physics to healing our relationship problems later in this chapter.) And the philosopher Aldous Huxley concluded from his studies of Western science and Eastern philosophy that "oneself as a separate ego enclosed in a bag of skin is an hallucination which accords neither with Western science nor with the experimental philosophy and religions of the East."

Just the suggestion that we may not be separate selves makes most people quite anxious. But Albert Einstein had a profound awareness of our gross misunderstanding of who and what we are, and suggested a possible solution:

> *A human being is part of the whole that we call the universe, a part limited in time and space. He experiences himself, his thoughts and feelings, as something separated from the rest—a kind of optical illusion of his consciousness. This illusion is a prison for us, restricting us to our personal desires and to affection for only the few people nearest us. Our task must be to free ourselves from this prison by widening our circle of compassion to embrace all living things and all of nature.*

Indeed, the reason we blame others—particularly our partners—for our unhappiness is that we do not recognize the two central aspects of our True Self: (1) that we are not separate, but interconnected to each other and the universe; and (2) that we are powerful beyond measure.

When we do not know our True Self identity, it affects whether we feel worthy, capable, or lovable. It determines whether we believe we have power to affect our relationships, or whether we experience things and people as happening to us. And most important, it affects how we interact with others and the quality of our relationships. In other words, when we do not know our True Self, we are destined to live in the inevitable misery of ego-based relationships. But when we choose to become aware of the True Self, then we are one step closer to living a spiritual marriage or relationship.

When we begin to realize our interconnectedness, that everything we think, feel, say, and do affects those around us in some way, then we begin to own our magnificent power to influence all our relationships. We awaken as if from a bad dream, no longer able to view ourselves as victims to others' feelings, behaviors, or actions. Now awakening to our True Self, we are able to move from ego-based relationships to more peaceful and happy relationships.

INSIGHTS FROM NEW PHYSICS

So how are we all interconnected? If you read the introduction of this book, you will have learned of my personal epiphany in which I discovered the implications of quantum mechanics and particle physics—that which I refer to as the new physics. In contrast to the classical physics of Sir Isaac Newton, who focused largely on what is observable with our five senses and that which can be measured, the new physics suggests certain truths about the invisible qualities of relationships. Whereas Newton measured gravity and discovered all sorts of things that changed the course of science and how we see the world in which we live, there were certain limitations and inaccuracies to his vision. With Max Planck's theory of quanta in 1900 and Albert Einstein's theory of relativity in 1905, science made huge leaps in our ability to see that our old way of looking at the world (Newton's vision) was just not comprehensive enough to understand the larger reality of the universe.

Essentially, with Planck's discovery of the quanta, a particle that is significantly smaller than an atom, he showed that there is an enormous part of the universe that is invisible to us and that there is tremendous power residing in that which is invisible and cannot be observed. I believe it is this power that people have often called "God," although often externalized.

The old physics of Newton not only has been unable to explain certain natural phenomena, but it also perpetuates the myth that we are powerless. We are just a cog in the big machine of the universe, where knowing enough about the past means we can predict the future. In this sense, we and everything else is predestined, having neither freedom nor power. The new physics, in contrast, helps us see the truth of our godlike nature—and this happens at quanta level. The quanta, which is the smallest known form of matter, is 10,000 to 10,000,000 times smaller than the smallest atom. At the quanta level, scientists now believe that matter and energy are virtually indistinguishable, and not in the fixed solid state we commonly think of as matter. Our bodies, as well as every other form of matter, are composed of 99.999 percent "dancing energy," where subatomic molecules are popping in and out of existence moment by moment. At the subatomic or quanta level, the particles are more like tendencies to exist. It is at the level of thought, or consciousness, that we may influence the nature of creation of all types, which is what the shamans of the world have known and practiced for centuries.

An example of how scientists came to regard the Newtonian view of the universe as no longer accurate was in their investigations of light. For many years of research, light had been perceived as wavelike and was proven to be such by Thomas Young in the early 1800s.

But then, in the early 1900s, Albert Einstein, in another experiment, proved that light behaved as particles rather than waves; that is:

....

....

....

The scientific community was terribly excited by this discovery, for light, formerly perceived as waves, had now been discovered to be comprised of particles. But just as they began to accept this new interpretation of light, other scientists attempted to replicate the old experiments, and light was again proven to be waves. Undaunted, the scientists wanted to repeat the second set of experiments to once again prove that light was made up of particles. And as you may have guessed, light was found to be made up of particles.

How could it be *both* particles and waves? The results of these experiments showed the scientists something very revolutionary about the nature of the universe itself: that—at least in the case of light—there was something that existed in both states simultaneously, as renowned physicist Neils Bohr had explained in his theory of complementarity. They then determined that the results—or their proof—was based on the means by which they were making their measurements. *They discovered that the nature of reality, in effect, was determined by the observer's expectations and how he designed the experiment, and that a fundamental change in reality could be effected by a change of mind.* And further, Arthur Compton developed yet another experiment that caused light to manifest both as waves and particles—at the same time!

The results of these light experiments literally forced the scientific community to alter its view of how the universe works. At the same time, they realized that Newton's universe did not have to be overthrown, but it turned out to be only part of the story—the part available only to our five senses. But more important, they began to look at the significance of the subjective nature of perception: if the qualities of exterior reality (such as the existence and nature of light) were dependent upon the observer and how he designed the experiment, what qualities does reality have without an observer?

These questions and conclusions began to topple the old Newtonian way of conceiving the world. Physicist David Bohm, mentioned above, contends that it is no longer useful to think of anything as field and particle in a fragmented or reductionistic way, but rather as an "unbroken wholeness." He suggests that any element contains enfolded within itself the totality of the universe: This concept of totality includes both matter and consciousness and has come to be known as the universe's "implicate order"—hence, the title of his book—*Wholeness and the Implicate Order*. And Neils Bohr sees a similar universe to the one conceived by David Bohm. Bohr suggests that:

> *What we experience is not external reality, but our interaction with it. This is the fundamental assumption of complementarity. . . . [A]n independent reality in the ordinary physical sense can be ascribed neither to the phenomena nor to the agencies of observation.*

So, contrary to the Newtonian perspective, quantum physicists believe that there is no such thing as an objective observer or experiment. Our perception of any object, as Lincoln Barnett wrote in *The Universe and Dr. Einstein*, "is simply the sum of its qualities, and since qualities only exist in the mind, the whole objective universe of matter and energy, atoms and stars, does not exist except as a construction of the consciousness." Furthermore, they believe that *there is no separation between the one observing and that which is observed*. Instead, the instant you have observed something or someone, you have interacted with it or them, and you both have changed in significant ways. Things and people do not exist independent of us, but rather always in interaction with us. This means that *our spouses, children, parents, bosses, and coworkers are not separate realities acting upon us*. We have influenced in various profound ways how they respond to us, and, at a deeper level, we are part of them and they are part of us.

What does this mean in terms of our relationships? For me, I saw this radical shift in thinking as an enormous step toward changing how we even think about our relationships. Essentially, new physics became my window or lens to seeing how I could finally, ultimately, help others heal and transform relationships that were mired in the conflict, disappointment, and pain of ego-based thinking into the joy, peace, and happiness of the spiritual relationship. How? Consider this idea: If our active creative participation with the universe, whether consciously or unconsciously, is involved in everything that *seems* to happen to us—especially in terms of our relationships, then everything that is happening in our relationships, even the parts that make us most unhappy, are ultimately something we are participating in creating. *Our emotional pain, our rejections, and our deprivations—as well as our moments of happiness and love—are the results of our states of mind rather than an independent reality that is acting upon us.* When he was at Princeton, John Wheeler, one of the more notable physicists of our generation, suggested that this power extended even to the foundations of the universe:

> *Today I think we are beginning to suspect that man is not a tiny cog that doesn't really make much difference to the running of the huge machine, but rather that there is a much more intimate tie between man and the universe than we heretofore suspected. . . . The physical world is in some deep sense tied to the human being.*

And this led him to a profound and shocking conclusion: "May the universe in some strange sense be 'brought into being' by the participation of those who participate? The vital act is the act of participation."

Wolfgang Pauli, another Nobel Prize–winning physicist, explained the connection between what exists inside us and what happens in what we perceive as the outside world: "from an inner center the psyche seems to move outward in the sense of an extraversion, into the physical world."

Again, the implications are enormous: We can no longer consider ourselves to be separate, powerless, or victims, for we always play some role in our interactions. Our separateness, powerlessness, and victimization must therefore be an illusion. Every time we blame another person, we are saying to ourselves and to the world that we believe ourselves to be separate, and therefore powerless and a victim being acted upon by other forces. On the other hand, when we awaken to ourselves as cocreators and as active participants in our reality, we see that we are constantly choosing, and therefore creating, our personal reality. And if we do not consciously make those choices, then we are unconsciously choosing to live according to the ego's illusion. In this illusion, a happy marriage is not possible. And yet, if we let go of this ego-based thinking, and accept responsibility for how we participate in the creation of our relationships (its problems as well as its moments of joy), then the path to a spiritual relationship is free and clear!

USING THE NEW PHYSICS TO TRANSFORM OUR RELATIONSHIPS

Can you imagine how every relationship in the world—not only with our partners, coworkers, and family members, but also between different nations, races, religions—would change if we eliminated the illusion of separateness? What if we all decided to choose to live in full consciousness from the True Self? We would own our power to continually create peace and joy in every relationship. *Every thought we think, every belief we hold, every interpretation we make of what we perceive, leads to every emotion and action we take. We are, therefore, very active cocreators of every relationship in every moment of interaction, whether in person or in our minds.*

Toni brought me a poignant example of how we participate in the creation of our relationships, in this case for the worse. Before coming in to see me one day, Toni had had a little interchange with her husband, Tim, in which he snapped at her, and then the spat seemed to be over. But it was not over for Toni, who dwelled for the next two days on how Tim had talked to her. In her thoughts, she continually argued her case about how horrible he had been to her. When they had their next interaction, without Toni saying more than a word or two, Tim went into a rageful tirade about how awful she was, calling her foul names, and leaving her feeling crushed and powerless.

While Toni and I went over the sequence of events, Toni began to wonder: "Would Tim have attacked me so viciously had I not been building my case against him in my mind?" At first this may seem to be blaming the victim, this time herself. Toni had done nothing actively to bring this about or to deserve her husband's abuse, and had not even verbally expressed her unhappiness with him. But Toni was also aware of how much Tim was affected by her internal states, knowing the interconnectedness of seemingly separate minds. She was convinced that it was her two days of rehearsing in her mind revenge against Tim that had created his vicious attack on her, pulling it into her life the way gravity attracts objects in space. Physicists tell us that any particle communicates instantaneously with any other particle—anywhere in the universe. Toni had no doubt that her resentful message toward Tim had gone forth. She saw herself as a cocreator of her relationship and was beginning to see how she was not a victim at all. Instead, she could shift her way of thinking about how she participated in the dynamic with her husband. She knew that if she began to think of Tim differently, not as her attacker but as the man she loved, then his attacking manner would stop. And it did.

When we are not conscious of how this process of cocreation works—as Toni was not at first—we cannot help but cocreate our partner's feelings of security and insecurity via our thoughts because the other person's mind cannot be thought of as a separate entity. We all know how in the honeymoon phase of most relationships there is great joy and love, for each person is only thinking the best about the other. The same process operates in reverse when a relationship sours—we create our own and contribute to our partner's unhappiness because we are thinking the worst of our partner, often in a state of unrealistic and inflated expectations.

The Swiss psychoanalyst Carl Jung, who happened to be a close friend of the physicist Wolfgang Pauli quoted above, understood this "in here–out there" nature of reality when he wrote:

> *The psychological rule says that when an inner situation is not made conscious, it happens outside, as fate. That is to say, when the individual remains divided and does not become conscious of his inner contradictions, the world must perforce act out the conflict and be torn into opposite halves.*

Therefore, the "out there" actually begins as the "in here," and acts as a reflection of what we believe inside, although it is often unconscious and is therefore perceived as a separate objective reality acting upon us. After all, if what we view as tangible and real is only dancing energy—molecules popping into and out of existence, influenced by our mind—perhaps, as physicist John Wheeler suggests, in our act of participation we are the creators not only of our personal reality (the world we perceive), but perhaps even the physical universe itself. If we begin to think in this way, we begin to see more clearly that our true identity lies within the True Self as part of a unified field of consciousness, with its limitless power to bring misery or healing into our relationships of all kinds, perhaps more so than we have ever dreamed. It is clear that there is never a time or a place where we are not participating in creation, sometimes consciously, but more often unconsciously.

In ego-based thinking, we tend to believe that other people are doing something *to* us, making us feel often like victims of others' influence; but the reality is that it is well within our power to create what it is we are longing for. And if what you want is a relationship that is happy, joyful, and peaceful, then all you have to do is shift your thinking accordingly. Joseph Weizenbaum, who was a scientist at the Massachusetts Institute of Technology, saw how "science promised man power . . . but, as so often happens when people are seduced by promises of power, the price is servitude and impotence. Power is nothing if it is not the power to choose."

When we become aware of and consciously become attuned to natural law, we see our essential interconnectedness. And when we take complete responsibility for every aspect of our lives, we learn to exercise our choices consciously in every moment. Thus the power that created our suffering becomes the same power we can use consciously to create joy in our lives, and especially in our relationships.

However, it is not easy to give up the ego's perspective that someone else is responsible for our happiness or misery in our relationships. We feel as reluctant to change our beliefs about who we are as it was for people to accept that our planet is not the center of the universe or that the force of gravity exists. Even Isaac Newton, the one who outlined the laws of gravity, originally had great difficulty in believing that such an invisible and irrational power existed. He wrote in a letter to the classical scholar Richard Bently:

> *[T]hat one body may act upon another at a distance through a vacuum without the mediation of anything else, by and through which their action and force may be conveyed from one to another, is to me so great an absurdity that, I believe, no man who has in philosophic matters a competent faculty of thinking could ever fall into it.*

Any relationship can be heaven, or it can be hell. Most of us know varying degrees of both. But we usually see others as having the power to bring us the heaven or hell, except for the moments we happen to be more aware of our true identity. The end of suffering and the advent of joyful relationships, then, will come from an awareness of who and what we truly are and embracing this godlike essence that we all possess—each and every one of us. If we insist on believing in the common illusions that we are powerless and separate, then we will continue to be at the mercy of our relationships. On the other hand, when you are able and willing to recognize and accept the truth about your innate power and your interconnectedness with others—even with the entire web of life—then you become the master of how you feel in your relationships, letting them flow from an endless supply of love. With this shift in thinking, you will know to ask yourself questions, such as, "How am I contributing to this storm?" With this new awareness you can learn both how to quell the storms of your relationship and how to stay centered, in spite of those storms.

ACCEPTING OUR DIVINE ESSENCE WITHIN

The idea that we are more than a body may trouble some Newtonian scientists, and others may think this idea is just more New Age hogwash. And then there are others who embrace the idea with open arms, knowing it as true in the very core of their knowingness. But some of the loudest dissenters may be those speaking from a theistic religious perspective.* The idea that we are part of what we call the Divine may sound like blasphemy, even though the scriptures of all religions, including Christianity and Judaism, contain many passages, often overlooked, which clearly support such a perspective. The true blasphemy, however, is to deny our divine inheritance.

In the creation story of Jewish and Christian scriptures, God is portrayed as being the Creator. And furthermore, God creates out of his mind's spoken desire: "And God said, let there be light . . . water . . . firmament," and so on. And creation concludes with God creating mankind "in his own image and likeness," not vice versa, as Freud believed people do. According to the Old Testament, therefore, we are created as Creators as well, able to create in the same manner as God; that is, with our minds or consciousness. In the creation story, we are also endowed with the same qualities that we normally attribute to God: that is, omnipotence (all powerful), omniscience (all knowing), omnipresence (present everywhere), and, in essence, love itself. We will discuss more about each of these attributes later, but, first, let us look further into the teachings of various religions, where God is seen as Love, and we are of the same creative essence or spirit as God.

Judaism:

Love is the beginning and end of the Torah.

God created man in his own image and likeness.

I AM that I AM.

*Theism, the idea of an external diety, when philosophically understood, is much like a watchmaker who makes a watch, winds it, and then leaves it to run, only occasionally intervening to wind or clean it.

Christianity:

God is love, and he who abides in love abides in God, and God abides in him.

I and my father are one. . . . You can be as I. . . . Greater things than I have done, ye shall do.

We are all sons of God and joint heirs with Jesus Christ.

I am the vine and you are the branches.

Know ye not that ye are the temple of God, and that the Spirit of God dwelleth in you?

Hinduism:

The individual soul is nothing else in essence than universal soul.

Deep within abides another life, not like the life of the senses, escaping sight, unchanging. This endures when all created things have passed away.

Buddhism:

Be lamps unto yourselves. Be a refuge unto yourselves. Seek not for refuge from anything but the Self. Desires and tendencies pass away. Only the Self abides.

He that loves not, knows not God. For God is love.

Islam:

On God's own nature has been molded man's.

Sikhism:

God is concealed in every heart; his light is in every heart.

It is interesting to see how the same themes run through each of the world's major religions: That God is love, and that we are of the same creative essence or spirit as God. John the Scot put it simply: *God is the loving energy with which we create*. And yet, the ego part of our mind fights in every way any acknowledgment of such an identity, whether in physics, psychology, or in religious thought, and seeks to preserve our sense of separateness, littleness, and powerlessness.

Who and what we are is so magnificent that it far exceeds our wildest imaginations and dreams. We are at our core spirit expressed through a body. As such, it follows that we contain all those qualities that we have typically disowned, and have projected outward onto a theistic up-in-the-sky god, separate and apart from us: full of an endless supply of love. We are omnipotent (all powerful), omniscient (all knowing), and omnipresent (present everywhere), and we are Love itself. Since it is only an illusion that we are separate from all of this, we have never lost any of these qualities—we just think we have. In essence, nothing limits us more than our beliefs—be those negative or positive. So as you begin to consider how you can change your relationship, letting go of the limiting concept of self and accepting the bigger reality of your True Self, you will become more and more aware of your beliefs, your thoughts, and the connection between the two.

In touch with your True Self essence, you will learn to use a previously untapped source of power within—not only to transcend your own personal suffering, but also to heal any parts of your relationships that are ego-based.

MIRACLES WITHIN OUR REACH

Relationships are a place where the greatest emotional and spiritual growth can occur, *if* we learn to use them for that purpose. Perhaps that is why most religions and spiritual paths emphasize that the way to the Divine is through loving our fellow humans—unconditionally and without exclusions.

Relationships of all kinds provide us with the opportunity to enter the "advanced spiritual growth" university, if used in that way. And with each lesson learned from the challenges presented, we rise to more and more moments of heavenly joy and peace. We need these challenges on earth to be our best. This principle seems to run throughout nature. For example, when I was in junior high school, a student found a cocoon containing a moth fluttering endlessly to get out. The teacher suggested that we keep the cocoon so that we might all observe what would happen. When after several days of nothing but fluttering, one boy in the class wanted to help the moth get out. So he took his pocket knife (which was considered safe to carry in those days), and scored the cocoon ever so lightly all the way around. As we came into class two days later, the moth began to break open the cocoon. But when he did, he fell to the floor—unable to fly—either in search of food or to get away from predators. Due to the ever-so-light scoring of the cocoon with the knife, the moth had broken out of the cocoon before his wings were strong enough to fly.

Similarly, baby chicks must be allowed to stay in their shells until they are able to peck them open. Otherwise, they will not have enough strength in either their necks to peck for food or in their legs to walk. And without the challenges presented in our special relationships, most of us do not learn to free our barriers to love, and remain in separateness to love.

It is only because we have denied our innate identity and potential that we cannot see that we are all potentially capable of doing miraculous things attributed to people, such as Moses parting the Red Sea and bringing food from the sky, or Jesus walking on water and raising the dead, or the documented "miracles" performed by various Avatars. Those Avatars, including the currently alive Sathya Sai Baba of India, have many reliable and scientific witnesses of instances where they have healed the sick, raised the dead, been unaffected by lethal poisons, appeared in more than one place at the same time, materialized diverse objects, dematerialized and rematerialized themselves, changed the weather, communicated without words, known a stranger's past and future, and so on.

Having witnessed many of these events myself, and having spoken with numerous highly reliable witnesses, I believe that these Avatars are at the core not essentially different from any of us, but are actually here to remind us of who and what we all inherently are. We just live so far removed from the knowledge of what we truly are. When we cease denying our own powers by deifying them—whether in the case of historical or current figures—we can discover, as Jesus said, that "even greater things than I have done, you will do." It is possible that we can awaken our own Christ consciousness or Buddha nature, just as they did.

I journeyed to India several times to learn from Sathya Sai Baba, other master teachers, and the people of other cultures, and carried with me Sai Baba's words ringing in my ears: "love all, serve all." I went because, if there was a Christlike figure living on earth during my lifetime who, according to many reliable witnesses, was able to perform the kind of miracles attributed to Jesus and Moses, I wanted to see him directly myself. To witness such a person live would further convince me that consciousness creates physical reality, as many physicists now say. I found this reputation to be true, but found his message even more important than his miracles. He did not desire to get people to worship him, but rather to recognize that we are all part of God, as exemplified in a conversation he had with one man.

Sai Baba asked a man, "Where is God?" To which the man replied, "Everywhere." "No," Sai Baba said, "Where is God?" And the man responded by pointing to Sai Baba. Sai Baba then retorted, "There is God," and he pointed to the man.

To witness miraculous events that are not limited by the body, time, or space, or even to hear about them, can be very anxiety arousing and may cause us to declare adamantly that "I don't believe that can happen. It has to be a trick. It must be a sleight of hand!" When I heard of Sathya Sai Baba's miracles, I wanted to witness him firsthand, and I did.

I saw Sai Baba materialize objects, including holy ash, perfectly fitting rings, and other objects for his devotees. I also witnessed a young man with muscular dystrophy whom I had seen in a wheelchair for days, unable to sit in the chair without being strapped in securely, suddenly stand up and walk normally in response to Baba's healing energy. In fact, continuing to see this young man walk and talk normally in the days that followed was disturbing to my sense of what is real and to a worldview where some things are possible and others are not. I found myself looking even more closely, out of my deep inner threat, hoping to discover that it was just a hoax. But I came to believe that it was only my limiting belief system that stopped me and others from living these miracles daily. If we are able to acknowledge our true identity as part of the Divine, then miracles would become the natural order of things. Their absence in our lives simply speaks of how far we have fallen into the illusion of separation. In this way, Indian culture has probably remained closer to the truth than most of the West. Once a fundamentalist Christian and a Hindu were having a heated debate, in the midst of which the Christian exclaimed, "And I suppose you don't believe in the divinity of Jesus either!"

The Hindu quietly replied, "Why should I deny Jesus' divinity? I have never denied it any other man."

If our core identity is part of the Divine, then our creative potential is infinite, as brain researchers now believe. Again, this is not our egos that have this infinite potential, but our True Spiritual Self essence.

When we are connected to our capacity to love by recognizing our godlike essence within, we can solve our problems in our relationships, quite often without struggle and pain. The pain comes because we keep trying to solve problems at the ego level. Pain, therefore, should be seen as just a sign of our resistance to learn, a signal, though sometimes a jolt, to wake up and become aware that we have reverted to trusting the ego's solutions to problems, which it always complicates. When we act from a spiritual perspective, problems are solved without conflict, for all the knowledge and guidance we need to solve any problem is readily available. All we need to do is to open ourselves to Love, without reservation, and it comes forth at just the right time.

Albert Einstein recognized that "our problems cannot be solved at the same level at which they were created." The ego cannot solve our relationship problems, for they were created at that level. Only the True Self that is spirit can operate at the higher level to bring a solution that is truly workable for joy and peace. When we know our True Self to be spirit, there is only peace, both within and with others. Attack and defense become increasingly impossible, for neither make sense anymore. Since nothing is outside of us, there is nothing outside that can harm the True Self. When we awaken from the illusion of separateness, nothing poses any threat to our peace of mind or the peace in our relationships. Only the body, perceived as separate, can be threatened; our spiritual self, connected to the Divine in the universe, cannot be threatened.

THE TRUE SELF AS LOVE ITSELF

If, as various religions have told us, God is Love, then we, being the same essence, would be Love also. Inside us is an infinite supply of Love, so we do not need to seek it from the outside. Seeking it implies that we believe we are separate from it, depleted and not whole, and intensifies our feeling of scarcity and emptiness.

On the other hand, we can easily become aware of our loving identity as our core essence any moment we choose to consciously extend love. Giving Love serves as a wonderful reminder that we already have an abundance of Love within. Anytime we feel a need for Love, all we need to do is to extend it and we will experience Love—inside of us, not something separate from us.

When we discover our True Self identity, we realize that we are more spirit than body. We also discover that loving unconditionally is natural. We desire nothing in return for our love because, as St. Francis of Assisi said in his famous prayer, "it is in giving that we receive." Giving from the heart and receiving are the same thing. This is the kind of unconditional love that we saw in the Sir Gawain story, and this is what forms the basis of a spiritual marriage.

In a spiritual marriage, we are centered and equally unperturbed by praise and criticism, yet always capable of compassion. From a strong and centered place, which only loving thoughts can provide, we can accept what is so without judging it, fighting against it, or being disturbed by it. We can see past the surface personas of people, and see their inner spirit and core essence. When we live in the knowledge that we are Love, we accept others as they are without trying to change them. In such forgiveness and acceptance, we find we are truly happy, for we are never disappointed in anyone or in anything.

When we are present with whatever is happening, we no longer feel needy. We no longer see the world through our perceived scarcity, searching for what we think will fill us. We clearly see that the very search for outside solutions to our misperceptions of incompletion is a flight into ego-based illusion. More than ever before, we can be present in our own lives—even when our circumstances are difficult. Everything, including all the people we meet and every situation we find ourselves in, are situations in which we can discover our true identity as Love itself.

When we do not try to change others to our liking, we create a deep and fulfilling sense of oneness with everything and everyone. This is the promise of a spiritual marriage. In fact, when you think about it, it is only in those moments when we actually do experience a sense of oneness and recognition of our deepest essence that we experience real and total happiness.

Barbara, for example, had lived most of her adult life feeling possessive and jealous in any relationship she appointed as special. But, once she began awakening her True Self, she began to change. In her new romance with Bart, she encountered a test of her resolve. Early in their relationship, he went away on a hiking trip, calling Barbara several times to say hello and check in. In his reports about his trip, he would make references to "and we did this" or "we did that." Barbara immediately experienced a pang of jealousy. Who was Bart with? Another woman? The jealous feelings soon became annoyance and hurt—why hadn't Bart invited her along on the hiking trip?

As she began to acknowledge her feelings—the hurt, fear and jealousy—she also began to acknowledge to herself that Bart had probably been afraid to tell her who was accompanying him on the trip. She tried to move into a state of full acceptance of Bart and the situation, no matter what it was. She would wait for him to return and then talk.

When Bart returned and came to see Barbara, he told her right away that his friend Jeanne, a very experienced hiker, had gone along on the trip. Barbara, feeling no jealousy or threat, said, "Great! How could she get that much time off at the last minute?" Then, instead of a fight ensuing, a flowing conversation followed for a couple of hours, ending with Bart exclaiming, "Barbara, you are such an incredible, wonderful woman!" Then they made love, experiencing more closeness than ever before.

Since Barbara had not projected her jealousy onto Bart, and did nothing to try and change him, their relationship was able to grow deeper in love as each of them experienced their True Self identity as Love.

The only thing that stands in our way is our sense of our isolation and littleness, of our suffering and pain. The process seems to be that first we recognize the illusions that make us suffer, and then we let them go—and with them our judgments and attachments to others—and then our state of Love fills and overflows from the sense of spaciousness we've created. But this is a choice that must be made again and again, moment by moment.

It is most important to remind ourselves, especially after portraying such beautiful images of our potentiality, that we are all dealing with the human ego. We will make choices for this heavenly state one moment, but five minutes later, we may unwittingly follow the ego's voice and plummet into misery again, feeling "done to" and discouraged. The most important thing for us to remember is that we can choose the higher road of the True Self, again and again.

CHAPTER 3

The Power of Thought to Heal Relationships

"You are what you think. All that you are arises from your thoughts. With your thoughts you make your world."
—The Buddha

"As a man thinketh in his heart, so he is."
—Jesus

A RADICAL SHIFT IN THINKING

If you're someone who has always believed that God or the god power is outside of you, how do you suddenly see or uncover your divine power within? How do we make this leap of faith? We must think about ourselves, our relationships, and our world around us in a new way, and historically, such a dramatic paradigm shift is at first difficult to accept. Consider the Copernican Revolution, which was profoundly significant in the evolution of mankind, shaking us out of one-dimensional thinking. In an instant, humans were asked to revise their vision of the world and no longer think of the Earth as the center of the universe, acknowledging that the sun is at the center of the solar system. Yet it still took many years for people to widely accept that the sun did not revolve around the Earth, that the Earth was not the center of the universe, and that there was an invisible force called gravity! People were ostracized, persecuted, excommunicated, and even killed for going against the tribal beliefs of the time. That is how powerfully attached we can be to one way of conceiving or viewing our world.

I suggest that we are now in the beginning of an even more profound revolution—the recognition that the human mind is not restricted to the brain and the body. Instead, there is a growing recognition that the mind reaches forth to the world about us through a unified field of consciousness, exercising effects at multiple levels in every aspect of our lives. This is often referred to as the nonlocal mind. While this reality has been understood by occasional masters and shamans and certain "primitive" tribes, only now are we on the brink of a major paradigm shift in the larger, human tribal mind. We now have more people willing to share openly their personal experiences, as well as mounting scientific studies that are propelling this revolutionary understanding of mind, finding evidence of the far-reaching effects of our thoughts on plants, our bodies, on seemingly nonconscious matter, and on other people, most notably for healing.

As you've seen in the previous chapter, it is the findings of the new physics that have decoded our interactive creative potential, and therefore our capability of being happy. The modern-day physicists have proven that our seemingly separate minds are actually a part of a larger universal mind. As the renowned physicist Erwin Shröedinger stated it, "Mind is a *singulare tantum*. The total number of minds I have been able to observe in the universe is one." If Mind is One, if there is no objective reality separate from it (as the physicist Heisenberg understood it), then our thoughts are constantly creating in synchronistic manifestations all about us. This universal mind contains all the power of the universe. *When we think a thought in our seemingly separate minds, the infinite power of Mind responds by using that power to manifest aspects of it that can be observed.*

It is becoming common knowledge that minds with compassionate thoughts can boost the immune system, promote healing, lift depression, bring happiness, and even strengthen us physically. *A Course in Miracles*, a comprehensive psycho-spiritual work, says: "There is no such thing as an idle thought. For what gives rise to the whole world you see can hardly be called idle." Does this mean that if I have a murderous thought about someone, that person will die? Hardly! But it does mean that powerful negative energy will have an effect on your self, and cause a ripple effect in those around you, and even the larger, collective world consciousness.

Andy, one of my clients, could not believe that his continual negative and pessimistic thoughts about work and his private, critical thoughts about his partner, Alice, could affect her in any significant way. No matter how much she insisted that she was deeply affected by his words, Andy discounted the connection between his thoughts and their effects on Alice even though he acknowledged that his thoughts created a depressed and unhappy state for himself. Like Isaac Newton, Andy could not believe that he could affect another across the house.

I decided to give Andy and Alice a dramatic demonstration of how all of us have the ability to affect those around us; I have used this exercise with numerous couples and demonstrated it to large audiences. First, so that Andy could experience in his body the effects of his thoughts, I suggested that he stand and extend his arm straight in front of him.

Next, in order to assess his relative strength, I then pressed down on his arm, asking him to resist. I then asked Andy to focus on any of his critical thoughts about Alice or his fear thoughts about work, and tested the strength of his arm again. It was very weak, virtually flopping down with my pressing down with only one or two of my fingers.

Next, I asked Andy to think a compassionate thought about anyone, suggesting that he remember a time when he felt his heart go out to anyone with love, expecting nothing in return. Again I tested his arm, and it was rigid with strength.

Then I suggested that Alice stand in front of Andy, but with her back to him, so she could not see him, and I had her put her arm out in front of her. After creating a private signal system with Andy as to which thought to think (i.e., positive or negative), I tested Alice's arm as Andy focused on each thought. When Andy was thinking thoughts of compassion, Alice's arm became strong; when Andy focused on critical or fearful thoughts, Alice's arm became weak. She couldn't explain why there was a difference. Finally Andy was beginning to see and believe that all of his thoughts indeed affected Alice!

But we did not stop the exercise there. I now instructed Andy to continue to think his fear thoughts or critical thoughts, and I instructed Alice to focus on thoughts of compassion. I first tested Alice's arm, and it became strong—no longer affected by Andy's negative thinking. As she continued to focus on her compassionate thoughts, Andy had more and more difficulty staying with his critical thoughts. Next, I tested Andy's arm: as his negative thoughts subsided, his own arm began to gain strength.

The higher energy of compassion overrode the lower energy of fear, not only protecting Alice from Andy's negativity, but also beginning to bring healing to Andy's mind as well! This is the inherent power of our thoughts. They not only affect how we feel—physically and emotionally—but they also affect the minds of others, especially those to whom we are most close and intimate.

Would you consider, then, that every so-called idle thought is hardly idle at all, that it is a powerful creative force extending from our bodies, out to others and the universe, affecting every aspect of our lives, including our relationships? This interconnectedness of all that exists in the universe has profound implications for us and our relationships. Let us look closer at how we can use our thoughts to switch out of ego-based relationships and open our hearts, minds, and bodies to all that is contained in the spiritual relationship.

USING THE POWER OF THOUGHT

While I was in graduate school in Boston, I was fortunate to have had Dr. Victor Frankl as a visiting professor for a seminar in existential psychology. Dr. Frankl, a Viennese psychiatrist and the founder of logotherapy, had also been a Nazi concentration-camp survivor, and had written a number of widely read books that grew out of his experience in the death camps, including *From Death Camp to Existentialism, Man's Search for Meaning* and *The Doctor and the Soul*. He told of the horrible circumstances in the camps, and how some people survived while others did not. Some got sick with malaria, while others remained healthy. Some ran into the electric wire and electrocuted themselves, while others chose to remain alive, even in hopeless circumstances. Some were tortured or even killed by the guards, while others were actually befriended by the same guards. Many were understandably miserable, while others amazingly remained cheerful and positive much of the time.

He became very curious as to what made such a drastic difference among people who were all living in the same circumstances—often a life-and-death difference. So he began to talk to many of the other prisoners to find out who they were, and what was going on inside them—particularly what they were thinking about. He found that some thought only despairing thoughts about the future. Others lived for the hope of reuniting with loved ones, or looked forward to tasks they wished to complete, such as writing a book, creating a business, or finishing school. Some constantly complained about the atrocities and the miseries they experienced in the camp, while others kept a cheerful spirit, finding something—anything—to be thankful for, even if it was only to have a little morsel of bread with their watery soup, or that the guards were not as cruel to any of them as the day before.

Out of his observations and dialogues with hundreds of fellow prisoners, Dr. Frankl came to his most important conclusion: *Even in a concentration camp where all external freedoms are stripped away, there remained one freedom that the Nazis could not take away: No one can control what we think in our minds!* He further concluded that it was what people thought that substantially distinguished the survivors from the nonsurvivors. The circumstances were the same, but the thoughts people dwelt upon in their minds were different.

Since that time, as I have observed my personal relationships and those of the people I worked with, I concluded that *what we think often does far more to influence the nature of our relationships than what we say or do.*

Over fifteen years ago, in order to test this premise, I tried an informal experiment with my wife over the course of two weeks, without her knowledge. I do not recommend that you do *this* experiment, however. One day, I thought only positive thoughts about her while I was away at work. I dismissed any negative thoughts and only focused on loving and caring thoughts, and thoughts of appreciation and admiration. And I focused only on good memories of times we had enjoyed together. On the next day, I thought only negative thoughts about her—critical thoughts, judging thoughts, grievances, complaints, hurts, resentments, and anger. Then, I continued alternating this pattern each day for two weeks.

The results were far more dramatic than I had anticipated. On the days I had thought only positive and loving thoughts about her, I found that when I opened the door to our New York apartment, where we lived at that time, she would bound to the door to greet me with a hug and kiss. Some days, she might have a cold drink in hand and lead me off to the sofa where we'd sit and discuss our day together.

On the days when I focused on only negative thoughts, she would be nowhere to be found when I entered. I would call out to her cheerfully, but would get only a grumpy response from the far end of the apartment. When I found her and we started to talk, we would inevitably quickly end up in some kind of spat.

At first, I concluded that thinking those thoughts must have set me up for a different orientation and mind-set prior to seeing her. While this was no doubt true, I was amazed to discover another factor as well. When we sat down to talk about the experiment, my wife was at first delighted to learn that the past two weeks had been only an experiment. Next, when I asked her to reconstruct as accurately as possible what *she* was thinking about *me* on those days, we discovered, amazingly, that when I was thinking positive thoughts about her, she was also thinking thoughts of appreciation and love toward me. And on the days I was thinking judgmental, critical, and resentful thoughts about her, she was thinking the same kind of thoughts about me! It seemed that what the physicists are saying, that our minds are not separate, but joined together in a larger unified field of consciousness, was indeed true. Even though we had not even spoken on the phone on those days, and were a distance apart, she resonated with the kind of thoughts I was consciously choosing to think about her. I wondered, *"Are our thoughts, both conscious and unconscious, always having an effect for good or ill on those about us?"*

If we pause to reflect on it, we see that everything actually begins as a thought; for was there ever anything that was created that did not first begin as a thought? The thoughts we think actually determine our whole personal reality! The notion that thoughts are immensely powerful and are the beginning of all creation is seen in the wisdom of the ages. In the creation story in the Bible, creation began with: "And God said, 'Let there be . . . '," which is a thought. The Gospel of John begins: "In the beginning was the Word . . . ," which is a thought! The Buddha said, "With our thoughts we make our world."

And yet the power of these thoughts can create ill as well as good by keeping us anchored in the counterfeit self, or ego, as we saw earlier, thereby creating and continuing our relationship problems. It's up to us to make a conscious choice to use these powerful tools to help us awaken to our True Self while transforming our relationships at the same time! This is the most direct way to influence our relationships most, immediately. Our thoughts always speak of what we think we are, either the littleness and limitations we believe we are, or when such thoughts are undone, the grandeur and power of our true essence.

Social psychologists tell us that the average person has approximately 25,000 thoughts each day. Some studies suggest that it could be as high as 72,000 a day, depending on how one defines a thought. Perhaps of most significance is that as many as 90–95 percent of those thoughts are the same ones we think repeatedly day after day. Some of these thoughts will be positive (loving, accepting, peaceful, happy, thankful, grateful, etc.) and some will be negative (fearful, judging, resentful, worried, guilty, angry, etc.). As you begin to become aware of your individual thoughts, you will also become aware of certain characteristic thought patterns. These are thought themes that you dwell upon repetitively, sometimes for years, each producing its characteristic result in your life. We all have these thought patterns; often, people who have kept diaries across many years are astonished to read their entries from a decade or two before, finding the themes frightfully similar to their recent entries.

But of course, it is the negative thoughts that we have to be most watchful of, for these are evidence of the ego at work. Such negative thoughts as fear make us anxious or angry and cause adrenaline to surge in our bodies. Powerless and critical thoughts bring depression by changing the serotonin level in our brains. Failure or worthless thoughts bring failure; rejection thoughts invite rejection, comparative and judging thoughts make us miserable, jealous thoughts make us anxious and depressed, and the list goes on. And, as is the nature of the ego's thinking, we may find ourselves constantly thinking, judging, analyzing, criticizing, projecting, reliving, or even rehearsing conversations in our minds with people we do not like. Sometimes these negative voices in our heads are so pervasive that if we ever seem to have a modicum of peace at all, it is quite temporary and easily displaced. The reason for this is that our thoughts are always having an effect of some kind! I call these negative thoughts "enemy thoughts"; in this way, we can begin to isolate, identify, and then expunge these destructive ideas from our heads!

Our soldiers in Vietnam had the highest rate of combat neurosis of any war in American history. The reason for this is that they most often did not know who the enemy was. While it could be a soldier in uniform like in other wars, often the enemy could be a grandfather, a mother with a baby in her arms, or a six-year-old child who could throw a grenade into their jeep. Not being able to identify the enemy is what drove the soldiers crazy, sometimes to the point of shooting innocent people.

Likewise, when we do not know which of our thoughts are enemy thoughts, it destroys the happiness in our relationships of all types. We experience diverse forms of anxiety, depression, and victimization because we are not aware that our pain began with our enemy thoughts. We then blame the other person or circumstances for our unhappiness. While most people would never invite an enemy into their homes for dinner, we do so unwittingly with our painful, negative thoughts. It's like inviting the Trojan horse within our gates, thinking it is a gift, remaining unaware that it is filled with enemy soldiers who are ready to take over the city. We entertain such thoughts not only for dinner, but allow them to stay as a houseguest, perhaps for months or even years, thinking that the source of our suffering is caused by something or someone outside our own minds. *A Course in Miracles* puts it succinctly when it states, "My thoughts alone cause my pain."

Like many people, I believed when I married for the first time that what happened had nothing to do with what I was thinking or feeling, since I believed my thoughts were private and only influenced my experiences if I acted upon them. From this perspective, I moved through my life the same way I dealt with the weather: I experienced a variety of situations and some of them happened to be loving or rejecting, nurturing or critical, giving or punishing, but all of them, like the weather, were completely out of my control. Things *happened* to me, including what happened in my relationships. Such a distorted perception led to the end of my marriage, as it has for so many others.

After remarrying, I continually and increasingly have learned that I am a major cocreator of all aspects of my relationships. I may not always want to see the scope of my responsibility and effect, but when I think critical or deprived thoughts about my wife, I not only feel worse, but she becomes more critical as well, and more rejecting and depriving toward me. On the other hand, I have also seen that when I let go of my critical thoughts and choose to think accepting thoughts about her instead, not only do I feel better, but my wife behaves differently—more loving, more accepting, more giving. After continuous testing and experimentation, I can now see without a doubt that the world that I have created in my mind becomes the world that I experience. This does not mean that she did not bring her own qualities and history with her. But what I do with them is a major influence for good or ill and certainly determines how I feel.

All joy and all suffering start with thoughts; depression and joy start with thoughts; abundance and scarcity begin with thoughts; health and sickness begin with thoughts; heaven and hell begin with thoughts; even those powerful placebo effects of drugs begin as thoughts. Can our thoughts, then, not affect every aspect of our relationships, since thoughts are the seeds of perceptions, emotions, and actions?

How often do we feel sad, frightened, depressed, anxious, or unhappy in a relationship, but do not know why? Or perhaps we get stuck at the level of blaming the other person for our unhappiness. If, however, we are able to identify the thought patterns that we have been entertaining, perhaps unconsciously, we can usually identify the source of our unhappiness. Similarly, if we feel joyous, optimistic, and happy, our thought patterns will expose that source as well so that we can repeat it. Our thought constellations are a central factor in what transpires in our interpersonal relationships, even affecting, to various degrees, whether our partners are loving and kind or rejecting and hostile. And, of course, our thoughts translate themselves, sometimes instantly, into bodily responses of health or sickness, and into success or failure in many situations, whether sooner or later. Even our brain chemistry is changed immediately in response to each of our thoughts and the feelings that follow. Dozens of studies not sponsored by drug companies have found cognitive therapy to be at least equally and often more effective than antidepressants in alleviating depression—and it is longer lasting.

As long as we think the thoughts we have always thought, with the frequency with which we have thought them, and as unconsciously, our lives and our relationships can never consistently improve, for we will be imprisoned in the ego mind's way of thinking. Until we become the master of our minds, we cannot take charge of our feelings or our relationships, and we will experience ourselves as being at the effect of others—essentially an experience of victimization.

THE VICIOUS CYCLE OF INTERACTION

We have been taught the three Rs, the sciences, and even computer technology, but most of us have never been taught how to be in charge of what we think, when we think it, and the length of time we spend thinking our various thoughts. Nor have we been taught to see that each one has a profound effect in our lives, for every mood of joy or sadness does not just happen by accident. Rather, it is first created by a thought, sometimes a conscious one, while at other times it may be a repetitive and less conscious core-belief system.

When my client Jennifer, a senior executive of a major corporation, came to see me, she had become very frustrated with her life because "she had no peace." And even though she "loved [her] husband and son desperately," she felt all they did was create more pressure for her. However, once Jennifer began to break into her vicious cycle, examining her thoughts, she began to recognize the fact that her thoughts had a great deal to do with her not having a consistent peace of mind. She agreed to keep a log for a few days of all the thoughts that disturbed her inner peace. Together, we practiced the thought-monitoring technique (described in the next chapter), and she came back to her next session with a few situations in which it seemed as if her husband's behavior took away her inner peace. But as we discussed these situations, she began to see that it was not his behavior that took away her peace, but her interpretations of his behavior and the things that she thought about it. She started to realize that the anger she was expressing and the resentment she was holding was an attack upon *her* inner peace and did not change the outside condition of her husband as her ego thinking had promised her.

At first she thought that only such dramatic interactions took away her peace. So I asked her if she ever felt a loss of peace otherwise, whereupon she became aware of expectations and disappointments with her mother. Next, she realized that she used a negative news report about something happening to a child to start a litany of worry about the safety of her own son. And further, after she referred to work as a place she enjoyed, we then discovered that there was a loss of peace there as well. She constantly felt pressured and anxious, and suddenly awakened to the reality that when she felt either, her peace flew out the window. She had not realized that she could do the same work diligently, but without pressure and worry. Suddenly she thought, "Oh my God! I live under constant pressure everywhere!" And then, referring to the log she had been keeping, she exclaimed, "I could be filling books with thoughts that take away my peace!"

Jennifer, like most of us, had not been aware of how constantly she lived in the ego state and unwittingly harbored the thoughts that destroyed her peace. She had become accustomed to a mediocre level of "happiness" common to many people, and was now beginning to awaken to the unlimited potential of the Spiritual Self for pervasive joy and happiness, once her thoughts were mastered. For with each disturbing thought she banished, it was another moment of peace and happiness. And the more she monitored such thoughts, the happier she was with her husband and son.

Let us look at a diagram that will help to illustrate how our thoughts work in what I refer to as the "Vicious Interaction Cycle of the Ego." Once you understand this cycle, you will see how by learning to monitor your thoughts, you can begin to transform your relationship from ego-based to spiritual. Of course, this entails the awakening of your True Self.

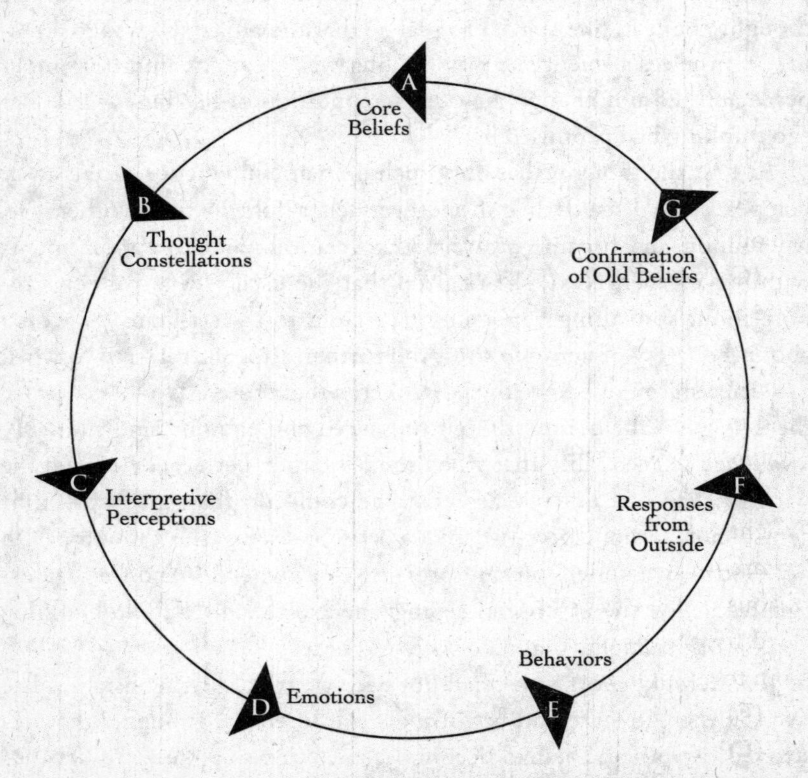

FIGURE 2: Vicious Interaction Cycle of the Ego

Look at the diagram, and focus first on

(A) CORE BELIEFS—which are outgrowths of our conclusions drawn from our childhood experiences about ourselves, about others, and about life, such as "I am worthy or unworthy," "I am lovable or unlovable," "I am capable or incapable," or "I am safe or in danger," just to mention a few. These beliefs also contain the ego thoughts of being born into a separate body, and therefore thrive in the illusion of separation, such as "I will inevitably be abandoned" or "I will definitely be rejected." Such beliefs are like computer software programs that generate the same relationship patterns throughout life, unless they are changed. These beliefs give rise to our repetitive . . .

(B) THOUGHT CONSTELLATIONS. If we make a careful analysis of both our beliefs and thought patterns, we find that the repetitive thought constellations we have each day actually rehearse our beliefs, thereby making them even more entrenched in the individual personality, much like rehearsing lines in a play. The more we rehearse them, the better we know them, and the more we live them.

The *core beliefs* combined with our *thought constellations* give rise to our

(C) INTERPRETIVE PERCEPTIONS. Our perceptions cannot be objective and therefore never are, for they carry an instantaneous and synchronous interpretation of an event growing out of our belief systems. These perceptions, therefore, always contain our personal meanings and interpretations, which are hardly objective. Our *interpretative perceptions*, then, give rise to our

(D) EMOTIONS. Our emotions never just happen, or, as some people might say, "I just feel that way." Instead, such a person is simply not aware of the thought, belief, or interpretive perception, whether conscious or unconscious, that triggered the emotion. Our *emotions*, fueled by our *beliefs, thought constellations*, and *interpretive perceptions* join together to determine our

(E) BEHAVIOR, which elicits a

(F) RESPONSE from what we perceive as the outside world. Such *response* usually serves as a

(G) CONFIRMATION of our old *belief system*. And the vicious interaction cycle goes on and on, often for a lifetime, unless we gain the awareness of how to change the vicious cycle and choose to do so. Most people live their lives of "quiet desperation" in this vicious cycle without awareness of how to break out of it; and many who are exposed to the awareness of how to, do not choose to or simply argue for the position of its being impossible. And when you live here, in the ego-based cycle, you perpetuate your confusion of identity—the ultimate cause of your relationship problems. Therefore, in order to reunite with your True Self and thereby be able to make a conscious choice to create a spiritual relationship, you must learn how to break into this vicious cycle of interaction.

BREAKING INTO THE VICIOUS CYCLE

When we begin to observe our thoughts and realize we are cocreators of our relationships, the ego experiences threat, for its very existence is now in jeopardy, since it feeds on being listened to and believed in. Like Hydra, the many-headed monster of Greek mythology, our ego will grow a second, more threatening head whenever one is cut off or jeopardized. So let us look at each part of the cycle in more depth, in order to anticipate this interference of the ego.

Most of our typical and repetitive thoughts and subsequent behaviors grow out of our **core beliefs (A),** those fixed conclusions we drew as children about ourselves, about people, and about the world—and particularly about who and what we are. Again, these core beliefs can be either negative or positive; and we need to be most concerned with the negative. The negative beliefs are those that come from the disturbing ego voice and therefore need to be dismissed. For example, if you were loved unconditionally, you probably have come to believe that you are loveable. This positive belief has therefore become part of your foundation for having happy, satisfying relationships: you believe and trust in love. If, however, you were judged, neglected, or criticized frequently as a child, then you may have come to believe that you are inferior, imperfect, and not worth very much just as you are. As a result, your relationships are probably founded on the negative belief that you don't deserve love. When you carry such a belief, it becomes difficult—often impossible—to actually experience love. The negative core belief cancels out the reality.

If you were treated like a prince or princess, you may feel entitled, having come to believe that the world should revolve around you and cater to you at all times, often overlooking other people's feelings and needs. If you were given affirmations about your abilities, you might trust your capacity to learn or perform, or conclude that you are inadequate if praise, approval, or belief was lacking. If your basic needs were not responded to with some love and consistency, you might believe that the world is not a trustworthy place for your needs to be met. Or, you might come to believe that people are loving or rejecting, trustworthy or depriving. If you were abused, emotionally or physically, by close family members, even neglected or overprotected, you might conclude that people are dangerous, especially in intimacy.

Our experiences, then, help to reinforce our sense of ego separateness or strengthen our awareness of the True Self.

Let's follow a core belief to its end. For example, if you were criticized a lot as a child, and came to **believe (A)** that you are rejectable and not OK as you are, then your **thought constellations (B)** will include repetitive **thoughts** that support and powerfully rehearse and reinforce such beliefs. You may remember times when you were rejected, and as the ego loves to do, anticipate situations where you know there will be a repeat of the pain in the future, or you may focus on something you believe is rejectable about you. Then your **perception (C)** will likely be colored by a rejection **interpretation.**

As we saw earlier, physicists tell us that there are no objective perceptions. All perceptions are interactional, and include our interpretations, for as the Nobel Prize–winning physicist Neils Bohr put it: "What we experience is not external reality, but our interaction with it." In this context, perceptions are profoundly influenced by our beliefs and the thoughts that sustain them. Therefore, if you believe you are not loveable, and that you are rejectable, then you are likely to view others' behavior as confirmation of your belief. And if you **perceive (C)** a statement or behavior as criticism or rejection, then your **emotion (D)** is likely to be hurt, fear, or anger. Your **behavior (E)** will follow suit in that you are likely to be defensive, retaliate in anger, take flight, or shut down. Any of these behaviors will effect a **response (F)** from the perceived outside, which, unless the other person is capable of remaining very centered with a lot of inner security, is likely to be a counterattack, defensiveness, or flight. This will then serve as a **confirmation (G)** for your old belief that you are not loveable or that you are rejectable.

Such a vicious cycle can go on ad infinitum throughout our entire lives, disturbing all our relationships, unless we become aware of our beliefs and our thoughts that sustain them. And most basically, such thoughts and beliefs help comprise our erroneous identity at the false-self level where we mostly live. In the next chapter, we will focus on highly effective ways, newly available to us, of changing the software of our beliefs. Yet we often need a way to begin to break into that painful and nonfunctional vicious cycle now, in the moment of experience.

CHANGING OUR THOUGHTS

Since everything begins at the thought level, it follows that the first place to intervene in the vicious cycle is at the source—our thoughts. Thoughts can be changed before they are manifested in countless visible ways. When we practice observing and changing our thought constellations, we have a most effective process through which all subsequent change can occur.

Before looking at some very powerful and practical techniques for doing such thought monitoring, first note how making such changes in our thoughts changes the whole vicious cycle. Note the effects of changing our thoughts as illustrated in the figure below. Think of the diagram as three-dimensional, and that the outer circle is actually above the other circle, representing a transcendent perspective.

First, we can now make the perceptual shift more easily, for we have stopped the rehearsal sessions that support our negative beliefs. Next, the emotions, behaviors, and responses just follow suit.

By simply changing our thought patterns, we can make a shift out of the old system at the ***thought constellation*** level *(B), and we move into a* ***new circle*** *(1)* by changing our thoughts, *which begins to create a different reality for ourselves.* If we can become conscious of the thought patterns that have been repetitive for us, and that have been contributing to our pain and suffering of any kind, then we can elect to change any of those thoughts, initially by choosing to let such thoughts not take root in our minds.

Please look at the new, outer circle in the diagram as you read, continuing with the same example of a belief that "I am rejectable":

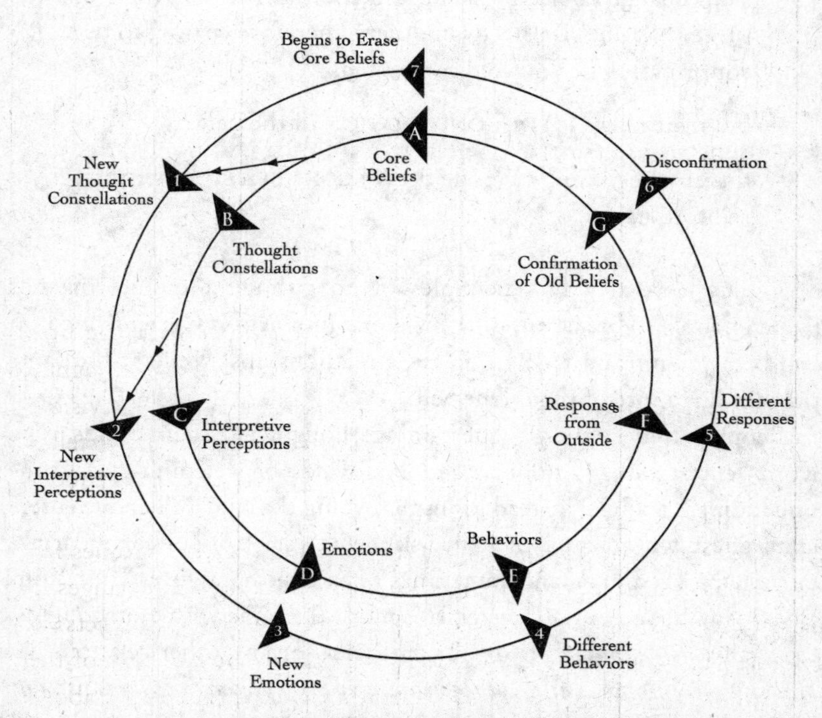

FIGURE 3: Transcending the Vicious Interaction Cycle

— If you have ceased rehearsing the old, negative core belief that you are rejectable by changing **(1) THOUGHT CONSTELLATIONS,**

— then your **(2) INTERPRETIVE PERCEPTIONS** of the world are likely to change as well, giving rise to visions of acceptance or love rather than seeing most experiences as evidence of rejection. If you are perceiving acceptance instead of rejection,

— your **(3) EMOTIONS** are no longer likely to be pain and anger, but perhaps joy and happiness instead. And if those emotions have changed,

— then your **(4) NEW BEHAVIOR** is likely to be kind, loving, and friendly, rather than fight, defense, or flight.

— Your changed behavior is most likely to invite very **(5) DIFFERENT RESPONSES** from others, therefore ceasing to be a confirmation of your old core belief,

— but instead is a **(6) DISCONFIRMATION** of the belief,

— thereby beginning to erode the **(7) CORE BELIEF** rather than reinforcing it.

Let us look at a few examples of how thought monitoring has helped people to break out of the Vicious Interaction Cycle of the Ego and bring significant changes in their relationships, while at the same time finding more of their True Self.

People often speak of entertaining thoughts in their minds. The word "entertaining" implies a certain attitude of welcoming and continuation for a while, instead of just a fleeting thought. When we entertain a guest, we welcome them in, ask them to stay for coffee or a drink, or perhaps for dinner, and sometimes as an overnight guest. Occasionally we invite one to stay longer. It is much the same with our thoughts, especially about ourselves or our partners—or any other relationship. *It is those thoughts that we allow to linger by welcoming them into our minds that have their persistent and continuing effects.* On the other hand, thoughts, even very negative ones, if stopped, reversed, or substituted, cease to have any lingering effect. And the sooner we stop such thoughts, the sooner we curtail the negative effects in our lives. In fact, even the frequency of their appearance in our minds quickly begins to decrease with continual thought monitoring.

Negative thoughts, which are all of the ego, are much like weeds in our flower gardens. When we have not weeded in a long time, the need for the next weeding comes more quickly, for the roots and seeds from the weeds have helped produce new weeds. On the other hand, when we have weeded frequently for a while, we can wait longer in-between weedings because the weeds do not sprout up so quickly. Similarly, ego thoughts that have been left unmonitored occur with vicious frequency, while those that have been consistently monitored and dismissed cease to reappear with such frequency. Gradually, they occur more sporadically.

Take Jon, another client who singlehandedly transformed a horrible marriage into a peaceful and happy one. Jon came to see me because he was having panic attacks every afternoon at the thought of going home after work. He opened his first session by saying, "Doc, I think I must be married to the world's biggest shrew." As he talked further, I began to see what he meant. His panic was based on the fact that he did not know what his wife might do when he got home. Would she start cursing at him as he walked in? Would he be hit in the face with a dirty wet dishcloth? Would she punch him for something she had been thinking about that he had done in the distant past? She had been known to throw cups of coffee or bowls of soup in his face at the table. Clearly, she was extremely unhappy and focused all of her unhappiness on her husband. He concluded, "Doc, you've got to help me." I responded, "How do you most want help?" to which he replied, "I would like help to make this marriage into a happy one, if possible. If I can't succeed, I want help in being able to get out."

After clarifying that his first choice was to save his marriage if it could be a happy one, I asked, "What are you willing to do to make your marriage happy?" to which he replied, "I'll do anything, Doc. I just don't know what to do." I then asked him, "Would you be willing to do an unusual exercise as an experiment for the next two weeks—one which might seem a little strange?" "Sure," he said.

I then outlined the experiment to him. I suggested that when he began to think of going home and started to feel the first signs of panic, that he observe the fear or dread thought, consciously and willfully let it go, and replace it with a memory of a good time with his wife. He said, "Doc, that's the dumbest exercise I ever heard of. But since I said I'll do anything, I will do it." Then he added, "I'll have to go way back to find a good memory, maybe back to our first year of marriage." He paused to retrieve some good memories. Eventually he came up with only three, all from twelve years before, and apologized for not finding more. I assured him that three would be sufficient, and we ended our first session.

He came back three days later and began his session by saying, "I think my wife must have a touch of that bug that has been going around. She seems a little more subdued than usual." I did not attempt to connect this to the experiment at this time. Four days later, he was back for his next session, saying, "This weekend was unusual. There were no arguments. I don't mean to say that all our problems are solved, but it sure was the easiest weekend we have had in years. My wife has always said that she would never go to see a shrink. I wonder, could she have started to see one secretly and didn't tell me?"

Again, instead of making any connection to the experiment, we just talked about whether he had been successful in doing the experiment. Three days later, at his next session, he said, "This is the longest time we have had without some kind of extreme outburst on my wife's part—the longest in years. (Thoughtful pause.) Could it be that exercise I have been doing?" Now he became curious as to whether he was actually having a positive and healing effect on his relationship—and he slowly became convinced since this was the only thing different that he could identify. Then he asked, "Do you mind if I keep doing the experiment? I know the two weeks are up, but since it seems to be working, can I keep doing it?" I assured him that he certainly could do it as long as he wished, and that I practiced and would continue to practice very similar exercises for the rest of my life.

As he continued his experiment week after week, and then month after month, doing it quite conscientiously, his relationship with his wife began to change dramatically. "She's not perfect," he said. "She still gets mad sometimes and sometimes she's impatient. But there is none of the extreme behavior that had been common before."

Sigmund Freud posited that strong irrational fears should be treated as wishes. We know that dogs smell fear in a frightened person and are more likely to attack such a person. Fear, therefore, seems to work like a magnetic force field, often attracting that which is feared into one's life—if not overtly, it is experienced as real in our minds. Likewise, loving thoughts which are genuine seem to attract love.

Jon came to see that by changing his thoughts he had healed his own mind, and had helped to bring healing to his wife's mind as well. Also, as he dropped his fearful thoughts, he no longer attracted his wife's negative behaviors to himself, but his loving thoughts brought more love into his life as well. This simple exercise literally changed the dynamic of their relationship, transforming it from one mired in fear and resentment to one of accepting love.

I suggested a similar experiment to a couple, Michael and Michelle, I worked with some time later. The husband, a physician, was something of a skeptic, but agreed to do the exercise. He returned the next week with his wife, ecstatic over the change in their relationship during that week! Then he paused, began to slump in his chair, and the corners of his mouth drooped as he said sadly, "But I would have to be godlike to do that all the time." He went on to talk at length about how he believed it would be impossible for him to continue it successfully. I replied, "Godlike is exactly what you are. That's why you could do it this week and can continue to do it and get similar results, if you so choose. If you did it once, you can do it again and again."

But Michael was unable to accept this truth and as a result he stopped the exercise and shortly afterward left therapy. I have no doubt in my mind that unless he was able to find help elsewhere, to this day, he remains in the state of unhappiness that was more familiar to him. It was clear to me that what Michael most feared was not the work involved in doing the constant thought monitoring, but his intrinsic god power. What he was not ready to accept was the idea that he could create with his thoughts what he wished for; in his case, a happy marriage.

Michael and Michelle are not alone. Sometimes we get so attached to our self-image as little, weak, and victimized, that it feels intensely threatening to let it go. Until we are ready, we will remain in our state of suffering, which will likely increase until we cannot take it anymore.

THE TERROR OF KNOWING OUR TRUE SELF

As we awaken to our divine nature as omnipresent, omniscient, omnipotent, we will rise above the counterfeit self and abandon our identification with our ego and our illusion of separateness, and this can happen quite effortlessly. However, it's often when we consider owning all the godlike qualities of the True Self, that we get stopped in the process of creating a spiritual relationship. We get stopped by our feelings of fear, perhaps even terror. We may fight in countless ways to keep our old limited view of who and what we are. We ask ourselves, as Marianne Williamson phrased it so beautifully, "Who am I to be brilliant, gorgeous, talented, fabulous? I ask you, who are you not to be? You are a child of God. Your playing small doesn't serve the world. There's nothing enlightened about shrinking so that other people won't feel insecure around you. You are born to make manifest the glory of God that is within you."

But as you know, life is not a straight road, and we as humans are not static. We are constantly changing and interacting with the world around us. In this way, the ego constantly tempts us, trying to distract and deceive us—it does not want us to stop believing in its supposed power, and it certainly doesn't want you to believe that you—as the True Self—are powerful beyond measure.

One day as I was on a commuter train and writing this chapter in my notebook computer, there was a man sitting across from me with two of his friends. He complained loudly and authoritatively about every aspect of his life, including his business associates and his family members, during the entire hour-long train ride. But what I could hear clearly underneath his complaints was an unhappiness in his voice and a feeling of powerlessness, even though he also bragged about his great business success. And when I looked into his face I saw the scowl lines of unhappiness and despair that had been etched into it through long years of negativity and fear. I was certain that his personal reality was a world of suffering and continual fear, that he believed himself to be in danger of being victimized by people in an unfair and powerful world, ranging from coworkers to his wife and children. His creative power was being misused in this act of miscreation, for it convinces him that he is basically powerless over the happiness or unhappiness in his life.

Our omnipotence creates in countless ways, even the delusion that we are powerless. By such denial, we do not see that we create our relationships, whether they are happy or conflicted. But when we begin to work with our potential to create differently, some people particularly resist the idea that they have created their lives and relationships. By being afraid of taking responsibility for their unhappiness, they remain stuck in their patterns, never realizing once that if they could only accomplish this they would immediately, just as easily, begin creating a better life for themselves.

One of the first steps to creating a spiritual or happy relationship is by addressing two of our greatest fears in ego-based relationships: (1) the fear of losing the other person, and (2) the fear of losing one's self. While we all tend to vacillate between these two primary fears to some degree, a person may express one or the other more predominantly in a relationship. But when we begin to recognize our divine capacity to love unconditionally, we actually solve both fears at the same time: (1) the more we accept our divine natures and our interconnectedness, the less we fear losing the other person, and (2) the more we genuinely love the other person, the less we fear losing ourselves because we have found our true loving selves by extending love.

In the chapters that follow, you will learn a number of techniques that will help you discover your True Self, reinforcing your connection with all others in the universe and inspiring your trust in the love that is the Divine within. You will learn not only how to own the power of your True Self, but trust in the path of the spiritual marriage. When you start to use these practices, you may find the ego mind engaging in a thousand different ways to try to get you to stop using them: you will not find the time, it will be too hard, blame someone else, you will be too tired, or you "don't believe in this crap." You may also simply decide the practices are not working, or "I can't do it." Others will forget to use the practices in a consistent way, even though they intend to do so. And still others may find they have the urge to put down the book even before getting to the practices.

I have felt such urges on numerous occasions when I have been reading any material that challenges my ego's perception of who and what I truly am. Many patients are more comfortable going into a therapy in which they analyze their problems for years and seek to find out what is wrong with them. Such patients and therapists are uncomfortable with any process in which awakening and empowerment could take place more quickly—sometimes in the twinkling of an eye. Sometimes people will flee couples' therapy if the therapist challenges in any way their belief that they are the victims of their partners. Some psychoanalysts may even interpret a patient's wanting relief from their suffering more quickly as a resistance to the process.

These and countless other resistances are evidence of the ego's fear of our losing identification with the false self we think we are. It is not only comfortable with our suffering, but also is threatened by our release from it. But the only power it really has is the power we give to it—and that is something completely under our control. The ego part of our minds will experience an enormous threat anytime we begin to own more of our power, our love, and happiness. It will oppose our positive strides toward awakening in every possible way. Psychotherapists have observed such reactions for decades, noticing that when a patient has just made progress or is on the verge of it, the person will find excuses to be late, miss sessions, cease using sessions productively, have nothing to talk about, or will sometimes even quit the process.

Recognizing this human tendency, the existential psychologist Abraham Maslow wrote a chapter "On the Need to Know and the Fear of Knowing" in his book *Toward a Psychology of Being*. After discussing many diverse ways in which we are afraid to examine ourselves and our resistance to carrying out positive growth-enhancing practices, he notes (emphasis added):

> *We find another kind of resistance, a denying of our best side, of our talents, of our finest impulse, of our higher potentialities, of our creativeness. . . . It is precisely the* god-like in ourselves *that we are ambivalent about, fascinated by and fearful of, motivated to and defensive against.*

To accept the innate godlike power of our Spiritual Self is very frightening to the ego mind, and we will often fight for the viewpoint that various things are impossible and that our powers are limited. Such power is actually the opposite of the ego, which feels its boundary to be of the body. But remember, our ego has no power beyond that which we give it, and in the moments when we come to this full realization, then the ego will cease to exist, or at least for that moment will lose its primary place in our thoughts. By recognizing our own potential divinity, we will lose nothing but our mistaken sense of littleness, the feeling of being out of control of our lives, and our fear and suffering in relationships.

The connection between our thoughts and our lives is inseparable. The degree to which our thoughts are out of control is the degree to which our lives and our relationships feel out of control. Just as we can easily understand that an athlete or musician cannot perform well if his thoughts are out of control—that is, not focused—so it is true in every arena of our lives. A person with angry thoughts is likely to be an angry person. A person who houses fear thoughts is likely to be a frightened person; and, as we saw above, this often attracts like a powerful force field what he is afraid of into his life. A person with a disorganized mind is likely to be disorganized in his life. A person with hopeless, judgmental, guilty, or powerless thoughts is likely to be depressed. And on it goes, all affecting how our relationships progress.

Whatever we think, not just about ourselves but even about others, always boomerangs instantly. If I dwell on a loving thought about someone else, I feel instantly joyful. If I dwell on an angry or resentful thought about someone else, I have attacked my own inner peace and it is annihilated instantly.

This ancient proverb summarizes it beautifully and simply: "As a man thinketh, so he is." The same truth was given clearly and poetically by the Buddha when he was speaking about one who is a true master:

With single-mindedness
The master quells his thoughts.
He ends their wandering.
Seated in the cave of his heart,
He finds freedom. . . .

Your worst enemy cannot harm you
As much as your own thoughts,
unguarded.

But once mastered,
No one can help you as much,
Not even your father or your mother.

It is the thoughts in your minds that affect most profoundly your marriages and other relationships. Do you think thoughts of judgment or thoughts of forgiveness? Do you think thoughts of deprivation or thoughts of gratitude? Do you think thoughts of fear or thoughts of trust? Let us look now to ways you can learn to be more in charge of the thoughts in your minds. The thought-monitoring exercises that are described in the next chapter will help you not only to become more in control of the quality of your relationships, but will literally show you how you can be happier in those relationships.

CHAPTER 4

Breaking into the Vicious Cycle

The Thought-Monitoring Exercises

"You are much too tolerant of your mind wanderings, and passively condone your mind's miscreations."
—A Course in Miracles

GOING UPSTREAM

In order to heal our relationships, we must necessarily go upstream, where the problems begin. By this, I mean that each of us as individuals must work on ourselves individually and the thoughts we harbor in our minds in order to help heal ourselves as couples. How can we heal any relationship without first healing our own mind, since we always take our mind and its thoughts with us? This process is like trying to clean up a polluted river: You cannot purify the water downstream when there are sources of pollution that are still active upstream. We must find the factories, farms, or towns that are dumping the pollution and stop it at the source. Such it is with our minds, specifically our thoughts.

The commitment to change usually begins with such thoughts as "I'm tired of my relationships always being so unhappy!" or "I'm sick and tired of being sick and tired!" or "There has to be a better way than this one that brings so much frustration and pain," or "I want inner peace above anything else." Yet most people's first attempt to make a change is by trying to change the other person, which is the least effective approach of any we could take. You can especially see this as the primary approach in troubled relationships. Such attempts continually result in our feeling increasingly powerless and frustrated, for this places all the power for relief from our pain on the other person; and in so doing, we fall back into the ego level of functioning.

Trying to make behavioral changes usually fares only a little better. Often, certain behavioral changes are helpful to begin the process, such as stopping drinking, or stopping verbal or physical abuse. However, most people need enormous support (such as AA provides for the alcoholic) in order to stop the behavior long enough to work on the basic issues inside oneself. Controlling a behavior without dealing with the thought constellations at the source is much like trying to dam up a creek by holding a few boards in your hands. You can succeed for a while, but it becomes exhausting, and almost impossible to continue without a lot of help. For instance, if you've never been a good listener and then suddenly decide to change your behavior and promise to really listen, it's more than likely that after a few weeks of being an attentive listener, you will stop. Why? Because you have not addressed the original problem that underlies your weak listening skills: the negative core belief that no one listens to you. In other words, this core belief evolved into your nonlistening behavior, and the only way to really change the behavior is by uprooting the negative core belief. *You* have to change your mind about being not listened to and instead decide that people will listen to you!

It is also quite ineffective to try to change an emotion. If we suppress our fear or anger, for example, it usually comes out elsewhere, such as in a physical symptom, or a "bitchy" attitude, or as a displaced attack on someone less frightening. Our emotions are most helpful when we use them as red flags alerting us to notice what thoughts we have been thinking. When examined, it is clear that the emotion does not come without some form of thought preceding it. If you're feeling unloved or lonely, for example, don't try and convince yourself to *feel* differently, shirking off or disowning the feeling in order to feel better. Rather, look at *where* this feeling may come from—although you may discover some circumstantial trigger in your life at the moment, it's more than likely that you have been carrying around the internalized feeling, as if it has become part of you, part of your makeup. Use your emotion to go upstream to discover the source of your suffering. As you will see in the coming chapters, our emotions can be used as our friend, helping us to identify the sources of our thought constellations, interpretive perceptions, and negative core beliefs, all of which fuel our particular vicious cycle of interaction.

Maria, for example, was very unhappy with her husband, Bob. She worked so hard in her job, trying to save money so they could buy a house and start a family. The commute from Westchester to New York was wearing her down, on top of her long hours at work. She resented Bob getting home earlier and having time to go to the gym; she also resented him for not earning more money so that she didn't have to work so hard. In fact, it seemed that Maria had arrived at a point in their relationship when she rarely had a positive or loving thought about him.

Bob was also angry at Maria much of the time. He complained that he felt so judged and criticized that he had no other choice but to feel angry and defensive. As a result, both Maria and Bob felt unloved, blaming the other for his or her unhappiness.

Yet neither was aware that what they were thinking about the other throughout the day was the major culprit for these problems. They did not see that their thoughts about each other set up the whole scenario of how they perceived each other, how they felt, and how they behaved. They were stuck at the level (in the ego of the counterfeit self) of blaming each other. With their minds so out of control, they could not be happy in themselves or with each other.

Once you have made the commitment to change and heal your relationship, and begin to try to create happiness in that relationship, your first step is learning how to recognize the ego and its voice. And the clearest, simplest way to do this is by learning how to monitor your thoughts. This is the most basic way of breaking into the vicious cycle of interaction created by the ego part of our minds.

As we have seen, the basic cause of our relationship problems has nothing to do with money, sex, our gender differences, or whether we replace the toothpaste cap. It is not even about who has control. Instead, the cause of all conflict, pain, and suffering in our relationships stems from our basic confusion about who we are. We think we are just the little "i," the ego, or just a body with all its limitations. It is the voice of the ego part of our minds that creates all of our conflict and suffering. Yet if we do not learn how to recognize this enemy, how can we create peace? If we do not know what is causing the pain in our relationships, how can we attend to it creatively and make different choices? It is, therefore, of utmost importance that we know just what the ego is, and how to recognize its voice. That way, we learn how to deal with it constructively by differentiating it from our True Self. How can learning to control the thoughts in one's mind be superficial when all creation begins at that level?

The solution to most problems is quite simple; but as we saw earlier, it is that inner voice we call the ego that makes them seem complicated in order to keep us in suffering and despair longer. Let's look closer at this enemy thought in our midst—the ego—so that we know how to recognize its signs. Once we become aware of the ego, it loses its power—immediately!

THE PARADOX OF THE EGO

I use the term "ego" differently from most of our popular Western connotations. Many believe that the ego is the personality of the person. In actuality, that which we believe to be the "I" does not even exist. Instead, it is essentially those layers of illusion that cover our true nature, our golden essence, our divine self. It is the ego's voice, therefore, that creates this confusion about our identity—about who and what we truly are—it's the ego's voice behind the counterfeit self, fueling its illusions and fears and creating all of the problems in our relationships.

The ego is just a word, a symbol; it is not a physical entity. It is not a force acting upon us, but basically an erroneous thought system in our minds. It is an elaborate conception used to justify and support our belief about ourselves as separate and victims of others and circumstances, and in need of external things and people to fill and complete us. Thomas, one of my older clients, carried the common illusion that pretty women are more loving than less attractive women. So he married Katherine, expecting her to fulfill all sorts of his needs: he assumed that she would be caring, loving, lighthearted, and charming—that she would take care of him emotionally, and be his helpmate.

Unfortunately, Katherine, though quite physically beautiful, was unable to meet any of Thomas's needs. After three short months of marriage, Thomas discovered, much to his surprise, that Katherine was not that warm or loving; she was actually quite withdrawn and being physically affectionate was difficult for her. Now, aside from Katherine's not being "perfect," Thomas's real problem was not Katherine, but his own disappointment and anger toward Katherine.

Where and how is the ego involved here? The ego is at the root of Thomas's need for beauty, care, and tending to; his desire to *be* loved. It is his ego voice that makes him believe that Katherine's beauty will automatically deliver these qualities. If Thomas were more in touch with his True Self, he would not have made such an erroneous assumption. First, though he may still have been attracted to Katherine's outward beauty, he would have been able to see her as emotionally unavailable and physically reserved. Second, and more important, he would not have gone to Katherine in order to be loved. He would carry the love, the warmth, and the ability to take care of himself within himself. He may or may not still have wanted to marry the beautiful Katherine, but he wouldn't do so under the ego's delusion that she would be his source of love or his helpmate.

Yet for all of its power to cause problems, even destroy some relationships, the ego is actually quite powerless. This is the great paradox: The ego has absolutely no power of its own, possessing only the power that you give to it by listening to it and by believing in its voice. Only by coming to recognize the ego and its ways of thinking accurately and completely can we choose *not* to listen to it and to cease continuing to experience its erroneous advice. Once recognized, we simply make a choice to listen to another voice—the voice of our deepest self. In this way we break into the vicious cycle of interaction (created by the ego), and get at the roots of our relationship problems. As you will see later in the chapter, you will learn not only how to disempower this ego voice, but also how to replace its voice with powerful affirmations that help you create the spiritual marriage you so desire.

In the ego state where the belief that we are all separate reigns, we also believe that the world is divided between the subject ("I") and the object (what is "not I")—or as psychoanalyst Harry Stack Sullivan put it, "me" and "not me." Obviously, some of this "me" and "not me" distinction is necessary for reasonable functioning in the world. The problem comes, however, when we take too literally and seriously this distinction of individual differences that the ego insists upon, not viewing this sense of separateness as simply a mental construct in an attempt to make the world more manageable. Yet, it is precisely this self we fear losing that we need to lose before we can find our True Self and create happy relationships! Such wisdom was stated in the Bible in the phrase "he who loses himself will find his Self."

The ego mind will go to painful lengths to preserve that which is actually insignificant and unimportant, but which it tries to convince us is essential. Consider such familiar examples such as "If my husband does not buy us a house in the right neighborhood, I can't be happy." Or "If Lucy does not make the honor roll, my friends will think I'm a bad parent." Or "If my wife won't have sex with me when I want it, it means she doesn't love me." Or "If I don't continue to be a beautiful head turner, then my husband will stop loving me." The ego wants us to question our inherent self-worth, our lovableness, our essential goodness. It wants us to question and doubt our commitments to the people we love; it wants to undermine our trust in our fellow human beings, including ourselves.

Yet, remember, the ego's power is all an illusion, and a sure sign of this mirage is the panic that results when the ego feels as if its illusion of separateness is in danger of being questioned. Whenever you begin to feel in your relationship either lonely and isolated on the one hand, or smothered and overpowered on the other, know that it is the ego trying to make you believe you are separate and incomplete. As a result, we alternate in our relationships between fears of loss and abandonment and fears of losing the separate self that we have constructed in our minds.

Everything the ego promises as fulfillment, security, happiness, power, or love ultimately becomes its opposite. In fact, every solution it offers to our relationship problems creates more of the problems it promises to solve, and often creates additional problems as well. For example, we may criticize or attack someone for not giving us the love and attention we want. Yet if we pause to look at our experience, we see that such an approach usually pushes the person further away from us—it certainly doesn't invite love. Or we may believe we can preserve love by clinging and grasping, but our experience shows that this, too, usually makes people pull further away. As such, the ego is the great deceiver. Instead of helping us find what we seek, the ego's actual motto might as well be: "Seek, but don't find, but keep believing that you will somehow find it where it is not." Is this not an insane voice?

This paradox is much like my son's little turtle. We usually move him from the tank to the sink to feed him, preventing the scraps from remaining in the tank, which requires more frequent tank cleanings. Whenever he sees me beside his tank, he thrashes about madly, wanting me to pick him up, take him to the sink, and feed him. When I find the special treat of fresh insects to feed him, and drop them into his tank right in front of his nose, he will continue thrashing, trying to get me to pick him up to feed him even though the real treat is right beside him. Like him, we do not see the love that is present, right inside of us—essentially our core identity—for we are busy looking for it out there.

Like my son's turtle, my good friend Frank West went through an analogous, yet obviously more heartwrenching, experience during his marriage. As he describes it himself, "About twenty years into my marriage, I became aware of an acute dissatisfaction with my life—an unhappiness that in my mistaken perception I attributed to faults and deficiencies in my wife. The only option I knew of then was to have an affair. And it was with a woman of gentleness, kindness, and what I perceived as a capacity for providing me the affection and love I believed I needed and lacked.

"As I approached the moment of decision as to whether I would leave my wife for this other woman, I was extremely conflicted, evidencing deep anguish. My wife was aware of my struggle to decide, aware that there was another woman in my life, and certainly aware of my anguish.

"A defining moment in our marriage occurred one evening when, upon again perceiving my pain, she said to me, 'I love you and I do not want to have you absent from my life, but if it would bring you peace—then go to her.'

"This was said, not in hate or resignation of defeat, but with a tone of a genuine wish for my happiness. In that moment, I experienced with shock that I was being given a gift, a gift of which I had never been aware of experiencing in my life to that moment. The closest I can come to describing what I received is this—a love with no conditions attached.

"I said it was a defining moment for it was a moment that gave me the freedom to choose—and what else could I choose but to respond to the love offered me? Thereupon followed a period of healing, which I have since learned is always true once love has been extended or received."

This story, described here verbatim as it appeared in a letter to me, always moves me to tears. The power and passion of the love Frank discovered amidst such emotional turmoil captures not only the essence of empowering love in the spiritual marriage, but also the power of such love to heal even the deepest of wounds, close the widest of chasms.

When Frank was gravitating toward the other woman during his affair, he was listening to his ego's voice as it told him, "you need this," "you don't have this," etc. When his wife confronted him with her true, unconditional love, its power broke through the ego voice in Frank's head.

It is the ego's voice that gives all negative emotions their strength, and convinces us to see these feelings as real, helpful, and even necessary. This is why we hold on to our hurts and grievances, and build numerous walls to keep ourselves away from a loving closeness to others, attempting to protect ourselves from future pain.

The answer to this ego paradox, and a practical, tangible method of disempowering it can be found in the power of thought. We are not consciously aware of so many of the thoughts that disturb our relationships, nor do we view them as the source of the problem. These exercises help us increase our consciousness and see the connection between what we think and what is transpiring to make us unhappy. Then, just as flowers grow beautifully when weeds no longer choke them out, once we get our disturbing thoughts out of the way, we find that our natural state is happiness.

If you can learn to monitor your thoughts, you can learn to recognize the ego voice and the thoughts it produces that distract you and put your relationship in turmoil. The following exercises can be used for any situation and any focus in one's life; we are giving specific attention here to the role of thoughts in our relationships.

PRACTICE 2:
The Thought-Monitoring Exercises

As you begin to practice these thought-monitoring exercises, you increasingly become the ruler of the kingdom of your mind, and will feel increasingly in charge of your relationships, for you will begin to have a more direct experience of your True Self. In addition, by being in charge of your thinking, you will not only heal all of your relationships, but also be relieved of depression and anxiety, take charge of your health and career, and control decisively whether you experience joy or pain in your life. Do not each of these affect our relationships in significant ways? The mind must be gradually and systematically brought under control, much like taming a wild horse, if you are to ever feel in charge of your life.

THOUGHT-MONITORING EXERCISE 1:
BECOMING AWARE

The purpose of this exercise is to become more conscious of your negative thoughts and to become an objective and nonjudging witness to them.

The exercise itself is very straightforward: Carry an index card around with you for a few days with an easily accessible pen or pencil. Observe all your thoughts carefully, particularly those about yourself, your partner, your parent or child, even your boss—or anyone you experience as disturbing you. Every time you become aware of a negative thought of any kind, whether a fear thought, judging thought, depressing or sad thought, a rejected thought, a scarcity thought, and even a resentful thought, simply take out your card, take a deep breath to focus and break into the cycle, and place a check mark on your card, saying to yourself silently or aloud: "*There* is one of *those* disturbing ego thoughts."

Don't judge the thought or yourself for thinking the thought. Instead, merely identify it, and place a check on the card.

If you are in a place where it is difficult to get out your card to place the check, such as driving your car or sitting in a meeting, just pause, take a deep breath, and picture yourself taking out the card and saying the phrase silently to yourself, "*There* is one of *those* disturbing ego thoughts." Then imagine yourself placing a check on your card.

Think of one who hurt you, rejected you, deprived you, yelled at you, criticized you, or toward whom you carry a resentment. Think of one toward whom you hold critical or judging thoughts of any kind. You shouldn't have much difficulty in identifying a person. It could be a spouse, a child, a parent, a friend, a boss, an employee, a clerk at the dry cleaners, or even a rude driver on the road.

Decide which relationship you would like to improve, without being at the effect of the other person. Decide whom you would like to have a positive effect upon and which relationship you want to heal or improve. In particular, look for any negative thoughts about any person or relationship. You can even focus on wanting to change those relationships that are hurtful.

Once again, as you identify any negative thought about that person, or about yourself in relation to that person:

Take a deep breath . . .

Say, "There is one of those disturbing ego thoughts about ______."

And place a check (✓) on your card.

Just the act of picking up the card, taking a breath, and placing a check mark begins to elevate you to the observer's position, separating you, the thinker, from the negative thought. The process of being the objective witness begins to significantly increase your awareness of your "enemy" thoughts. It breaks into the automatic pattern of negative thoughts that you are accustomed to thinking. Just being a conscious observer helps many people to think negative thoughts less frequently, very often resulting in a significant shift in your relationship. Don't be surprised if you find the number of check marks on your card decreasing with practice just because you have become the conscious nonjudging witness to your disturbing thoughts.

A Common Sabotage: The ego voice inside your mind will often protest: "But it's true!" The ego is trying, with all its might, to keep you believing in the erroneous thought and wants you to begin to doubt yourself. Do not be distracted by the voice: You do not have to debate whether or not the voice is speaking the truth. Simply label it an "enemy" thought that is trying to disturb you or your relationship.

THOUGHT-MONITORING EXERCISE 2:
IDENTIFYING THE THEMES

This exercise is designed to help you become aware of the various repetitive negative thought constellations you have in your mind, so that you will know which thoughts you are to look out for in your thought monitoring.

In preparation for this exercise, set aside a day (or two half days) for keeping a log of as many of your thoughts as you can. It does not matter whether it is a work day or a leisure day; it is important that it be a day in which you are most likely to succeed in getting down a lot of your thoughts. One day is quite sufficient if you remind yourself that 90–95 percent of your thoughts are constellations you repeat daily.

You will not be able to write down all the details of your thoughts since you think much faster than you can write. However, you can write down the gist of each thought. Also, if you find some thoughts repetitive, instead of writing them down each time, you may simply tabulate them by placing tab marks beside the thought each time it is repeated. At the end of the day, you can go through the log of your thoughts and begin to classify the various themes of your recurring thoughts.

Here are some examples of thoughts and their themes:

Thoughts about yourself

I'm no good.

I'm scared ______ will happen.

Negative thoughts about your bodily appearance.

Negative thoughts about your health.

Guilty thoughts.

Judgments about yourself.

Thoughts that you are powerless to change things in your life.

"Should" thoughts.

Thoughts about your life

Nothing ever works out.

Thoughts of hopelessness.

Despairing thoughts.

Thoughts about others (partners, children, parents, siblings, boss)

Resentful, disappointments, angry, rejecting, depriving, yearning from that person, critical or judging, victimized thoughts.

Thoughts about the past

Guilt, remorse, regret, If only I had, I should have, I could have.

Thoughts about the future

Fear, anxiety, idyllic yearnings, yearnings for people, yearning for things.

Once you've assembled your lists, ask yourself these questions:

—What is the ratio of positive thoughts to negative thoughts? Were you surprised by the frequency of your negative thoughts?

—What are the categories of negative thoughts, and which are the most frequent?

—Is there a tone in the voice of *your* thoughts that you recognize? Does it remind you of anyone in your life?

—What is the emotion you are aware of feeling when you have the thought?

—Who is the focus of your thoughts?

—How many of these negative thoughts are about you or about your partner?

—Are they about some other relationship?

—Do you notice any effects from these thoughts on your relationships—how you feel toward the other person, how that person relates to you, and how you perceive that person?

Finally, make a list of your categories of negative thoughts. Print or type the list so that it can be easily scanned. You are *not* to read and reread it carefully, for that would be rehearsing the negative thinking.

You can now use the list as a daily process to prepare yourself for the *Five-Step Thought-Monitoring Process* (below). Start the day by just glancing at the list and declare, "These are the disturbing ego thoughts that I will vigilantly monitor today." You could also add the suggestion, "I will be able to identify them quickly and easily and apply the thought-changing exercise successfully."

Setting your course for the day is much like setting your course on a sailboat. As the Chinese philosopher Lao-tzu once said, "If you continue in the same direction, you're likely to end up where you are headed." While this may be a warning that we might need to awaken and change directions, it is also a reminder that we can consciously set our course as well—and then are more likely to end up where we have chosen to head. Then, throughout the day, whenever you become aware that your inner peace is disturbed in any way, you are more likely to be able to identify the thought that was behind the perturbation.

THOUGHT-MONITORING EXERCISE 3:
THE FIVE-STEP THOUGHT-MONITORING PROCESS

NOTE: *Remember to Use All Five Steps!*

This Five-Step Process is the central and most important of the thought-monitoring exercises to help you take charge of your mind. It is an exercise that I regularly use myself, and one that I expect to use indefinitely—as long as I am here in a body. Not to use this or some other effective process vigilantly will allow the ego thinking of the mind to take over once again, taking us back into the hell of our disturbed relationships and suffering of all kinds.

Let's follow the situation of two of my clients, Andrea and Kevin. Andrea, a 45-year-old stay-at-home mom, often found herself disturbed by what she claimed was her husband's criticism of her. "Anything I did was not good enough. If I disciplined the kids, I wasn't strong enough. If I tried to help the kids with their homework, I was being too overbearing. If I made a suggestion about how he might feel better if he ate less junk food, I was being too intrusive. No matter what I did or said, Kevin always judged and criticized me."

But as Andrea began to monitor her own thoughts, she realized that most of the time, she was already judging herself—before her husband had even opened his mouth. She found that she was anticipating his criticism! She also learned that though she couldn't control his behavior, she could control her thoughts. And when she stopped thinking critical thoughts of herself (or projecting them onto Kevin), he became much less critical of her. She had begun the first step to accessing her power to give herself relief.

Step 1: When your inner peace is disturbed in any way, ask yourself:

"What was I just thinking?"

While a simple question, it is based on the profound understanding that the disturbance of your peace of mind began with your thoughts. This question can immediately take you out of any position of victimization and back to the full empowerment of your True Self. You become instantly aware that it is not the event, circumstance, or people and what they did or did not do that created the disturbance, but *what you are thinking about the event, circumstance, or people* and their behavior. If you already know the disturbing thought, then you have already done the first step.

Step 2: Once you have identified the disturbing thought, pause, exhale completely, and take a deep breath while saying to yourself:

"There *is one of* those *disturbing ego thoughts (or enemy thoughts)*. It only brings pain!"

Step 2 is a very important one—and it's important that you use the phrase: "*There* is one of *those*." The problem is that you can easily identify with the negative thought. Instead, now you are becoming an objective witness to your thoughts by externalizing them with the designations, "there" and "those."

Again, do not struggle with the thoughts or argue with them, and certainly do not judge them! That would be giving undue power to the thoughts. The goal is to be more like a biologist looking at bacteria through a microscope. You do not take your hand and mush it around in the bacteria. Instead, you observe it through the microscope.

Your goal in this step, therefore, is to make a distinction between you as the thinker and the thought you are thinking. You are not to identify with the thought, but rather, see the thought as something to observe, identify, and label by putting an enemy uniform on it, and then make decisions about what to do with the thought.

This is precisely what needs to be done with all your negative thoughts as well. By saying, "*There* is one of *those* enemy thoughts, just here to disturb my peace," you have extricated yourself from being enmeshed with the thought. Now, you the thinker begin to experience yourself as distinct from the thought.

Many failures at thought monitoring take place because this step is skipped over. When a person observes his or her thoughts, but still remains identified with them, the problem persists. Let's use Andrea and Kevin as an example. If Andrea simply says to herself, "Oh, here I am thinking all these critical thoughts about myself again" and doesn't identify the thoughts as enemy thoughts capable of disturbing her peace of mind, then she is now only observing what she is doing and therefore will continue to do it. It's likely she will feel even worse because she now sees herself harming herself, and continuing to do it! So, be sure to include Step 2!

Step 3: This step has two parts, equally important:

Part A: Each time you do the exercise, remind yourself of the truism: "*What I focus on will surely increase.*"

By doing so, you remind yourself of how the universe works. "It will increase internally as my personal reality; it will increase in the outside world, or most often in both ways." Even though this separation between the "in here" and "out there" does not really exist, I find it helpful to think of it both ways. This helps transcend any illusions of redeeming value in focusing on the disturbing thought. Instead, it just reminds you how the universe works—it's Natural Law.

Part B: After you remind yourself that the thought you are focusing on will surely increase, we then say "*Do I want this thing I am focusing on to increase? If I keep thinking about it, it surely will!*"

Such a pointed question usually prompts us to answer, "No way! I don't want this to increase!" You will then feel motivated sufficiently and inspired to take the next step. Remember, you do not even have to debate whether it is true or not, for often the ego voice may speak up when you attempt to dismiss the thought, saying, "But it's true!!!" Knowing that the thought is bringing you pain and that it will increase if you focus on it is enough.

This happened to Andrea. When she asked herself, "Do I want Kevin to be critical of me?", her ego screamed, "But it's true! He is critical of me!" But when she remembered that this step has nothing to do with whether the thought was true (i.e., whether or not Kevin was indeed critical of her), she could declare with strength, "No! I don't want this thought to increase!"

Such a step helps you to begin to accept the interactive component to minds. Andrea was not being acted upon by Kevin so much as she was cocreator *with* him. Later, Andrea began to see that her thoughts about her husband reflected a core negative belief that she carried that "she was always criticized." By catching this thought about Kevin and clearly declaring that she did not wish it to increase as her reality in any form, she had already begun to erode the belief as well.

On rare occasion, the ego will seem to reign for a while, making you want to hold on to the judgment or other negative thought, even though it brings pain. This is when the ego mind convinces us to "cut off our nose to spite the other's face." But if you just experience this desire without judging it, you will usually get tired of the pain rather quickly and be willing to go to Step 4.

Step 4: *Actively and willfully dismiss the thought with an executive order, using an action word.*

You might use one or more of the following words or phrases: "Stop!", "Cancel!", "I banish that thought!", "I choose to let that thought go." "I dismiss that thought!" One computer person I knew liked the word "delete." Someone else said she liked the word "exorcise" since her thoughts felt so demonic. It is only necessary that it be a phrase that is decisive and active! Don't get into a struggle with the thought. Andrea felt powerful as she said, "I banish that thought because I'm clear I don't want it to increase."

Step 5: *Fill the space where the negative thoughts were with an affirmation.*

It should be a positive thought or affirmation that is preplanned and readily accessible without having to scurry about trying to find an appropriate one in the middle of the exercise. Aristotle long ago observed that "nature abhors a vacuum," which means that if there is an empty space, something is inclined to rush into it. So, if we leave an empty space where the negative thought has been, especially until we become accustomed to a quiet mind and habitually are the witness to our thoughts, the negative thought could rush back in.

The affirming thought you use to fill the space can be anything you choose, but it should be something you believe and will not argue with in your mind. Andrea chose two phrases with this step. She said, "I want peace" and "At my core, I know Kevin wants peace." She made it a point to state them emphatically so that they would not just be empty rituals.

Other examples of affirmations some people have used are "I am love," "I only deserve love," "This person only wants love," or "At my very core I am Love." Or you can just focus on your breath going in and out, or a full concentration on the task at hand. Catholics could recite Hail Marys and Hindus could chant one of the names for God. Other spiritually minded people may use something like "God is Love and so am I," your favorite chant, or the words of an inspirational song. Nonreligious people may repeat the words "peace and calm" to themselves a few times.

It is most important that you have a prepared affirmation so that you do not have to go searching for it in the midst of trying to dismiss a troubling thought! You might take a moment to decide right now what your affirmation will be.

Once learned, the exercise will take only about 20 seconds to accomplish silently in your mind. The ego part of our minds will try anything to get us not to use a process that can bring much more joy into our lives, including saying, "It's too much work," "I can't learn all that," or, "it will take too much time and effort." Instead, *read the following summary quickly, and note how fast it can be done*:

1. Upon feeling a loss of inner peace, ask yourself, "What was I just thinking?"
2. "*There* is one of *those* disturbing ego thoughts."
3. "If I focus on this thought it will surely increase. Do I want this thing I'm thinking to increase? No way!"
4. "I banish that thought!"
5. Quickly state your affirmation one or several times.

Andrea found that for two or three days, she had to do the thought-monitoring exercise a number of times—often just a few minutes apart. But then, the critical, judging thoughts appeared less and less frequently. After a couple of weeks of diligent thought monitoring, they only appeared occasionally.

She found she had fewer and fewer incidents where she felt criticized by Kevin. And over the course of several weeks, as the thought monitoring eroded the belief (that she should be criticized) behind the thoughts, she actually stopped attracting any critical behavior from Kevin at all. The two of them had discovered a wonderful peace!

A VARIATION ON EXERCISE 3

After using the *Five-Step Thought-Monitoring Process* for a while, some people find it effective to use the following shortcut method:

Your brain is easily programmed to respond to a key word. Just as negative words or associative experiences may easily push our buttons, we may also use a consciously programmed connection for good. Pick a word you would like to use. It might be "peace," "free," "calm," "love," or even "God." It is any word to assign this authority to. Next, close your eyes and breathe a few times to focus your attention. Then instruct your unconscious mind to heal the disturbance anytime you say your word: ———.

So, when you have done steps 1 and/or 2—"What was I just thinking?" and "There is one of those disturbing ego thoughts"—just say your word. For many people this is sufficient. For others, you may need to practice the full five steps for a longer period of time before trying this alternate practice.

THE EBB AND FLOW OF THE PROCESS

Some people will try the thought-monitoring exercises and find they work for a while, but then they seem as if they stop working. Others may find that the exercises do not work from the beginning. If they were to look closely, they usually realize that they are leaving out one or two of the five steps instead of using all five each time. For example, they might not be becoming the distant witness by observing the thought, but remaining fully immersed in the thought, leaving out Step 2, "*There* is one of *those* ego thoughts." Or they are not reminding themselves that if they focus on the thought it will increase. Others may not give a full executive order to actively and decisively dismiss the thought. *Attention must be paid to all five steps of the process to ensure success.* You will understand the truth of this if you take the time to understand the significance of each of the seemingly simple steps.

Some may have trouble with the process because they judge themselves for having such negative thoughts. Only the observation of our thoughts without any judgment is useful, for only in such observations are we free to make decisions to think otherwise. When we judge ourselves and our thoughts, then we become immersed in the bad feelings that result from the judgment and we cannot make healthier conscious choices about the thoughts we entertain.

For example, my client John had constantly experienced his bosses as exercising control over him, much the way his father had when he was a child in Ohio. Two different partnerships in Chicago were ended in order to get away from controlling people. On the other hand, he tried desperately to control his wife, frequently threatening divorce in an attempt to gain control over her. He lived a life of control or be controlled. He entertained thoughts of fear, anger, retaliation, revenge, and guilt. Gradually he developed an array of physical symptoms, including overall muscle fatigue, irritable bowel syndrome, and severe anxiety and a debilitating depression.

Now John's physician in New York City prescribed an antidepressant and referred him for therapy with me where, rather quickly, he became aware of the central influence and creative capacity of his thoughts.

As John began to hear my observations on his thoughts, he began to observe some of his own thought patterns, and then began to use thought-monitoring exercises vigilantly. First, he became aware of the abundance of fear thoughts he entertained about his body and its health—Was he going to develop colon cancer? Was he going to die?

Next, John became conscious of his critical thoughts about his wife: She was so impulsive and irresponsible! All she wanted to do was spend his money! Didn't she have any regard for how hard he worked? Didn't she care about him?

Once he went through these thoughts about his wife, he began to see that his wife's spontaneous energy, her get-up-and-go attitude was something he had always admired. He was always the one who had been afraid of being impulsive, overcompensating by planning every detail of his day, week, month, and year!

Once he was able to see how his frustration with his wife was really about his own fears, he began to notice at work his fear thoughts about his partner. All of his fears began to unravel as he observed that his partner was not *really* a threat; John just *thought* she was a threat.

At first motivated by his desire to get off his medication quickly, John began to monitor his fear thoughts and resentful thoughts diligently, releasing them and replacing them with positive, affirming thoughts. He saw again and again how he was the creator of much of his anxiety and worry. He realized that his wife was not irresponsible and careless; it was he who was afraid of being that way himself. As he shifted the responsibility from her to himself, he also began to see her differently: She was so magnetic! He admired her energy, enthusiasm, and zest for life!

John was desperate to know that these positive changes in how he began to feel were not from the medication; he needed to feel the power within—not feel that something outside him was controlling his life once again. So he weaned himself from the medication as he continued to do the five-step thought monitoring several times a day. And not only did John's need to be in the "control or be controlled" system fade away, but also his anxiety, depression, and physical symptoms as well.

Every change in thought produces a change in the body chemistry, and the neuropeptides, those chemical messengers, scurry through the body at lightning speed to communicate the change. Every change in thought, therefore, changed the serotonin imbalance that had created the depression; the body chemistry righted itself with right thinking. The quality of his marriage and his work relationships began to change impressively since his wife and coworkers ceased feeling criticized and judged by him. Essentially, the more he began to be in control of his thoughts, the more he felt genuinely in control of his life and his relationships, and his fears became tiny specks on his internal horizon, rather than looming dark clouds blocking his vision.

However, John's progress, like most people's, was not a consistent and direct path. He would have intermittent times of forgetting to monitor his thoughts, and his anxiety and depression would return immediately. Such experiences, however, actually helped him to integrate the truth of the importance of his thoughts, for in seeing the shift back into the negativity and suffering coming so easily with a change of thought, he also saw that the movement out of suffering was just as rapid with a change of thought! He learned that it was he who made the choice moment by moment! With diligent practice, he increasingly became the master of his mind and therefore of his body, his relationships, and his life.

Be creative in stopping your destructive thoughts, for these exercises are not the only effective ones. One day when I was taking my exercise walk, I became aware of thinking critical and judging thoughts about someone that were disturbing my peace. My attempts to use the Five-Step Process were not working as they usually do. I opened myself to inner guidance about what to do, and a funny little rhyme came to me that I chanted in rhythm as I walked:

If I focus on this crap,
I will certainly adapt,
So I'll let my judgments go,
Let my stinking thinking go!

As I continued to chant in rhythm with my steps for the next five minutes, I found that my whole mood changed. I realized that if I focused on the crap I would begin to adapt to that as a way of viewing myself in the world, as one who can only have crap. I would see myself as a victim. That was the incentive to "let my stinking thinking go." Then, once the negative was cleaned, I chanted the opposite:

If I focus on the love,
I'll rise up to heights above,
So I'll let my fear thoughts go,
Let my stinking thinking go!

By doing this, I recognized that in my transcendence, I find joy and peace. So if there is ever a time the Five-Step Thought-Monitoring Process does not work for you, use my chant or be creative and come up with your own. One client told me that she sternly commands the ego voice: "Shut up!" And she says it works for her!

WHEN YOU HAVE DIFFICULTY IDENTIFYING OR ACCEPTING YOUR "ENEMY" THOUGHTS

Some people may find that they are only occasionally aware of their enemy thoughts, and may wonder how to identify them, as in Step 1. Your emotions and physical sensations are an excellent resource. When you feel your inner peace and joy disturbed in any way by anything, use that feeling or body symptom like a red flag popping up and signaling you to attend to it. Are you clenching your jaw? Do you feel a tightness in your belly? Indigestion? Do you feel overly anxious or worried? Do you feel particularly lonely or unloved? Use these feelings as a signal, to pause, take a deep breath, and ask yourself the question: "What was I just thinking that would cause me to feel (anxious, worried, hurt, rejected, afraid, angry, etc.)?"

Our feelings can often block our view of the thoughts that take place just below the level of consciousness, and we need to scratch below the surface to expose them. A great majority of the time this process will work, for when we are sincerely interested in knowing our thoughts, most often they will emerge into awareness.

By starting with the thoughts you are aware of, and adding to them the ones you identify by using your disturbed feelings as a flag, you begin to become increasingly conscious of more and more thoughts. Remember to be patient with yourself. If you have not monitored your thoughts before, then you will not likely be an instant expert—unless you are feeling desperate for a better way. But with diligent practice your ability will increase quickly. Each time you do it is a success. Practice increases the frequency of success.

When we commit to, or have some success in identifying the enemy thoughts of the ego mind, and begin consciously to change them, thereby feeling more loving and empowered in our relationships, the ego voice may try even harder to dominate our minds with enemy thoughts, or make us start feeling it requires too much effort to keep such awareness of our thoughts. The ego mind never tells us, however, that if we do *not* monitor and change our negative thoughts, we will be even more exhausted and miserable in our relationships. The peace the ego voice offers by tempting us to give up the effort to be conscious is actually the opposite, for the result is suffering instead.

The ego's first line of defense is to introduce blame and guilt: it wants us to project our feelings and thoughts onto someone else instead of taking responsibility for them ourselves. It is an enormous threat to the ego way of thinking to acknowledge that we have created our moods, our disturbed relationships, our failures, or our symptoms—therefore someone is to be blamed! So, according to the ego's system, if we are experiencing problems in our relationships, it's the other person's fault. We are simply the victims. Instead of viewing our new awareness of what we have created as an opportunity to own our internal god power, the ego mind sees such awareness as an opportunity to blame ourselves. Instead of seeing that we can now consciously use the source of power that created our suffering to create peace and joy, the ego would have us blame ourselves instead. But since this self-blame feels unbearable, we will then project the guilt and blame on the other person. But once again the ego presents only part of the picture for it does not tell us that by blaming our pain on others we are also throwing away our own power to be happy in our lives and relationships. Essentially, the ego mind's solution promises safety, but pushes us into a state of victimization.

However, if we allow ourselves to be victims, blaming others for our pain and suffering, we are simply letting the ego voice derail us in our journey to the True Self and the spiritual or happy relationship. By seeing our own role in how we feel—whatever the emotion or thought—without any blame or guilt, we keep our connection to our True Self intact. Only the observation of our thoughts without judgment is useful, for only in such observations are we free to make decisions to think otherwise. When we judge ourselves and our thoughts, or when we judge others, then we are distracted into the bad feelings resulting from the judgment. As part of the vicious cycle, it becomes more difficult to make healthier conscious choices about the thoughts we have been dwelling upon.

Consider the example of Cynthia and Robert, who came to see to me for couples' therapy because they lived "in total misery" together. Robert told me that Cynthia was someone whom everyone hated, including himself. She was passive aggressive, constantly undermining him. He was staying with her only for their children's sake. Cynthia, however, told me it was Robert who was the evil person in their marriage; she described him as verbally attacking her and calling her horrible names in front of their children and friends—with little or no provocation. They both believed that it was the other person who was creating the unhappiness in their marriage.

I counseled them, however, to temporarily forget about the other person and solely concentrate on changing their individual perceptions of their own responsibilities in the marriage. Cynthia immediately accepted the premise that she had the power to change their relationship. She accepted both the belief in her inherent connection to the divine interconnectedness of the universe, as well as the belief in the power of thought to change her experience. As a result, she soon began responding to Robert's criticisms with kindness instead of defensiveness, anger, or hurt feelings. And immediately she saw a change in his behavior: He attacked her less often and with less intensity, and they both seemed to back off, letting peace enter their relationship where before there was only tension and fighting. When I asked Robert what he was experiencing, he told me his wife had become less threatening to him, and as a result, he felt safer in the relationship.

But soon Cynthia began to complain, wondering, "Why should I have to do all the work? Why can't he do some of it as well? I shouldn't have to put up with any of his bad behavior." *With that thought*, she reverted back to being a victim; her ego mind began trying to convince her that the problems in the relationship were Robert's fault. As a result, she ceased practicing kindness toward him, and the relationship quickly spiraled out of control, plunging them into hell again. As a couple they regressed to their former state in which Cynthia would question, doubt, and undermine Robert's every action and word, and Robert would lash out at Cynthia in violent verbal assaults.

After a couple of weeks, however, Cynthia had an insight. Having briefly experienced a somewhat more peaceful relationship and remembering how it had come about when she took responsibility for her behavior, Cynthia stopped listening to her familiar victim voice telling her that she was being treated unfairly, and once again returned to more useful thoughts. She realized that even though she could make the choice to leave, she would not do so yet. She would experiment once again with her own power to make a difference, both for her own centeredness and to see if it would also bring healing to Robert. She now saw that it was her own fear that prompted her unloving ways, and that fear was also probably behind Robert's actions and behavior as well. The more Cynthia learned to be compassionate toward herself, focusing on compassionate, loving thoughts, the more she was able to extend these same thoughts to Robert.

The situation once again quickly stabilized with Robert. Cynthia was then able to see how she had created both her own happiness and unhappiness merely by changing her thoughts. Cynthia realized she actually preferred to be in control of her life and not at the mercy of outward circumstances—such as her husband's punishing behavior, and that they both benefited from her changed attitude.

It happened to take some more time before Robert's fears healed enough for him to be willing to risk extending loving kindness toward Cynthia as well, but when he did, his own healing began.

Taking responsibility for our own thoughts is the central means by which we can affect anyone else. When we heal ourselves, we are no longer adding gasoline to the fire, and we create around us an atmosphere through which others can contact their own potentials of healing. The more we become conscious of our thought patterns, the more we are able to see that we, through our thoughts, are the doer and cocreator.

We can then see that often we are the creators of our own anxiety, our own fear, our depression. We are also the creators of our own joy, peace, and happiness. We also see that we are always cocreators of our relationships—whether they are happy or disturbed.

When you learn to monitor your thoughts you will begin to see that your relationship has not just happened *to* you, making you feel like a victim, although it may appear that way on the surface. By putting enemy uniforms on the ego thoughts that disturb you, you learn to recognize the source of your suffering—especially in your relationships—and then no longer entertain them in your mind, letting them interfere with the natural flow of love and peace emanating from your True Self. As you've seen above with Cynthia and Robert, when you are not conscious of the thought constellations that have produced your emotional, interpersonal, or physical expressions of pain, you will tend to experience the pain as happening to you from an external cause.

When you begin to take responsibility for your thoughts and therefore begin to feel differently in the world, you may feel some resistance—this is natural—it's the ego at work again! Be aware of what you're feeling, and don't chastise yourself or be critical or judgmental. And if you feel guilty for the happiness you have created, know that your guilt is more an indication of your need to do further thought monitoring—particularly your guilty thoughts. It's not an indication that something is wrong.

In his profound classic little booklet *As a Man Thinketh*, James Allen notes with simplicity:

> *Suffering is always the effect of wrong thoughts in some direction. It is an indication that the individual is out of harmony with himself, with the law of his being. The circumstances which a man encounters with suffering are the result of his own mental inharmony. Man has but to right himself to find the universe is righted. Let a man radically alter his thoughts and he will be astonished at the rapid transformation it will effect on the material conditions of his life.*

Owning your creative potential may just feel unfamiliar until you grow more used to it. So don't throw out the baby with the bath water—what a terrible waste of life and love that would be! The more you become conscious of your thought patterns, the more you are able to see that you are the doer and creator of your reality and your relationship.

When you experience the happiness, which comes from monitoring your thoughts, you will have increasing difficulty in tolerating your customary suffering. This immediate experience of relief and tangible happiness becomes a powerful motivator to return to thought monitoring on a regular basis.

Again, if your goal is to create a spiritual or happy relationship, then you must make a conscious decision to act and think from your True Self, again and again and again. The thought-monitoring exercises are clear and simple ways to help you make this decision on a daily basis, or even moment by moment.

As your mind is healed, the result radiates and spreads to the people around you, even those you do not see or know. You will see a difference in your children, your mate, or your coworkers when you shift from focusing on what is wrong with them, to thoughts of loving acceptance. By consciously observing and practicing focusing your mind, you will rediscover the magnificence of who and what you are at the core and connect to the divine spirit within yourself and your partner, which of course, connects you to All That Is.

In the next chapter, we will look at another way to break into the vicious cycle. Practice 3, Making a Perceptual Shift, and Practice 4, Seeing Others As Mirrors, allow us to literally change the dynamic of a relationship in the moment of interaction, giving us a powerful, tangible experience of the True Self and its capacity for Empowering Love.

CHAPTER 5

Choosing Love, Not Fear

Making the Perceptual Shift
Seeing Others As Mirrors

"We do not see things as they are,
we see things as we are."
—The Talmud

A SIMPLE SHIFT, A PROFOUND RESULT

At an elementary school in Harlem, where 80 percent of the students live in poverty, Stephanie, a ten-year-old student the size of a fourteen-year-old, was in the principal's office. This happened at least once daily because of her disruptive or violent behavior in class and in the hallways. She would kick or bite a teacher, and even throw desks across the classroom. Her disruptive and violent behavior was so unpredictable that she could never be taken on field trips. However, after her teacher participated in a ground-breaking program to reduce violence in students, four short months later Stephanie took her first field trip with her class, going to Carnegie Hall for a concert. She behaved beautifully, and she and the others had a wonderful time together. It soon became increasingly rare that she had to be sent to the principal's office anymore for any disciplinary measures. Her violent behavior was fast becoming a thing of the past.

How did Stephanie experience such a rapid, life-altering change in her behavior? As part of the violence-reduction program called the

Perceptual Shift Empowerment Program, which I designed, Stephanie's teachers, guidance counselor, principal, and even the office secretary who interfaced with Stephanie every day, participated in four learning modules. The one relevant here is that instead of focusing on the student who was prone to act out violently, making them angry, frustrated, and needing to control her, they shifted their perceptions to focus on the frightened little child inside her ten-year-old body. Once the adults were able to look beyond Stephanie's behavior and focus on the fear that resided just below her surface turmoil, they were able to respond to her with loving kindness instead of anger and disapproval. By seeing her fear, the adult helpers were able to let go of their own fears in dealing with such a difficult child. For the teachers' group, seeing Stephanie differently allowed them to create different feelings, which in turn brought different ways of behaving toward her, which in turn cumulatively began to heal Stephanie's fears of further hurts from adults. As the teachers' false perceptions were healed, Stephanie healed, and as a result the whole class began to heal.

After participating in the twenty-week program, many teachers at this New York public school experienced similar dramatic results with their recalcitrant students by learning to make a "perceptual shift." Students who were formerly viewed as incapable of learning were now seen as extremely capable, which made a noticeable difference in the way teachers worked with them. Students with violent behavior problems or administrators whose behavior was seen as noncaring, were now viewed as frightened and appealing for help and for love.

The teachers stopped yelling and using physical force to try and control the children, and changed their perception of and thoughts about the kids—from viewing them as needing control and judgment to needing their love and help. They also used diaphragmatic breathing exercises, which I will discuss later, and consciously released any negative thoughts about each child, doing careful thought monitoring. As a result, potentially destructive violent behaviors were nipped in the bud, children learned much more satisfactory ways of behaving, and teachers began to feel more confident in handling such situations, enjoying their work instead of dreading each school day. Everyone involved became much, much happier.

If Stephanie's entire world could change because of how her teachers and counselor perceived her, then why is perception such a powerful force? How is it that our perceptions of others and situations have such an influence on our experience of them?

These questions are at the heart of this chapter. Essentially, our perceptions stem directly from our thought constellations and the erroneous voice of the ego. A perceptual shift is the act of choosing to see someone or a situation differently. In the case of the violence-prevention program at Stephanie's school, it was the entire group of teachers, counselors, administrators, and to some extent the parents of the children, who participated in a perceptual shift. And as you see, the outcome was quite amazing; some may even call it miraculous! But it's clear that above all, the transformation for Stephanie and other students like her was real, tangible, and palpable, and affected every aspect of their lives.

In this chapter, you will learn another way to break into the Vicious Cycle of Interaction, enabling you not only to disempower the ego, but also giving you another tool to heal your relationships. By making a perceptual shift in the moment of interaction, you literally change the dynamic of your relationship in the moment of the experience—in an instant you can feel the very nature of your relationship changing, becoming filled with love and joy and peace! You will also learn a smaller exercise in which you learn how to stop projecting your erroneous ego thoughts and further assume responsibility for your relationship. By learning how to use others as mirrors, you are able to control your part of a relationship more strongly.

But before we go into these powerful practices for healing your relationships and yourself, I want to spend a little more time showing you how and why perceptions are so powerful to begin with.

OUR IMPERFECT PERCEPTION

The quotation from the Talmud that opens this chapter presents the ancient wisdom that perception is not a viewing of an objective external reality, but a projection of what is inside of us. Similarly, *A Course in Miracles* more recently states the same truth succinctly and tersely: "Projection makes perception." Quite simply, this means that the thoughts and beliefs inside of us are projected outward, coloring our perception of the outside world, its events, and our relationships in it.

How we perceive things does more to determine our personal reality and our experience of it than anything else. It is not what another person says or does, nor the events of life that make us happy or unhappy, but rather what we *think* about that person's behavior or those events. Just imagine: If the same event universally brought happiness, one could have a most successful industry of packaging and marketing it! Yet we know that when many people go through the same experience, each one's interpretive perception is often quite different.

For example, two children raised in the same family can grow up with very different perceptions of their family life. One takes the mother's guidance and nurturance as helpful and loving, thereby becoming open to learning from adults and authority figures. The second child takes her mother's guidance as intrusiveness, thereby growing up to resent and question authority.

As we've seen, the new physics also supports this notion by showing that there is no such thing as an objective reality that is separate and apart from us. The minute we have observed something, the physicists tell us, we have interacted with it and therefore influenced it. And there is no place where this interaction with what we perceive as outside of us is more true than in our relationships.

As a result, we do not—cannot—see other people in our lives with absolute objectivity. Nor do they have a reality apart from us, since we are constantly affecting our reality by what we believe, think, feel, say, and do. Each aspect of our inner world tints the glasses through which we look at the people in our lives. Let me give you an example.

Liz, a graduate student, had had an hurtful encounter with another woman, Sherri, in her class. Liz felt that Sherri had been unfriendly toward her. After class, Liz began to ask herself obsessively, "What is wrong with me that Sherri doesn't like me?" A few hours later, however, after much inner suffering, Liz overheard two classmates talking about how Sherri is bearing up so well given that her youthful husband had a premature heart attack and almost died. Sherri is in the midst of trying to keep up with school and take care of her three children while dealing with her fear.

With this information, Liz had compassion for Sherri instead of feeling rejected and rejectable. When she shifted her interpretive perception of Sherri, her reality was now quite different. Nothing in the world had changed, particularly Sherri; only Liz's interpretive perception changed, but that made an entirely different personal reality for her. While Liz had the good fortune to hear some facts about Sherri, which changed her perspective, we shall see that it is possible for us to do even if we are not presented with personal details or inside information.

Let us look at other patterns we may observe with our children. Sara, for example, was disturbed that her daughter was talking back to her with anger and disrespect a great deal of the time. "It makes me not even want to be around her," she complained to me. However, upon looking closer, we discovered that Sara had been routinely talking angrily, disrespectfully, and even contemptuously to her eight-year-old daughter—even in trying to stop her daughter's disrespectful behaviors. Her daughter could best be viewed not as a separate objective reality, but as a projection of Sarah's insides and behavior. Instead of seeing her own negative thoughts and feelings, Sara projected them onto her daughter.

Likewise, qualities in others that upset us, particularly in a spouse, are usually our own issues as well—and sometimes not even the other person's issues at all. Take Dana, for example, who came to therapy because she felt critical and angry with her husband much of the time. Upon reflection, she discovered that she was also very critical and angry with herself much of the time. And she further noted that her husband was not typically a critical or angry person, and that he continually reassured her that he was not feeling critical or angry with her.

She began to see that her critical and angry behaviors toward him simply reflected her own internal state.

Dana learned that she cannot change the world, but that she can change the world *she sees* by changing herself. Perception is then a vehicle for projection of who we *think* we are. And since most of us tend to live in the ego state of mind, these perceptions are necessarily imperfect, reflecting our confused sense of self, our counterfeit self. However, and as you will soon see, we can use the power of perception as a vehicle to transcend the ego and reconnect with our True Self, which is the way in which we can truly heal our relationships. But first we need to wrestle with the ignoble ego when it tries to convince us to hold on to our perception of the world in order to convince us to believe in the illusion that we are powerless, separate, and unloved. Again, the ego's perception of the world keeps us away from one another and from our divinity within. And when these negative thoughts are in place, there is no way our relationships can sustain happiness. Instead, they become precarious, triggering the need for love outside of ourselves, which in turn starts the cycle of judgment, blame, and guilt, dooming the relationship to failure.

Our task, then, in our world of illusion, is to consciously convert perception into a way of seeing through the eyes of the True Self, a form of spiritual alchemy. Once we live in the True Self, we no longer have a need to question our perception or experience of people or our environment. But until then, we need to remain vigilant to the ploys of the ego as it tries to shade our view of the truth.

Perception, in the world of the ego, is necessarily determined by each individual. It is common knowledge, especially in our courts, that multiple people viewing an accident or a crime report very different perceptions. One experiment was done in a classroom, where a robbery was staged. A man ran into the room, grabbed the teacher's purse off of her desk, and ran out of the room. Later, when the children were then asked to identify the robber, perceptions ranged from tall to short, from nicely dressed to disheveled, from caucasian to black, from male to female. The children saw whatever they were prone to see given their individual beliefs and subjective realities at the moment.

Most of us have had the experience of looking at the world through depressed eyes. Everything looks bleak, helpless, and hopeless, and misery prevails. On the other hand, with nothing outside having changed, if we view the world through happy eyes, begin to have a happy memory or entertain a loving thought, then everything becomes bright and hopeful. The only change has been the thoughts in our minds, yet our whole world is now different. A shift in perception can be this simple!

CHOOSING LOVE INSTEAD OF FEAR

If it is our interpretive perceptions that bring our pain and suffering, then how can we change them to move from an unempowered position, in which we feel like a victim at the mercy of the people in our lives, to an empowered and happy one, in which we take responsibility for our thoughts and behaviors, and choose to extend love? How do we accomplish this task without having to wait for another person or the world to change? Remember: *We are never seeing a separate objective reality when we look at another person.* Contemplate the fact that your perceptions are just as controllable as your thoughts and beliefs. What does this mean in terms of healing the problems in your relationships? As you know, a perceptual shift is the act of choosing to see someone or a situation differently. It is seeing through the surface personas presented to us that appear to be attacking, rejecting, or depriving. It is looking with X-ray vision to see that the undesirable surface behavior is only a manifestation of mistaken identity at the ego or counterfeit-self level. Since perception always includes interpretation, usually a judgment of some kind, then perception is not just a sensory experience, but includes thoughts as well and can therefore be changed.

Like the practice of monitoring your thoughts, making a perceptual shift requires that you take "response-ability" for your thoughts, feelings, behaviors—and the characteristics of your relationship. It's up to you to make this choice moment by moment. And essentially, making a perceptual shift enables you—in an instant—to choose love instead of fear.

In order to make a perceptual shift in the moment of interaction, you need to think of all emotions as being distilled down to two basic ones: **love** and **fear**. All the positive emotions, such as joy, happiness, delight, and affection, all grow out of love. Negative emotions, such as anger, jealousy, guilt, envy, hurt, and rage, all grow out of fear. In fact, the more intense or pervasive the negative emotion, the greater the fear that gives rise to it, no matter how bizarre, difficult, obnoxious, or vicious the person might be. In fact, the more obnoxious or vicious they are, the greater the fear that gives rise to it. You will commonly find such irrational and excessive outbursts in the borderline personality, who lacks confidence in his or her ways of coping. The extreme manifestation of such fear is in the paranoid schizophrenic or in the paranoid character.

Fear, being of the ego, is the world of illusion, but we experience it as if it were true every time we feel afraid. We are not always conscious of being afraid. In fact, an angry person will often deny fear, rather than seeing that his anger is just a defense against fear, and fear is then a defense against love. But if we are able to look with X-ray vision, see past the surface behavior of the other person (or ourselves), and see the fear that lies behind it, an important step has already been taken away from victimization. Remember the students and teachers from Harlem? The fact that Stephanie's behavior changed was a result of her teachers' and counselors' deciding to change their perception of her, choosing to extend love, not fear. Here is how it works.

PRACTICE 3:

Making the Perceptual Shift

EXERCISE

In the moment of interaction, when a person is behaving toward us in a way we do not like, we can simply ask ourselves, "Is it love coming from this person?" If not, there is only one other conclusion that is possible: This person is afraid and appealing for love. Instead of viewing this person as an ogre, see them as a scared little boy or girl hiding behind a paper tiger and who desperately wants love. In fact, the more ferocious-sounding the tiger, the greater the fear and desperation for love.

I find the simplicity of only two emotions especially useful in moments of intense interaction, especially when there is not enough time to recall or get to know a painful history that might give rise to the other person's behavior. The same X-ray vision applies to everyone in every situation: *without exception, whatever is not love is fear, and is an appeal for love and for help.*

The perceptual shift we need to make is quite simple, though very profound. When we see fear instead of attack, we are no longer afraid, and we are able to tap into our inherent capacity to love or be loving. If we do not perceive attack, we don't have to mount our defenses. We know that the displaced anger was just an expression of fear, and there is no reason to get caught up in it. We will know that when someone behaves in such bizarre ways, it only means that they do not know more effective ways of getting past their fear.

For example, Sam got up one morning to get ready for work. When he entered the bathroom to shower, he found that his wife, Karen, had left her makeup strewn all over the sink in which he would shave. Then, when he went to the kitchen for breakfast, he found the counter, stove, and sink covered with last night's dishes, pots, and pans. With this scene before him, he exploded into a tirade about how messy Karen is, how the one night he is not home to wash the dinner dishes, she can't do it! "I can't stand this chaos one more minute!" he shouted at her.

Karen, who had been reading the paper at the breakfast table, didn't say anything. Sam's complaints about her being messy were nothing new. But instead of reacting defensively or going on the counterattack about how controlling Sam was, she just listened to his tirade and focused on the fear in her husband: She remembered that Sam was particularly sensitive to anything that seemed remotely like chaos because the home in which he grew up was always total mayhem.

Karen was able to listen to his anger, knowing it came from fear, and gave him reassurance that she would take care of her mess. By making the perceptual shift right in the moment of their interaction, she did not feel attacked, and Sam's fears were assuaged not reinforced, giving him room to feel Karen's love.

If we enter into a defensive or counterattacking mode, even though the ego voice tells us this is the way we'll be safe, we are actually empowering the perceived attacker, increasing his fear and intensifying his defensive structure, and at the same time we are taking away empowerment from ourselves. We make ourselves unhappy, take away our peace of mind, weaken and injure our bodies, and exacerbate rather than heal the problem. It is often hard to remember that the choice is ours to make. Yet the choice we have moment by moment is between victimization or empowerment; pain or joy; hell or heaven; illusion or truth; the ego or our True Self.

The ego, the prince of fear, which always constructs defenses against what it perceives as threatening, will balk at this approach. It will scream: "But you will be destroyed! Danger! Get those defenses ready. Attack back or flee as fast as you can! And above all else, save face! You're a weakling and pushover if you don't defend or counterattack." To listen to *this* inner voice is the real danger, however. The ego never ever tells the truth about what will make us safe! Its solutions or defenses always bring more fear, danger, or attack. In fact, as noted earlier, it usually brings more of the very thing it promises to protect us from! Perhaps before agreeing or disagreeing with this statement, consciously empty your cup of preconceptions and beliefs, and take time to reflect on your own experiences to see whether this is true.

What we have, then, especially valuable in moments of crises, is a world filled with only two categories of people—(1) those who are able to extend love or (2) those appealing for love out of fear. All of us vacillate between the two categories. Both, however, provide us with opportunities to get in touch instantly with empowering love. When we are in a state of loving, we are manifesting our True Self essence, which is love, our divine nature. When someone is extending love, we can be in touch with love just by opening our hearts to receiving it. Perhaps even more important, if the other person is appealing for love out of his or her fear, you can also get in touch with love by extending love yourself to the person who is crying out for it. The fringe benefit is that it also ensures your happiness. You can never be bereft of love, for it is always there to give simply by deciding to do so, much like deciding to turn on a faucet connected to an eternal spring.

In this sense, *love is more a conscious decision than it is an emotion.* To get in touch with love is to be in touch with your True Self, for Love is what you are at your very core.

THE EFFECTS OF SHIFTING YOUR PERCEPTION

Tim and Carly were in a bad place in their marriage. After twenty years, Tim was deciding to leave his powerful job at a telecommunications corporation to do something that wasn't so spiritually, physically, and emotionally draining. The big bucks he had been earning were no longer enticement enough to make him stay. But every time he approached his boss to tell him of his decision, his boss begged Tim to stay, saying he was an invaluable asset to the company, and he owed it to the shareholders. So month after month, Tim put off leaving, despite feeling miserable.

Meanwhile at home, his relationship with his wife was suffering. They had recently begun redecorating a family room in their home, with Carly pretty much in charge of the project. When Tim came home one night, Carly explained how the contractor had at first refused to install a skylight in the new family room, saying that the arc of the ceiling and walls wouldn't allow for it. Carly insisted the skylight could be installed with a minor adjustment to the wall.

As Carly relayed this story to Tim, being somewhat proud of her accomplishment in successfully installing the skylight, Tim barked at her, "You're just unbearable!"

The insult cut straight through Carly, hurting her to the core. But instead of launching one of her attacks or defending herself, she took a deep breath and tried to focus on how frightened she knew Tim to be. By reminding herself of how dismayed Tim was feeling about himself for not having yet left his job after he had resolved to do so, she was able to stop herself from reacting. This was not easy, but it gave her a chance later on to have a peaceful discussion with Tim about his outburst. And Tim apologized.

The other person does not have to admit the fear or the appeal for love for this to be true. In fact, it is best if we don't try to convince other persons to see themselves this way unless he or she has asked us for help. It is also not your place to accuse him of fear and wanting love, for that would be another disguised attack or defense of your own arrogant little ego, taking the form of a judgment. In fact, such a response on your part is apt to be experienced as not loving, and would therefore create even more of a threat to the other person, causing more defensiveness rather than healing. You would be bringing in discord rather than peace, for yourself and the other person. Instead, you need to give top priority to making your own shift in perception, rather than informing the other person of his error.

If you can recognize the appeal for love for what it is, how can you deny that to anyone in need? And especially, how can you deny love to someone you profess to love? And how can you withhold love, when giving it is just as much, or even more, a gift to yourself to be stronger, happier, and at peace?

When you recognize fear accurately as an appeal for love, rather than being deceived by the surface appearance, your are empowering yourself to change the very nature of your relationship—in an instant.

WHAT HAPPENS IF YOU DO MAKE THE PERCEPTUAL SHIFT? (FIGURE 4)

A typical progression might be:

1. An early realization is that it might be possible to see something or someone in a different way.

2. Next, you might become aware of multiple possibilities of seeing, out of which you might begin to see yourself as the creator of your interpretive perceptions.

3. Then you may begin to choose consciously a different way of looking at a situation or person, finding the powerful result to be rewarding. Because you truly want peace and are tired of the painful advice the ego or false self offers,
4. you might even feel a strong determination to look at the situation or person differently.
5. You now begin to see with increasing clarity that you make up your own personal realities, and that you are not a victim living simply at the mercy of others the way you had previously thought or acted.

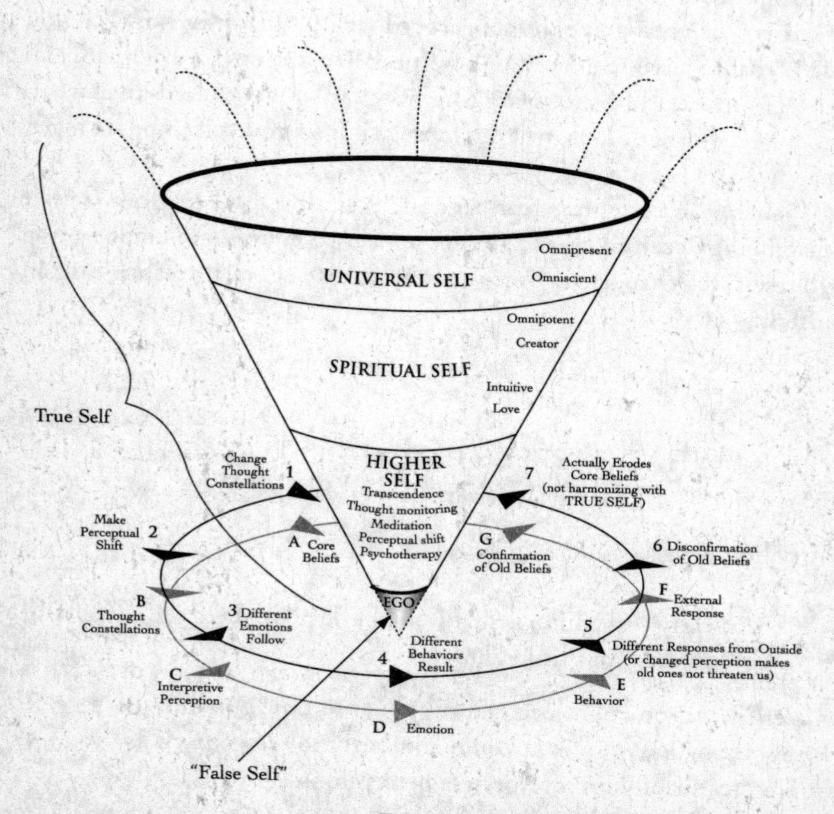

FIGURE 4: The Process of Awakening Self

If you can make a shift out of the old system at the thought constellation level (B) and/or by making a perceptual shift (2), you move into a new circle, which begins to create a different reality for you. If, for example, you no longer perceive attack, but instead allow a new perception, such as seeing the other person as being afraid, then you are no longer threatened. If you are no longer threatened, then your emotion (3) instead of being fear or anger is likely to be compassion. Your compassion will not likely result in fight or flight as before, but rather in some desire to reach out caringly in a different behavior (4). This caring behavior is less likely to invite a retaliation or defensiveness of some kind, so you may get a different response (5), which then is no longer a confirmation of your old belief, but rather, *disconfirms* it (6), therefore beginning to erase the original belief system. With the perceptual shift, you have an additional way to erase negative core beliefs.

If you make the perceptual shift, just as in changing your thoughts, you move into a higher self transcendence (note the bold upper circle running through the Transcendent part of the True Self, instead of staying at the ego level) and instantly move out of the Vicious Cycle of Interaction to start a new cycle, in which you are completely empowered and responsible for your thoughts and actions. If you do not perceive someone as attacking or rejecting you, but instead, just appealing for help and healing, how can you feel threatened? Instead, you are more likely to feel compassion, caring, and love. With such emotions, your behaviors will certainly be quite different, for instead of fight or flight, defensiveness or shutting down, you are more likely to reach out in some kind of caring fashion, whether in your thoughts, with your words, or with an overt action.

By being conscious of your perceptions, along with your thought constellations, you begin to realize that you indeed are a creator of the world you see. In this way, you may use your perception to see things differently and as a means of rising out of the ego's world of illusion and entering the real world of the True Self—the foundation for a happy relationship. In turn, you are then freed of your suffering and enabled to live in harmony with all the people in your life, especially your mate or partner. And isn't that the goal of your spiritual marriage?

To live in a harmony that is unshakeable, creating an abiding love that you can always trust?

TROUBLESHOOTING

One may wonder why such a simple act as making a perceptual shift is so powerful. Actually, it is at the core of the way the universe works, as we see in the new physics, particularly quantum theory. Basically, how we design the experiment determines what we will see, and the "out there" reality is dependent upon our interaction with it. If we just begin to get the principle that reality starts within and is projected outward, and that what we see outside is a reflection of our own insides, and not the other way around, we have a made a major leap toward empowerment, health, and happiness, and away from victimization. We are beginning to see our interconnectedness with everyone in the universe. We have taken a major step in transcending the counterfeit "self" toward the realization of our True Self, which is the basic way to heal and enrich all our relationships.

However, some people may not respond differently in the instant you change your perceptions of them. It might be that a person has very deep psychological wounds from childhood and may associate that pain with you, personally, especially if your past behaviors were critical or rejecting. Or you may represent such a hurtful person to them, and it may take a period of time for the cumulative effects of your perceptual shift to be evident in the outside response.

Sometimes the other person is so accustomed to a history of perceiving you and/or the world as attacking and threatening, that even though you make the perceptual shift, it may not result instantly in a different response from the other person. You may need to persist for a long period of time in order for the other person to let down his or her armor and begin to trust to see you differently. Instead of expecting the other person to be changed, you will need to remind yourself that you have already had a major success in making the perceptual shift yourself, lifting you from a victim position. Now, knowing you are already filled with love, and are not dependent on receiving it from someone else, you can be free to choose to continue extending love and compassion to the other person, as well as to continue to keep your own perceptions accurate in the new circle. By continuing to perceive accurately, and by continuing to extend love, the other person may gradually come to feel safe, therefore feeling less fear, which begins to allow love to come forth. Now healing occurs. And even more important, you have healed yourself, even if you don't see a change or healed response in the other person.

William and Joanna are a good example of how this level of healing can take time to occur. William came to see me because he had become so frustrated in his attempts to convince his wife, Joanna, that he did indeed love her. In his every gesture, Joanna only saw rejection and disapproval. If William was a little late arriving home from work, if he wanted to play an occasional game of golf with a friend, if he didn't give her the exact kind of hug she was looking for, Joanna interpreted his behavior as proof that he didn't love her.

At first, William was dismayed by Joanna's perception of him. But as she continued in her erroneous perception of him, he became angry, which is why he sought out therapy with me. Soon he began to understand the benefits of making the perceptual shift, both for himself and Joanna. As he was able to see her complaints not as attacks against him, but as her desperate appeal for love, he could more easily feel compassionate toward the frightened child within his wife. This shift in perception also made it easier for him to have loving thoughts about her and extend these toward her. Finally, he was able to be more genuinely reassuring in his love whenever she seemed to feel unloved.

Although Joanna had trouble believing in the truth of William's love for several months, she gradually began to heal, trusting in his love and letting it into her heart. It was at this point that she herself sought me out for therapy, so she could resolve the trauma and negative beliefs that had originally caused her to feel so unloved. In the meantime, William was able to stay centered and at peace, and no longer felt attacked by Joanna.

The internal effects are always instant. You will feel empowered immediately, allowing for your love to flow freely and instantly beginning to heal your relationship. As you no longer feel fear, but love instead, you become aware that love is always the universal antidote to fear and instantly displaces it.

You may ask, "What do I do if the other person persists in their hurtful behaviors and is not responsive to my perceptual shift?" First, it is most important to reflect on whether you are making the perceptual shift in order to try to get the other person to change. When you use this motive, your efforts will usually backfire, at the worst, or be ineffective, in the least. Even if the other person does not seem to change, you are already centered through your perceptual shift and empowered through extending loving thoughts, so that the other person's response, if different, is simply an added blessing, not an expectation or a necessity.

However, as we shall see, to have a spiritual marriage, both people must join together in their quest to relinquish the ego and bring joining in love rather than separation.

The perceptual shift process will not work when you try to get the other person to do it instead of you, or wait for the other person to change. Nor will it work if the love you extend is with the expectation that you change the other person or expect to get something back—if even a more sane or friendly response. Such "love" with conditions attached is not love, but rather a barter or manipulation only thinly disguised as love. All these avenues put you back in an unempowered position, for when all the power for relief and the source of love lies outside you in another person, you are left trying to get the other person to change, which you are rarely, if ever, successful in doing. Paradoxically, it works only when we extend love for its own sake, knowing a basic truth that it is *as you give, you receive: We do not give in order to receive*.

Once you have made such a shift in your interpretative perception, the rest of the cycle has to change, following suit. If you no longer perceive an attack as real, that is, actually existing, then there is no need for us to feel afraid. If you are not afraid, then you are not likely to be angry, or hurt. And if you are not hurt, afraid, or angry, why would you need to defend, counterattack, or take flight? And if you don't engage in such behaviors yourself, you are less likely to invite negative responses from the other person. Hence, the other person's response, instead of being used as a confirmation of your old beliefs, may now be a disconfirmation of an old belief; and as it moves around the circle it actually begins to erase the old belief and to help set you up on a new track for the next opportunity to see the truth of the appeal for love instead of the illusion of attack.

THE MANY BENEFITS OF MAKING A PERCEPTUAL SHIFT

A most important benefit of making the perceptual shift (seeing fear instead of attack, viewing it as an appeal for love, and then responding with a loving thought), is that it reminds us of our True Self, which is Love. If we are extending loving thoughts, we become aware that we cannot give something that we do not have and that does not come out of our true essence. How could we be giving it if we do not have it and if that is not what we are? Hence we must be Love itself!

The Wizard of Oz offers a universal image of the benefits of making a perceptual shift. When Dorothy and her friends finally find the great Wizard of Oz, they are terrified of the size, loudness, and smoke, until Toto, Dorothy's dog, pulls back a curtain with his mouth to reveal a little frightened man, frantically pulling levers for visual and auditory effects, turning cranks, and projecting his voice loudly through an amplifier. At that moment, all of Dorothy's fears simply disappear. With Toto's help, an important perceptual shift was made that totally renders the fear unnecessary, for it was based, as always, on illusion. Their perceptual shift made possible a radical change to a more real communication, which ultimately led them all to look within for that which they were seeking without.

While the perceptual shift will be much easier to make if we have practiced monitoring our thoughts and changed the Self-diminishing ones, we can always choose at any time to see someone or a situation differently, thereby breaking out of the vicious cycle so inherent in the ego state of mind. Making a perceptual shift, a change in our way of viewing someone, is a most powerful way to regain our peace instantly. This has enormous impact on all of our relationships, but especially our most intimate.

Christina, for example, was criticized frequently as a child by her mother. It was not loud or obvious, but was subtly expressed with some consistency. If she was dressed to go out on a date, her mother chided, "Why didn't you wear your yellow dress?" Or, "You always look so good in your pink dress; was it dirty?" implying that she did not look good in what she was wearing. Or it might have been, "I don't think you finished your chores, as usual. Is that so?" Or she would say, "Do you think you told him clearly enough how you felt about that?" And usually before Christina was walking out the door, she would find her mother racing toward her with a hairbrush, if not already pulling a brush through Christina's hair. Growing up in this environment, Christina came to conclude that no matter what she did, it was not good enough; something was always wrong or inadequate about her.

It was easy, therefore, for Christina to interpret her husband's behaviors as criticism, especially since he tended to speak authoritatively. So when Donald would say, "I felt ignored at the cocktail party last night," Christina heard, "You ignored me last night." She did not even see Donald's hurt and fear, but instead only saw a personal attack, feeding into a familiar and painful memory. As a result, her immediate response was a knee-jerk defense in the form of a counterattack. "How come you're always on my case?! You're not so perfect yourself! You could have come over and talked to me if you were feeling bad. But no, you always come back and complain to me later. I should know. Anytime we have a good time, you are going to come back and spoil it with one of your criticisms!"

So Christina's belief and accompanying thought constellations gave rise to her interpretive perception of criticism and judgment, which evolved to her emotions of hurt and anger, which precipitated her defensive attack, which in turn provoked an attack from Donald, which she then used as confirmation of her old belief that she is not okay and that people will inevitably criticize and reject her. This is her vicious cycle repeating itself over and over unless changed.

How then does Christina change this repetitive system? Does it help her to stuff her feelings of hurt and anger? Hardly. Suppression usually means that the feelings still lurk actively inside, looking for another and perhaps indirect way to come out. "I'll stuff it now, but I'll get you around the next bend," is the implied message of this ego defense.

Nor is it of value for Christina to live by her feelings, for this would simply be another way for her to feel out of control. Who feels genuine strength when she is run by her feelings? She needs to acknowledge them, accept and understand them, and then try to see what belief, supporting thought constellations, or interpretive perceptions gave rise to them.

The encounter movement of the sixties and seventies made us aware that suppressed and repressed emotions are not healthy. An emphasis in much of psychotherapy from that time was to get out the feelings, which helped to free us from unconsciousness, repression, and empty intellectualizations. Now we know, however, that simply getting out one's feelings is not an end in itself, but must be for the purpose of understanding which perception, thought constellation, and belief system gives rise to the emotion.

What if Christina tries to change her reactive behavior, and not attack Donald when she is feeling hurt and angry? Such a decision can be somewhat useful, for it probably won't provoke Donald into a counterattack. But it still leaves Christina holding on to hurt feelings without any way of dealing with them constructively. Also, trying hard to change a behavior continually is much like trying to dam up a small creek by holding boards in your hand; you can succeed for a while with much effort, but it is hard to keep it up because the stream just keeps on flowing with its pressure from the beliefs, thoughts, and perceptions.

Hence a change of thoughts or a change in perception is the most effective and efficient way to break into the painful unproductive cycle, far more than any change attempted at the feeling or behavioral level. If we change our thought constellations, we are more easily able to perceive differently. And if we perceive differently, then we both feel and behave differently.

Christina decided to make it a practice to make a perceptual shift. Instantly, she began to view Donald not as judging and attacking, but as coming from fear and appealing for love. Consequently, she is no longer at the mercy of Donald. She does not even see an attack, and therefore the attack does not exist. Nor does she have to wait for Donald to change and become more sensitive to her feelings in order for her to feel safe in his presence and to be happy. All this means that Christina, having made a perceptual shift, is not likely to be frightened, unempowered, hurt, and angry as she was in the vicious cycle. So, instead of fear, she feels compassion toward Donald. Her compassion is likely to lead to a quite different behavior than her counterattack in the vicious cycle. She now behaves in a caring, nonthreatening manner, which will undoubtedly elicit a drastically different response from Donald, since it is more probable Donald will not have to be defending and counterattacking, and will probably be more peaceful. His behavior will *not* serve as a confirmation of Christina's old belief system, which in turn sets her up in position for different thought constellations that will support a perceptual shift or new interpretation the next time. And even if Donald's response is not different, Christine is already a winner.

Most often caring behaviors that grow out of a genuine compassion are likely to elicit quite different responses from the outside world. Instead of counterattack or flight, we are more likely to see a softening and often friendly response, which then disconfirms the old core belief, and actually begins to eradicate some of it by letting in this new experience.

SEEING OTHERS AS MIRRORS: TURNING PROJECTION AROUND

An extension of our imperfect perception is the ego's tendency to project. We usually see the problem lying in the other person, not in ourselves. A common example is when a driver on the road cuts you off, and you blow your horn to call his attention to that dangerous fact. He blows his horn back, shakes his fist at you, or gives you the finger. You are to blame for blowing your horn; he does not see that he almost caused an accident by cutting you off.

This same dynamic exists in our relationships. If we feel rejected by our mate, we usually blame him or her for the rejection instead of looking at ourselves—attempting to identify how we might have provoked or invited the rejection. We might have been rejecting our partner and causing him or her to respond in like fashion. Sometimes, we may identify a behavior on our part that invited a negative response. Other times, we get negative responses even though we have done nothing. Many times, however, it is important to see what thoughts we have been thinking or what belief system we are unwittingly seeking confirmation for. Remember, we get back what we put out. To see another person as a mirror of what you are believing, thinking, feeling, or behaving is a way of breaking out of a fruitless pattern of projection.

A good friend told me of a wonderful example of using others as mirrors in order to find inner peace and save a friendship. He and his wife went on vacation to Scotland with another couple, close friends of theirs. Since they had planned to travel about, and since there are few if any hotels outside the major cities, they would be staying in bed-and-breakfast homes. And since such homes do not have uniform rooms, as do hotels, they decided that each couple would have first choice on the selection of bedrooms every other night.

On the first night there, they entered their bed and breakfast place, and the woman from the other couple insisted on her preference of room for the night. My friend agreed, thinking, "It's okay for her to have her choice first." But on the next night, the same thing occurred. My friend reminded her about their agreement, but she still insisted on her first choice of room, giving several reasons as to why she must have this particular room. Feeling a little annoyed, he let it go, thinking "We will get first choice of rooms tomorrow night." But on the third night, the same scenario was played out. This time my friend was quite annoyed, but the woman continued to insist on having her first choice.

He went to his room steaming inside, wondering whether he could continue the vacation with these friends, and of even greater concern, whether this behavior would destroy their friendship.

Being a spiritually minded person, he decided to apply this mirror exercise, whereupon he asked himself, "Where or how have I insisted on my own desires or preferences at the expense of someone else?" He said he quickly identified three different ways in which he had done this. They weren't exactly in the same way that this woman had done it, but nevertheless, he had insisted on his own preference at someone else's expense. He reported that once he identified these similarities, and made different decisions inside himself as to how he preferred to be, his anger and resentment toward his friend went away. And further, it ceased to matter to him whether or not she continued to insist on her preference.

I found it quite interesting to note that I had a parallel experience inside myself as I heard my friend tell this story. When he described the woman's selfish insistence, I became angry and judgmental of her in my mind. When he described his decision to see her as a mirror in order to look inside himself, I chose to do the same thing. Quickly, I identified several ways in which I had insisted on my own way or preference at the expense of someone else, seeing how my own narcissism had ruled. Then, once I made different choices inside myself about how I preferred to behave, my parallel anger and resentment went away as well.

Seeing others as a mirror of our own thoughts and beliefs and behaviors helps us to break through the illusion of separateness that the ego mind holds, which is why the exercise is so valuable. Otherwise, we could go on maintaining the illusion of separateness, and that there is someone out there who is separate and apart from me, and who is doing something to me. But, if we can see the person as a mirror of ourselves, the illusion of separateness breaks down, for that is me over there doing that thing as well. We can now see that it is not another separate person acting upon me, but rather, it is part of me over there! This exercise is part of taking responsibility for healing our relationships and creating a spiritual marriage.

By stopping our projections, we look within and therefore begin to take back our creative power to affect our special relationships with our partners, children, and parents. For example, I have often observed that when I feel unloved, the odds are great that I have forgotten to extend love. I have observed that when I feel like I am not being listened to, there is a good chance that I have not been a very good listener. I have observed that if I feel neglected, the chances are that I have been neglecting others. If I feel judged and criticized, it is likely that I have been critical in my mind of someone else or of myself.

Kenneth complained that his wife, Betsy, was such a messy person that it was getting more and more difficult for him to live with her in the clutter. When he began to look at himself, he discovered that, even though he did not keep a messy house, his desk was a mess, his workshop in the basement was a mess, and the garage where he kept his yard tools was also a mess. When he accepted his own areas of messiness, he was able to be more compassionate with Betsy around her messiness.

PRACTICE 4:

Seeing Others As Mirrors

1. Take a moment to think of a situation in which you have been disturbed by anyone close or distant.
2. Think of someone who has pushed your buttons or whose attitude or behavior really gets your goat. It doesn't usually take very long to identify such a person.
3. Next, think about what that person does that upsets you, the behavior you can't stand. And then ask yourself, "Am I like that in any way? Maybe I don't express it in the same style, with the same personality, or even to the same degree. But, how do I express that to any degree in a way that is at all similar?"
4. Try to acknowledge even a remote similarity.
5. Once you get in touch with those characteristics within yourself and own them as yours, too, see how you feel. Try not to judge yourself, but rather, accept these undesirable traits within you as just a fact.
6. Then, choose to deal with the issues inside yourself instead of trying to fix them in the other person.

Jesus is often quoted as saying that if we pick the log out of our own eye first, instead of focusing on the speck in our brother's eye, then we shall see him clearly—which means that we cease judging and see him as sinless as are we. On the positive side, if we can see the Divine spark in other people, and see the god self in each of them, then we can also see it more clearly in ourselves. What we see in ourselves, we will see in others, and what we see in others, reflects what we believe is ourselves. When we can see the other person as mirroring our insides, then we have begun to awaken to the world of the True Self. All the problems with others that grow out of our own projections and arise from the illusion of separation are thereby diminished or extinguished for that moment.

This exercise is particularly useful when the relationship problem persists. *When a problem persists for us, it often means that we have not yet learned some lesson intrinsic to that problem.* Perhaps we might have learned one or more lessons from it already, but usually another remains that we have not identified. When we can say, "This suffering in this relationship is now unbearable—I am ready to see what else I need to learn," then you are ready to see what may lie inside of you that is causing the problem.

You may be wondering, "How can I know what the lesson is that I am to learn from this problem?" Perhaps the following questions can be of help:

1. Do you experience others as rejecting or critical? Then you might ask yourself, "Have I dealt with my own rejections and criticalness?"

2. Do you experience others as controlling? You might then ask yourself, "Have I dealt with my own needs to control?"

3. Do you experience others as attacking? You might then ask yourself, "Have I dealt with my own attack thoughts toward myself and toward others?"

4. Do you keep feeling an absence of love in your life? You might then ask, "Have I been withholding love from myself and from others?"

Adrian, for example, had been married three times. In each marriage she complained that her husband would not listen to her; in each of these situations, she believed she was simply the victim of an inattentive and nonlistening husband. Three such men in a row!

Finally, she was willing to look at herself and was ready to learn whatever lessons were there so that she did not have to have another repeat of this situation. She began to see that she talked incessantly, which did not give the other person a chance to show that they heard. And in further reflection, she saw that by talking continually, she never gave herself the opportunity to be a listener. She got back the same nonlistening behavior she displayed. And once she became a listener herself, with her third husband, she discovered that he, amazingly, began to listen to her.

Similarly, David complained that his wife, Rachel, was always late, often by hours. Her lateness troubled him because he viewed it as thoughtless and inconsiderate of others—including himself. He had endured her behavior for years, and the pain became too much to bear, which is often one of our greatest motivations to change. After hearing a talk about problems and suffering being lessons not yet learned, he was now ready to explore what lessons he might not have learned from this situation, since he had been so unhappy for so long.

David was able to say to himself, "Since I am not late, what are other ways in which I might be thoughtless and inconsiderate of others' needs and feelings? How am I that way with Rachel in particular?" Once he had identified a number of ways in which this was true of him, and chose to begin to deal with these situations in a more considerate way, he ceased to be disturbed by his wife's habitual lateness.

The Dalai Lama expressed it clearly when he said, "spiritual practice involves transforming ourselves." Instead, most of us think our job is to transform others. When we take this route, we constantly fail and then feel increasingly like victims. Essentially, by not seeing others as mirrors of our own issues, we delay our enlightenment and happiness needlessly. On the other hand, when we transform ourselves by taking responsibility for who we are, we transform our relationships—for nothing is separate from us.

BEYOND PERCEPTION

It's imperative to remember that perception exists only because we believe we are separate from others and the universe. When we realize our interconnectedness with the universe, perception is no longer necessary because we simply know who we are and who everyone else is—that we are One.

Thomas Merton, the twentieth-century contemplative Christian mystic, has written about an experience he had one day in a busy marketplace:

> *Then it was as if I suddenly saw the secret beauty of their hearts, the depths of their hearts . . . the core of their reality, the person that each one is in God's eyes. If only they could see themselves as they really are. If only we could see each other that way all the time, there would be no more war, no more hatred, no more cruelty, no more greed. . . . I suppose the big problem would be that we would fall down and worship each other.*

It is inherently difficult for us human beings to see the divine reality in ourselves or in others. For that reason, we have to make a conscious decision to do so. But know that when we begin to heal, the healing does not stop with us, for the healing of our minds always reaches out to countless numbers of those about us, and they are the beneficiaries as well.

The converse is also true. When we engage in our old perceptions of attack and react with fear, and project these fears onto others, this also affects those around us. Unwittingly, we can increase their pain and suffering and delay their healing. This is true unless they are so strongly centered that they are unaffected by our projections.

By making a perceptual shift, we not only break into the Vicious Cycle of Interaction set up by the ego, we also further awaken our True Self identity and release our tremendous capacity to love. And as we learn to choose love over fear, we open ourselves to live freely in the Love that is All That Is. It's all up to your willingness to choose love over fear.

In the next chapter, you will learn yet another way of breaking into the Vicious Cycle of Interaction, stopping the ego at its source—our core beliefs. As you continue to monitor your thoughts and practice perceptual shifts, you will have automatically erased some of the negative core beliefs that drive your ego thinking. But the next practice, Changing Our Negative Core Beliefs, will put these beliefs to rest—for good.

CHAPTER 6

Going Further Upstream

Erasing Traumas and Changing Negative Core Beliefs

As you saw in the last two chapters, both thought monitoring and making a perceptual shift are two practices that allow you to break into your Vicious Cycle of Interaction, giving you a tangible way to heal your relationship and feel the power of a relationship based on empowering love. Another way to break into the vicious cycle and cement this healing is by uprooting the negative core beliefs that fuel your enemy thoughts and perceptions, which can cause you so much unhappiness. By breaking into the cycle at the level of your beliefs, you are rooting out the deepest layer of your negative-interaction cycle. In this chapter, you will learn how to erase your negative beliefs, replacing them with positive, life-affirming beliefs that reinforce your True Self identity and empower your spiritual marriage, creating peace and happiness for you and your partner. Let's take a look at how these negative core beliefs function in our lives.

THE VICIOUS CYCLE CONTINUES

We all have many beliefs, some positive and some negative. These beliefs play a decisive role in why we tend to repeat behaviors that are joyful and rewarding, or painful and disappointing. The negative thought constellations that we saw interfere with our happiness in a relationship are fueled by those negative beliefs we have about ourselves, relationships, and love in general. And while many of our beliefs might be positive, such as "I am lovable" or "I am smart" or "I am strong," many others are likely to be negative. Since it is the negative beliefs that produce negative and painful results in our lives and our relationships, these are the ones we will focus on here in order to allow more happiness and success into our relationships. But please take note: I am not suggesting that you focus on the negative beliefs for their own sakes, but to use our garden metaphor again, we focus on the weeds only long enough to pluck them out so that the flowers can grow more beautifully.

Our negative core beliefs (and the thoughts that come out of these beliefs) are the foundation of our counterfeit self. And underneath all of our psychological beliefs lies one belief that is basic to them all—that we are separate instead of interconnected with all others, the universe, or God. This basic negative belief, taking us out of our sense of Oneness with our True Self, gives rise to all other more specific negative beliefs. But as long as we experience the beliefs as many, we must deal with them separately.

Our negative beliefs usually come out of the conclusions we draw about ourselves, about people, about relationships, and about life. And as you go further upstream, following the tide established by these negative beliefs, you will often find traumas that you've experienced in the past. By "trauma" I am not limiting the meaning to tragic events, such as the death of a parent or sibling, sexual abuse by an elder, or a horrible accident, though such events are of course traumatic, creating intense pain that can be carried with you into the future. Instead, I use the term "trauma" in a more generalized way, referring to any emotional experience or continuing experiences—big or small—that have caused you pain that continues to cause disruption in your life, especially in your relationships. A trauma can be a dramatically painful experience, (such as emotional or physical abuse, the divorce of parents when you were a child, or the death of a close family member), or a trauma can be an ongoing painful time, (such as being criticized, rejected, ignored constantly, or not acknowledged throughout one's childhood or even your current relationship). An event or an ongoing painful time becomes a trauma when whatever caused the pain remains lodged in the mind and forms a block or barrier to your other, more positive emotional experiences. And just as there is a basic negative belief that we are all separate underlying all negative core beliefs, so there is a basic trauma of unlovingness that underlies all the others. All rejection, criticisms, neglect, judgment, excessive control, smothering, and abuse are different reflections of a profound experience of a lack of love—this is the ultimate trauma underlying ego-based thinking.

At some point, the conclusions drawn from the trauma seem to congeal into a belief system, which we then live by. These beliefs affect all our relationships in profound ways, but especially our closest ones. If, for example, we were treated unfairly as children, we may come to believe that the world—especially close relations—will treat us unfairly. Or, if we were not loved sufficiently—and how many of us were!—we may come to believe that there is a scarcity of love and that we are the most likely ones to experience that scarcity. We might come to believe we are bad, not good enough, not loveable, have little to give, are unworthy, rejectable, not enough in some way, or will be abandoned, and the list goes on ad infinitum!

Consider how Jeffrey's traumas led to his negative core beliefs. Jeffrey came to see me after his third marriage had begun to fail. Frustrated and disheartened, he was perplexed as to why all his relationships with women ended so miserably and seemed so impossible. As we began to trace the patterns of his relationships, he described for me how prior to each marriage, when the relationships were more casual and less intimate, he would be very affectionate, engaging, and enjoyed a lot of sex. But after he got married, he found himself behaving in contrast to the way he had prior to marriage, finding many ways to create emotional and physical distance. Then, like clockwork, he would find himself complaining about not having enough sex, not enough affection, and feeling unloved in various ways!

Each of his wives seemed to pick up the cues as to how to behave toward him to reinforce his belief that he was not getting enough—sex, affection, or love. And even when his wives did not behave in confirming ways, Jeffrey would interpret their behaviors as evidence that he was deprived. He would become critical and angry, frequently complaining that he was not loved or did not get enough sex—his responses only drove his wives further away.

But once he began to monitor his thoughts and become more familiar with his own thought constellations, Jeffrey could see that these negative beliefs were based upon childhood experiences: neither his father nor his mother expressed any affection—toward him or each other. Jeffrey was able to acknowledge that overall, there was an ongoing emotional deprivation in his family.

He then saw how this trauma of unlovingness played out in his beliefs: he had entered each of his three marriages with a three-pronged belief about scarcity in intimate relationships: there will be scarcity of love, scarcity of affection, and scarcity of sex. It didn't matter how his three wives had behaved! Jeffrey would still have found proof of this scarcity!

Another example of a seemingly innocuous trauma that created lasting negative beliefs happened with Sophie, who was raised in a household in which all roads led to achievement—whether it was law, medicine, or art. Sophie's parents and grandparents had established a long legacy of tremendous success and they put enormous pressure on her to do the same. As a result, she suffered not a trauma exactly, but a strong sense that she was only worthy if she did something successful. In a backward sort of way, her trauma can be seen as an absence of being loved simply for who she was as a daughter or granddaughter. Consequently, she developed the belief that she was worthless all on her own.

When Sophie married, she picked a husband who shared similar values to her family. Like Sophie, Stephen was driven to be successful and seemed to value her (and himself) based on the degree of their accomplishments. They each worked endless hours and rarely saw each other. Their only relationship time was to connect for a few minutes here and there, usually when they were already quite exhausted. And even so, they would usually talk about their business frustrations and successes.

After one and half years of marriage, they both began to feel lonely, isolated, deprived, and resentful, and blamed each other for their misery. Together, they thought separation was the answer. Thankfully for them, they didn't give up marriage so easily.

In our work together, Sophie and Stephen were able to see that they held beliefs that not only had programmed preordained results for them, but would continue to produce the same results with any other partners they might have. Once they learned how to erase their core beliefs with the exercises that follow in this chapter, Sophie and her husband were able to begin working less, spending more time together, and building a different and more satisfying relationship than either had ever known.

A belief works much like software in a computer program—until it is changed, it will do only what it is programmed to do. And further, we rehearse and reinforce each belief countless times with a portion of the 72,000 thoughts we think each day, which is why thought monitoring is so important. *Keeping and reinforcing our negative core beliefs in our thinking is why we continue to get the same results in our relationships year after year, and relationship after relationship!*

Therefore, if we want to heal our relationship from its unhappiness, criticism, blame, or guilt, then we must break the vicious cycle at the level of our beliefs, erasing the beliefs and the effect of the traumas that created and fuel them. If we do not change our negative beliefs and the underlying traumas, we will continue to play out the negative software that has printed out the same problems in our closest relationships. We can keep doing the same things, relationship after relationship, often for a lifetime. One reason that therapy for couples and families has often not been effective in the long-term is because these traumas and their negative core beliefs have not been erased. Core beliefs often work like a major logjam in the stream and interfere with many people's success in couples therapy. But when these beliefs are identified and erased, then much more can usually be accomplished.

Remember, when you identify and erase your core beliefs and traumas, you are going upstream to the source of your relationship problems. At times, you may feel like you are simply working on yourself, as if you're taking a detour away from the relationship itself. Not so. Processing your beliefs and traumas is essential to healing your relationship, and giving you the clean stream from which you will let your love flow freely and unencumbered. When you leave the trauma and beliefs in place, they act like barricades, preventing this flow of love.

CHANGING YOUR CORE BELIEFS

It is usually a difficult process for people to change their belief systems. People have spent years in various forms of talking psychotherapy or psychoanalysis trying to change those beliefs that have locked them into repetitive, but unproductive and painful patterns with only varying amounts of success since talking can often reinforce the problem.

For some people, talking out their traumas with an attentive, nonjudging and loving person is helpful, and can sometimes be quite sufficient to heal the scars of traumas. Other times talking may help, but may not clear out the roots of the trauma. Still other times continuing to talk about the traumas, sometimes obsessively, may even serve to rehearse the older pains, thereby locking them in even further, usually combined with some kind of blame. If repeatedly talking about your traumas has not released the pain, then it's probably time to explore another approach. Some forms of psychotherapy, for example, which rehash the past over and over may inadvertently reinforce or even build further the traumas and beliefs instead of releasing them.

People who have tried spiritual practices, such as meditation, have often been able to erase the pain of traumas and their resulting negative belief systems by melting them away, much like pouring water on crystals of ice. But most people need a stronger and more exact method for clearing out the upstream pollution of the past in order to have clean water in the stream of the present. With these exercises, we can actually erase the effects of the traumas and their negative beliefs energetically, and install a new belief we would prefer to live by. This process is like changing our software, and can happen quickly—sometimes in a few minutes! The quickness reminds me of a statement from the Book of Revelation in the Bible, "You shall all be transformed in the twinkling of an eye." Powerful and significant changes need not be slow and laborious. The time it takes is mostly due to our reluctance to get past our resistances to change. Such resistance even promotes the widespread belief that change must take a long time. But how long does it take to change a thought? Only an instant. And since beliefs are only congealed thoughts, they can change in an instant as well!

PRACTICE 5:

Erasing Traumas and Changing Negative Core Beliefs

Some core beliefs are so deeply entrenched that they are difficult to erase completely by breaking into the vicious cycle at the level of thoughts or perception. When you feel as if you are trying to put the brakes on a train (your thoughts), you may begin to realize that a powerful engine (the beliefs behind your thoughts) continues to push you in a negative direction. In such instances, you may need to use an approach that goes beyond the conscious, rational mind. This extra support comes from exercises that stimulate subtle energies in the body, or that help to synchronize the right and left hemispheres of the brain while you engage in a highly focused ritual. Once a recalcitrant belief is cleared out, and with it the effects of the trauma that inspired the belief to begin with, then you will be better able to return to thought monitoring, as well as find your path essentially more peaceful.

STEP 1: IDENTIFYING YOUR NEGATIVE CORE BELIEFS AND THE TRAUMAS THAT INSPIRED THEM

First, you need to identify the negative core beliefs that adversely affect your relationships, as well as the traumas that gave rise to them. Pains and traumas are often immediately contained or expressed through the body. For example, when there has been a major disaster in a country, such as an earthquake, a flood, or terrorist activity, the birth weight of newborn infants goes down significantly. Further, traumas we experience as children or as adults may be contained in the body for decades following the actual experience, unless one has used some effective means of clearing out the effects. Since these traumas are the original motivators for the negative core beliefs, and because they are retained energetically in the body, they continue to fuel the beliefs and the repetitive thoughts that rehearse them. In doing so, they act something like a glue, helping to keep the beliefs locked in place. If you are unable to identify a trauma, then focus instead on the emotion you are feeling. Connect this feeling to the belief behind it and release the emotion.

Some people are very conscious of the negative belief systems that impact on their relationships, wearing them right on their sleeve. They can quickly run through the sample list of some common beliefs below and instantly know which ones are theirs. Following is a list of some of the more common negative core beliefs that interfere or negatively impact relationships. If you recognize any of these as being ones you believe in, then you need to try and trace them to their origin of trauma—big or small—that created the belief in the first place.

Place a check by all the ones that seem at all like they apply to you and could possibly be affecting any of your close relationships:

- ☐ I am not loveable.
- ☐ I am undeserving of love.
- ☐ Love will smother me.
- ☐ Love will go away.
- ☐ I will inevitably be abandoned by those I love and want love from.
- ☐ I will not be listened to or acknowledged.

- ☐ Love is dangerous.
- ☐ People will not like me as I am.
- ☐ I don't deserve to be happy.
- ☐ I don't deserve to have a happy and loving relationship.
- ☐ I will inevitably be rejected.
- ☐ People will betray me.
- ☐ I don't deserve closeness.
- ☐ Closeness is dangerous because . . .
- ☐ I cannot be myself, or I'll be rejected.
- ☐ I must always please in order to have love.
- ☐ I will be left out.
- ☐ I am not enough.
- ☐ Life has to be a struggle.
- ☐ Relationships must be a struggle.
- ☐ Communication is contentious.
- ☐ Fighting is a way to connect emotionally.
- ☐ I will be controlled or overpowered by others.
- ☐ I must do what everyone else wants me to do.
- ☐ Love must come to me without my doing anything.
- ☐ I cannot be assertive with people who are special to me.
- ☐ I cannot initiate affection or sex, for I will mostly be rejected.

☐ If I accept love, I'll have to pay for it.

☐ Marriage is a trap or bondage.

☐ Marriage is boring.

☐ Marriage will bring me happiness.

☐ I will always be an outsider.

☐ I don't have much of value to give.

☐ To argue is to connect.

☐ Surrender means I will be controlled.

☐ And even more basic: I don't even want to have a happy life or relationship since I don't believe I deserve to have it or can have it.

These are just some of the more common core beliefs that many of us developed in early childhood—not so much in a conscious way that could be articulated, but automatically as a means of self-protection and emotional survival. Unfortunately, these beliefs, once in place, become the software we use to print out our lives. This is why so many of us keep getting the same negative results in our relationships, even though we consciously say we do not want them.

If any of these ring true for you, trust your conclusion and know that these are most likely beliefs you will need to eliminate in order to have a happy and fulfilling relationship. Just reading this list may cause you to think of other beliefs you might have. *Make a list of what they are.*

If you are still not aware of what your beliefs are, it is often helpful to do the following: Observe the dissatisfying and recurring aspects of your special relationships. If one of your issues is something that also seems to characterize your relationships or your life, happening over and over again, it's very likely that you have a core belief driving that outcome. You might ask yourself the following questions and place a check beside each word or phrase that seems like it would be true for you. Place two checks beside the ones that describe the way you often and repeatedly feel:

Do I repeatedly feel like I am:

- ☐ unloved
- ☐ rejected
- ☐ ignored
- ☐ not listened to
- ☐ depleted
- ☐ self-involved
- ☐ nonassertive
- ☐ deprived
- ☐ lonely
- ☐ mistreated
- ☐ demeaned
- ☐ not acknowledged
- ☐ attacked
- ☐ criticized and judged
- ☐ unfairly treated
- ☐ controlled
- ☐ powerless

☐ abandoned

☐ unable to express my feelings

☐ talking too much

☐ angry

☐ anxious or afraid

☐ selfish

☐ unloving

☐ withholding

☐ distancing (being distanced)

☐ desperate for sex or affection

If you experience any of these more than just occasionally, then they most likely represent a core belief that you live by. See if you can allow yourself to brainstorm with an open mind about what you might believe led to such recurring feelings or experiences. If you explore your repetitive experiences sincerely and openly, you will most likely arrive at several possible beliefs you live by. Add these to your list of beliefs.

Next, *now that you have identified one or more negative beliefs, make a list which you will work from, ordering them into the priority of their importance to you and leaving several lines of space between each one.*

Some people head the list with beliefs that disturb their relationships most in the present. Others prefer to clear out the traumas and beliefs from early life first, even if they do not immediately see a connection with their current relationship problems, and then do the later ones.

Finally, once the beliefs are identified, see if you can *determine what your painful childhood experiences were that could have provoked such a belief. Write these traumas beside the corresponding beliefs on your list.*

STEP 2: RATING YOUR BELIEFS AND TRAUMAS

Take your list of beliefs, and focus on the first one. Rate the strength of your belief on a scale of zero to ten. Zero means that you do not believe the cognition at all; ten means that you believe it deeply and live by it accordingly. Pick a number that seems accurate when you are most honest with yourself. If you pick three, for example, as the strength of your belief that you are unworthy of closeness, but you typically have little or no closeness in your life, you are probably deceiving yourself. Do your best to be very honest.

STEP 3: BELIEF AND TRAUMA-ERASING PROCESS USING EMDR

The next two steps can be used together or separately, depending on your preference. EMDR stands for Eye Movement Desensitization and Repressing, and was originally developed by the West Coast psychologist Francine Shapiro. She teaches the approach as one to be done only with a trained practitioner, which is usually the most effective way. However, I have devised a simplified version that many can use effectively and safely by themselves as a way to clear negative core beliefs and the effects of traumas.

This exercise includes two steps: (1) erasing the effects of your traumas, and then (2) erasing your negative core beliefs. It is usually most effective to erase the effects of the traumas first, before proceeding with the beliefs, since the traumas are what originally inspired the beliefs.

1) Traumas: Assessing the Degree of Disturbance

Use a ten-point scale to assess the degree of disturbance—ten being the highest possible disturbance and zero indicating no disturbance at all. If your trauma is a repeated experience of not having your feelings heard and acknowledged, note to what degree the disturbance is still with you today. After you have identified a number that seems accurate, such as eight or nine, then proceed with the following process:

2) Erasing the Effects of the Traumas:

1. Focus on the trauma or painful experience that you've identified in steps one and two.
2. See what images or memories may come to mind that represent that belief or trauma . . . . . (pause) . . . .
3. Identify whatever emotions you feel when you think of your belief or trauma and recall the images and memories that represent it . . . . . (pause) . . . .
4. Locate the places in your body where you feel those emotions and focus on those spots . . . . . . (pause) . . . .
5. With your head facing forward, move your eyes from the left to the right, at a medium pace about fifteen times.
6. Pause for a moment to note any images or feelings that might have been evoked. Sometimes there will be nothing. Other times an emotion or image is evoked. If the feeling is particularly strong, take slow deep breaths as you focus

on the feeling, saying with each exhalation, "I now release this feeling from every part of my being" . . . . (pause) . . . .

7. Now reevaluate. On the scale of one to ten, how strong is your disturbance now? See if it has come down a few points. If so, repeat the process again, followed by an assessment of your disturbance on the ten-point scale. Continue to repeat the process and assessment until you reach zero.

If you are unable to reduce your degree of disturbance at least one or two points each time, you should locate a trained practitioner to continue the process. (See the resource list at the end of the chapter for further information.) If the disturbing effects of your trauma have been cleared, scoring zero on the ten-point scale, then proceed with the same process to erase the core beliefs that grew out of your traumas. Most people will find the process quite effective.

3) Erasing Negative Core Beliefs

1. Evaluate the strength of your negative beliefs on the ten-point scale. One if you do not believe it at all, ten if you believe it very strongly.
2. Focus on the negative belief.
3. See what images or memories may come to mind that represent that belief.
4. Identify whatever emotions you feel when you think of your belief and recall the images and memories that represent it.

5. Locate the places in your body where you feel those emotions and focus on those spots . . . . . . (pause) . . . .

6. With your head facing forward, move your eyes from the left to the right, at a medium pace about fifteen times.

7. Pause and evaluate the strength of the belief on the ten-point scale. Continue the process as described above until you reach a score of zero.

Since there are often constellations of beliefs that are influencing our relationships in negative ways, you may need to identify and then process out a series of beliefs to experience the full effect of being free of the negative influences of your beliefs in your relationships. Some people, however, will begin to experience significant changes after processing out only one belief.

I would recommend that you do not try to erase more than one trauma or belief at one sitting. Spread them out, giving yourself time to assimilate the changes. Do not do the process in a cursory way, but with a focus, seriousness, and deep intent to release the trauma or belief.

STEP 3 ALTERNATE: ERASING TRAUMAS AND NEGATIVE CORE BELIEFS USING THE TAPAS ACCUPRESSURE TECHNIQUE

The Tapas Acupressure Technique was developed by a deeply spiritual acupuncturist and lovely person in California by the name of Tapas Fleming. While I have made a few variations on her technique, I think the basic core aspects of it are still central and do justice to her method.

While it is possible and often quite effective to do this process alone, I find it even more effective to have another person guide you through it. If you are part of a couple, you might take turns guiding each other through the process for each negative belief or trauma you wish to erase. Or you might take turns with another family member or friend who also wishes to erase one or more negative beliefs or effects of traumas.

1. Sit in a comfortable chair in a quiet place where you will not be distracted. Decide whether you are erasing a belief or the effects of a trauma.
2. As you did before, determine (a) the strength of your belief or (b) the strength of disturbance you still have with you from the earlier trauma or disturbing experiences. Pick a number on the ten-point scale that represents the strength of your belief or disturbance, a ten being the strongest belief or disturbance and a zero being the absence of any belief or disturbance. Write this number down beside your trauma or belief.
3. Place your thumb and fourth finger (ring finger) on the bridge of your nose at the corners of your eyes. While holding this posture, place your middle finger between and slightly above the eyebrows, commonly referred to as the third eye. Then, in addition, place your other hand at the base of your skull on the back of your head.

The posture may seem odd at first, but those positions stimulate powerful accupressure points. While holding the posture, please do all of the following steps. (These steps are ones you will use with yourself if you do this alone, or use them to guide another person through the process. If you are guiding another person, it is also helpful to hold the posture yourself since we are all interconnected.)

1. Take a few slow deep breaths to relax and to focus your consciousness on the negative belief or trauma you wish to be free of . . . . . (pause and breathe slowly and deeply)

2. See what images or memories may come to mind that represent that belief or trauma . . . . . (pause and breathe slowly and deeply) . . . .

3. Identify whatever emotions you feel when you think of your belief or trauma, and recall the images and memories that represent it . . . . . (pause and breathe) . . . .

4. Locate the places in your body where you feel those emotions, and focus on those spots . . . . . . (pause and breathe) . . . .

5. Say slowly and meaningfully the following: "I now release this belief (or effects of this trauma) from every part of my being" . . . . (pause and breathe) . . . .

6. And then say: "All the origins of this belief (or trauma) are healing now" . . . . . . (pause and breathe) . . . .

7. And then say: "Every place in my mind, body, and life that was damaged by this belief (or trauma) is healing now" . . . . . . (pause and breathe) . . . .

8. And then say: "Every place in me that got something out of holding on to this belief (or effects of this trauma) is healing now" . . . (pause and breathe) . . . . . .

9. And then say: "I forgive ____________ (my parents, my sibling, etc.), myself, God, or anyone else I might have blamed for this belief (or trauma)" . . . . . . (pause and breathe slowly and deeply) . . . . . .

10. And then conclude by saying: "I thank God for the healing that is occurring now" or "I am thankful for the healing that is occurring now" . . . . (pause) . . . . . .

11. Hold the posture as long as you want, and release it when it feels like the right time to do so. For those who like the posture and want to hold it a long time, note that it is probably best not to hold the posture longer than fifteen minutes or so, or it might make you somewhat spacy. Most people will hold it only a minute or two when the exercise is finished.

12. Now, assess the strength of your belief or degree of disturbance from the trauma on the scale of 0–10. Be very honest with yourself in picking a number. Cross out the old number and write down the new one. Then keep repeating the TAT process until you have reached zero.

Your goal is to bring the strength of your belief or degree of disturbance to zero. If you don't repeat the exercise until you've reached zero, the disturbance may be more likely to creep back up to a higher number. If you are not succeeding in bringing down the strength of your belief—with either EMDR or TAT exercises—it usually means that there are some significant reasons for holding on to the belief or trauma. Perhaps it is serving some protective purpose, or is connected with not feeling worthy—all from very early childhood conclusions. Often you can clear out these barriers by rubbing your heart in a clockwise circle, saying "I deeply love and accept myself, even though I have barriers against releasing this trauma (or belief)." Repeat the phrase three times and then continue with the EMDR or TAT process.

STEP 4: INSTALLING A NEW BELIEF

Just as you can grow better flowers after you have weeded your garden, so can you plant the seeds of positive, loving beliefs to replace the former negative beliefs that tied you to your traumas. Once you have cleared your negative beliefs, ask yourself, "What would I prefer to believe instead?"

If you want to remind yourself of beliefs that underlie the principles of a spiritual marriage, refer back to Practice 1 in Chapter One. The questions that pertain to a spiritual or happy relationship can be used as suggestions for installing positive, loving affirmations and beliefs.

Once you have identified the positive beliefs you would prefer to live by, do the process described below, using the ten-point scale to assess the strength of your new belief.

1. Focus on the desired belief.

2. Bring in any images that represent the desired belief. Let them be 3-dimensional and involving the senses.

3. Observe any emotion you feel along with the positive cognition.

4. Note where these feelings are in your body and focus on these places.

5. With your head facing forward, move your eyes from left to right about fifteen times at a moderate pace.

6. Evaluate the strength of your new belief on the ten-point scale and keep repeating the process until you bring your belief to a ten.

The process of erasing the effects of your traumas and changing your beliefs is—on the surface—very simple. However, once you experience a positive change and begin to become comfortable and familiar with your new, positive, loving thoughts, you will experience profound change throughout your life, but especially in your relationships. If you and your partner choose to engage in this process together, and you are thorough in clearing out all related traumas and beliefs, then you are more likely to enter a whole new world of love and deep intimacy. And anytime you as a couple encounter conflict or problems—and no relationship is without either—then you can fall back on the resource of your experience with love.

If we continue to dwell on the negative thoughts that would reinforce the old core beliefs, then it is possible we might rebuild the belief. Take a few moments to list any thoughts that you characteristically think would reinforce or rebuild the old belief. These are the thoughts to be vigilant of; identify them and use the Five-Step Thought-Monitoring Process (in Practice 2) to dismiss them. Regular and systematic thought monitoring of these thoughts will ensure that you do not reconstruct the belief that you have erased. Remember, thought monitoring is always essential! Any negative thought, unmonitored, continues to have a snowballing effect. But any thought that is dismissed will cease to have any negative effects.

THE EXERCISES IN ACTION

One might ask, "How does this work? How can one actually erase a core belief so quickly that he has lived by so many years?" "How can we so easily eliminate my inner opposition to letting go of the belief or disturbance?" If everything in the physical universe is just energy, vibrating at different frequencies, and if at the quanta level, where matter and energy are virtually indistinguishable, then it is easier to understand why our beliefs are not intractable nor immutable. If the negative core belief was made up by the ego, and the ego is just a fearful thought, not an entity, then a thought can be changed—even in an instant.

Here are some of the benefits people have observed from participating in these exercises:

- They are no longer disturbed by memories or thoughts of the trauma.
- They find that they can more easily monitor their thoughts around the belief.
- They find it easier to see differently people with whom they have intimate relationships, rather than with the automatic interpretations they were used to.
- They find their reactions to situations related to the trauma or belief no longer evoke the same emotional responses.
- The can deal more with present situations, rather than getting caught by what has happened in the past.
- They can make more sane decisions about how to react in the present.

When Fred and Caroline came to see me, they were on the verge of divorce. In the early years of their marriage, while living in Pennsylvania, they had experienced several years of trauma, after Caroline had a miscarriage. Both she and Fred fell into depressions, putting distance between them when they needed the other the most. In the years following, they had become increasingly hurt, fearful, and antagonistic toward each other and had reached the point where they weren't sure it was worth staying married. This is when they came to see me.

Wanting to give the marriage one last chance before divorcing, they decided to seek help, though not believing that much could change. In the sessions it became clear that each was quite wary of the other, much like puppies who have been beaten and are wary of people. Caroline openly expressed her serious doubts that they could remain together. When they both assessed the level of their trauma, or the degree to which they were still experiencing pain based on these past events using the ten-point scale, Fred discovered he was still experiencing a level nine in their relationship, and Caroline was experiencing a level ten. Since they shared the same trauma, they agreed to do the TAT erasing process together, which we were able to complete in one session, bringing the disturbance down to a zero for each of them. As they processed the miscarriage, they were finally able to let go of the pain, not forgetting it, but allowing it to lift so it would no longer carry such a deadly impact on their present emotional life. This kind of lifting was only possible through the tangible experience of the TAT.

In the next session, things between Caroline and Fred were noticeably different. When I greeted them in the waiting room, they were laughing and engaged in a very friendly conversation. When they came into the office, I noticed a lighter gait in Caroline's walk as well as a significantly more relaxed face. She looked at Fred with affection rather than with apprehension, fear, and anger. She opened by saying how much relief she had felt from our processing the trauma of their Pennsylvania years together. Fred eagerly agreed, and noted that there had only been one little episode of difficulty between them over the past week, whereas usually there were several painful and lengthy episodes.

Caroline then looked at Fred with deep warmth, totally missing from any previous sessions, and said, "I really want you to feel safe to tell me what you feel. I know that my anger has made you feel unsafe and you have shut down. It's only fair that you have the right to express yourself, too. I want you to feel comfortable to tell me anything." With these words, Fred relaxed even more in his body and his face, feeling and accepting the love that was coming from Caroline for the first time in years.

Within two weeks they had begun to talk in an unusually cooperative way about a house they would like to place an offer on, whereas, when still carrying the traumas of the past, they would not even think of considering such a move. At this point, their work moved rapidly and relatively smoothly as their trust, communication, and love deepened. Without clearing out the trauma, the work could have taken months to achieve even partial success.

But then another glitch appeared. Caroline began to find fault with Fred in a variety of ways. It seemed that many things he would do or not do would make her very unhappy. With further exploration, we discovered that Caroline had a belief that she did not deserve to be happy and that she could not be happy. Once this belief was changed, her judgments of Fred ceased, and they were able to continue their progress toward deepening their trust, love, and intimacy together.

Alex and Lucy are another example of a couple who were able to use the Trauma and Belief Erasing exercises to achieve profound healing in their relationship. They both came into their marriage feeling a strong sense of camaraderie. During their courtship, one of the ties that bound them together emotionally was their similar backgrounds. Unfortunately, they unwittingly based this intimacy on negative core beliefs that they shared.

Each of them had been raised in big families that were chaotic, noisy, and argumentative. Their parents were overwhelmed by trying to care for the many children, and run their respective homes; as a result, they barely kept their heads above water. As middle children, both Alex and Lucy were frequently ignored, falling between the cracks so to speak. As a result of this lack of loving attention, each of them had developed a common belief that family is a place where you will not be heard or acknowledged.

Once married, these common beliefs—instead of forging a positive bond—created conflict and discord. Even though both Alex and Lucy yearned for good communication and closeness in their marriage, their talking would quickly became so contentious that they felt increasingly estranged from each other, feeling unheard and unacknowledged. Again, their negative core beliefs were being confirmed in their relationship, reinforcing their Vicious Cycle of Interaction.

After many years of therapy, individually and as a couple, they called me in one final desperate attempt to salvage their marriage. Once we identified their mutual core belief, "I will never be heard," and several others that were related such as "I don't deserve to have a happy life or relationship," or "It's not safe to have a happy relationship," we began to identify the thoughts each carried that supported the belief, "I will not be heard." Next, they began to do the Five-Step Thought-Monitoring Process, focusing on those thoughts. This practice helped Alex and Lucy begin to see each other differently. Instead of viewing the other as the familiar depriver, each began to see the fear of not being heard. They both began to feel and be more compassionate to the other, extending love and a desire to be an interested, caring presence to listen, acknowledge, and respond lovingly.

This exercise began to erase the old belief and introduce a new positive belief in its place: "I can be heard." And while this helped give them a tangible sense of being happier in the relationship, they still needed to erase the effects of the traumas and the negative core beliefs. I then guided them as they did both EMDR and the Tapas Accupressure. Only then were they able to use their couples' therapy to begin to build a different kind of communication in which each really listened to the other and could perceive themselves as being listened to and acknowledged as well. From this place, they became quite committed to the spiritual principles enabling a happy marriage, with each of them taking responsibility for their participation in the relationship.

I hope that you can now see that you have the power to break into your Vicious Cycle of Interaction by both monitoring the distracting thoughts of the ego and erasing the effects of your traumas, and replace the negative core beliefs with positive, love-enhancing beliefs. We will turn now to see how we can further free our relationships from the Vicious Cycle of Interaction by making the perceptual shift.

In the next chapter, you will get even closer to your True Self and thereby create tangible happiness in your relationship. Just as simply as you chose to erase the negative beliefs, so you can choose to love—the quickest, most direct route to transforming your relationship from ego based to spiritual.

Resources: As mentioned throughout this chapter, there are several new technologies that provide us other workable methods, including EMDR (Eye Movement Desensitization and Reprocessing), Thought Field Therapy (TFT), Tapas Acupressure Technique (TAT), Emotional Freedom Techniques (EFT), and numerous others. If you have a broader interest in the field, you might read Dr. Fred Gallo's book on *Energy Psychology*, Gloria Arenson's book, *Five Simple Steps to Emotional Healing*, Or Francine Shapiro's book, *Eye Movement Desensitization and Reprocessing: Basic Principles, Protocols and Procedures*. You may also obtain more information about EMDR on the Web—www.emdr.com; and about energy psychology, including TAT at www.energypsych.org.

CHAPTER 7

Identifying Your Barriers to Love

"Love alone is capable of uniting living beings in such a way as to complete and fulfill them, for it alone takes them and joins them by what is deepest in themselves."
—Pierre Teilhard de Chardin

"We do not love people so much for the good they have done us, as for the good we have done them."
—Leo Tolstoy

THE ILLUSIONS OF COUNTERFEIT "LOVE"

Like the Golden Buddha, we are all made up of layers of clay. The body and the ego cover our loving core, and we are usually only given rare glimpses of the infinite potential inside of ourselves or others. Stuck in this limited perspective of the counterfeit self, we think that our clay ego body and its counterfeit "love" is all that we have—and we believe the same is true about everyone else as well. Just as the illusion of the ego disguises the infinite capacity of our Divine Nature, so too does this counterfeit self cut us off from our knowledge that we are Love. Remember the story of Sir Gawain and his bride? The kind of love that characterized their marriage is what I call Empowering Love, a form of love that is unconditional; that is about giving and not about receiving, that is about being in touch with the Love that we are.

Sadly, much of what we think of as love is not love at all, but the ego's counterfeit "love." And many of our culture's films and novels actually reinforce this misconception. Authors and singers continue to misguide us by describing forms of counterfeit love in films, plays, novels, and songs, and asking us to buy into this fragile, impermanent, and ultimately false idea. We leave the theater or put the book down thinking that someday this imaginary love will arrive and change our lives into the life we've always dreamed of. Or we return to our present relationship certain that it could never be the special kind of relationship that we know will be possible if only we were with the right person.

This counterfeit "love" not only undermines joy in all of our relationships, makes us miserable, and is the basis for discord, but it also actually weakens us physically, emotionally, and spiritually, and can even make us sick. On the other hand, genuine, or Empowering Love, the central aspect of our True Self, is dramatically different from most of the common behaviors, feelings, and attitudes that are associated with the word "love." This Love actually makes us stronger physically, boosts our immune system, heals emotional wounds and fears, transforms troubled relationships into ones that are joyous and fulfilling, keeps us from being adversely affected by any negative energy around us, and helps us find our core Spiritual Self, all at the same time.

In this chapter, we will begin to question the familiar meanings that we give the word "love." And we will see that our customary experiences of romantic love, passion, sexual attraction, and infatuation, when looked at more closely, often resemble manipulation, yearning, possessiveness, neediness, control, or barter. Even love we experience for our children may often include an underlying demand for control or certain expectations that they fill our own sense of emptiness, which is tied to our quest for happiness. The various forms of counterfeit "love" actually act as barriers to love. They make us feel emotionally bankrupt inside ourselves and in our relationships, and further sabotage our efforts to connect with our natural ability to love in an empowering, unconditional way.

Counterfeit "love" results from fear, scarcity, and need—all arising out of the ego belief that we are separate. On the other hand, the love from the True Self comes out of a feeling of abundance and completeness, for you know that you are part of the Divine in the universe, and thus can never be empty of Love. Empowering Love, the genuine form of Love, is spiritual love and forms the basis for a spiritual marriage. Since this love always strengthens and brings joy, it never results in pain or diminishes anyone in any way. When expressed sexually, it is a powerful experience of intimacy and of joining as One. On the other hand, weakening "love"—the counterfeit "love" of the ego—may bring temporary elation and excitement, and even a flash of sexual passion, but it never brings lasting joy. And when this form of "love" is the main basis of marriage, it inevitably leads to disappointment, despair, and misery—and often divorce, emotionally if not physically.

THE FORMS OF COUNTERFEIT "LOVE"

To be happy in our various relationships, it is of utmost importance that we become highly adept in recognizing the barriers to love that are blocking us from our loving core and our ability to love fully in our relationships. The barriers to love are illusions, just as all the thoughts and beliefs that stem from the ego are illusions. Therefore, they can be removed and replaced with thoughts and beliefs about Empowering Love. Once you recognize the forms of counterfeit love for what they are—false—then they no longer have any power over you. But that doesn't mean that it's always easy to stay aware and cognizant of their false nature. Instead, you have to be constantly vigilant, asking yourself frequently, "Am I being loving from a counterfeit perspective or an empowering perspective?" That may be all it takes.

1. Infatuation or the falling-in-love syndrome that we discussed at length in Chapter One is the first form of counterfeit "love." Based on the illusion of separateness and a fantasy of the beloved, instead of a real knowledge of the self or the other person, this form of love can hardly be anything but counterfeit. As long as we confuse such a state with love, it will serve to block our awareness of the real and Empowering Love that we are.

When we are attached to illusions of what we want to see, we don't see anything else. As is characteristic of perception, it is always colored by what is inside us. Jennifer, for example, wanted a partner who would take good care of her—materially and emotionally. When she met John, she knew he was the one. It was love at first sight. John was a successful lawyer, and seemed to have a very good chance of becoming a partner in the prestigious law firm he worked for. Blinded by her desire for financial security, Jennifer was oblivious to John's inability to be with her emotionally. She confused his sexual interest with loving and caring. Therefore, Jenny had unwittingly picked a partner who could be familiar to her—much like her father who was financially successful, but remote, self-involved, and unavailable. She could now repeat her lifelong quest of yearning for love, trying to get it from one who could not supply it. She fulfilled what Freud called the repetition compulsion. She didn't know John for she saw what she needed/wanted to see in order to repeat her lifelong struggle for love. Of course, she was also unable to see the divine spark within John, and therefore did not know him psychologically or spiritually. By relying on the falling-in-love syndrome to choose a partner, she not only unconsciously chose to ignore John's True Self, she also set herself up for disappointment. She married her fantasy, not the real person, and fell in love with the *feeling* of falling in love.

In the thrill of being "in love," it is very difficult to see the other person's True Self. We confuse our feelings of intense sexual attraction and excitation with love, and we think that by getting to know another's body we have gotten to know the person. Passion, so often associated with love, is most commonly associated with a strong and sometimes desperate attempt to possess the other person or to get something from the other person. Sometime it is a desire for the excitement of being with someone new, or other times it is for someone who is not fully available—as in the case with Jenny, above.

Quite often, then, passion could be a synonym for yearning to have a connection, but not embracing what is. Remember the ego's motto "seek, but don't find"? This is why many couples lose their passion when they know they have each other and when the bubble of their illusion has burst. Many find stimulation only in the conquest, trying to get someone who is perhaps not available emotionally. And even if the other person is available, some people will still perceive them as unavailable because it confirms their inner belief that love is unavailable to them—as was the case with Jenny. Or once they have been gotten, they will create a situation in which they feel bored or they begin to fight as a way to distract themselves from the challenge of real love and intimacy.

On the other hand, spiritual Love is about more than physical attraction or excitement or passion or longing. With spiritual Love, our body becomes the vehicle through which we can communicate the deep feelings we have for the other person in the most intimate, vulnerable, expressive, exposed, and powerful way. And it is also the clearest experience of how we receive back what we give to another person. By expressing the love we feel for a special other person in our lives, we feel that emotion expand within ourselves before we express that feeling to another—and thus we find the love we seek.

2. Appointing someone as special. As soon as we appoint someone as special, we set the stage for our own disappointment. For by deeming that person special, we are asking him or her to live up to our expectations of who we want him or her to be. We immediately are asking that person to be someone for us, instead of being who he or she is naturally. Often a feature of the falling-in-love syndrome, appointing someone as special is a basic form of counterfeit "love."

Out of our belief that we are separate, we confuse love with specialness. Then do we not live by the belief that if we find someone special we will be happy? We often believe that there is just one true love that will bring a marriage made in heaven. Are these not all myths, quite prevalent in our culture, but ones that do not hold true in our experiences?

Problems come with appointing anyone as special. We may think of our children as special, but when we do, we impose more of our expectations upon them as pressure. Or we live in fear of something happening to them. We also attribute specialness to parents or friends. But specialness, as we commonly live it, so often destroys love instead of increasing it; it means that we believe love lies outside us rather than within us. As a result, we feel we have to control, protect, criticize, and try to change the special person—instead of accepting and loving them without conditions attached.

Later in the book, I address a somewhat revolutionary idea: Why not choose to appoint no one as special? Wouldn't that mean we treat all people with the same unconditional love? Would we not love our partners more if we did not appoint them as special?

3. Seeing love as a commodity. Counterfeit "love" makes love a noun, a commodity that can be bartered. I have often asked audiences of hundreds of people, "How many have ever succeeded in trying to *get* love from someone?" No one has ever raised a hand. When we seek outside of ourselves for love, we have already separated ourselves from it, thinking it is that which we are not. The verb to "to love" cannot be captured and held anymore than "to see" or "to run." In an ever-expanding universe, God must also be seen as endlessly creating and expanding. And Love, as well, is just such an experience, because when we give it, it expands and multiplies. With the ego in charge, we tend to see others as "love suppliers." Our partners or spouses become less people and more objects who should give us the love that we believe we need.

But most important, when we think of love as a commodity, we tend to focus on getting, rather than on giving. If you are going to experience gain in love, then you cannot barter, but must give without expectation. This is the essence of Empowering Love.

4. Needing to control those we love. Counterfeit "love" confuses love with control. We often think our attempts to control another's behaviors, attitudes, feelings, values, morals, interests, activities, and bodies comes out of our love for that person. Hence we may want to know exactly where they are all the time, who they are with, what they are doing, and for how long. We may even try to control what they eat, how much they sleep, and how often they exercise! This is the result—and cause—of our fears and insecurities, and makes Love impossible.

One of my clients, for instance, had to constantly know where his wife was, calling her on her cell phone fifteen to twenty times a day. He wanted to control who her friends were, what she did with them, and when. Throughout it all, he would tell her how much he loved her. Yet his "love" was merely an attempt to control her out of his fear.

5. Confusing worry with Love. Worry is another of the ego's forms of counterfeit "love." Many believe that to worry about someone means that you love that person. Worry, however, is not love, but in reality a form of fear. The worry can be about a person's health, safety, future, or even that we might lose that person to someone else.

You may worry that the loved person will not be safe or that he or she does not take care of him or herself. You may worry that your children won't do well. When you worry, you are really showing concern about your own needs. You are afraid of potential loss or damage to your self-image, created by the ego mind. This fear ultimately displaces Love.

While some worry over people we care about is part of the human condition, we need to transcend such ego thoughts and let go of the barriers of fear and worry in order to love. You may also consciously choose to extend Love to the person about whom you have been worrying, which will immediately stop the worry since Love takes its place.

I have asked my closest family members to not worry about me if I am ever critically ill or injured: "Think loving or compassionate thoughts, or simply ignore me in your mind, but do not harbor worry thoughts." I do not want the effects of worried thoughts to negatively impact me if I am in a weakened state. Loving thoughts empower and bring healing, as we shall see later. Worry, on the other hand, has no redeeming value whatsoever since it only weakens us as well as the others around us; love displaces worry and fear, while worry and fear displace Love.

6. Needing our loved one's physical presence. Another form of counterfeit "love" confuses love with the need for another's bodily presence. In this case, the other person's physical presence is viewed as the literal embodiment of Love, which means that when your lover's body is not there, you feel that you are being deprived. There is a difference between enjoying being with another person and a *need* to be with that person. Needing to be with that special person is caused by the emptiness we feel because of our illusion of separateness (because we are not in our True Self awareness, but rather acting out of our confused sense of identity). If instead you were aware that we are all joined together as One, then you would feel your lover's presence even when his or her body is not with you.

But in the illusion of separateness, you tend to believe that another's physical presence will fill or complete you. Yet often when two people are together in this need state, they complain about each other instead of enjoying the time they do have together. For example, Jean often yearned to be with her lover Jamie. However, when they would get together, Jean spent the time unhappily, complaining about how Jamie was not there enough for her. Yet as soon as they were apart, she would pine away in loneliness, feeling miserable and abandoned.

ADDITIONAL BARRIERS TO LOVE

While all forms of counterfeit "love" are barriers to love, there are a number of additional barriers that are not forms of counterfeit "love," but rather result from loving in a counterfeit way. As with the forms of counterfeit "love," we need to identify and clear out these other barriers to love that we carry inside of ourselves. These barriers often stem from the negative core beliefs you examined in Chapter Six, or act as erroneous beliefs about love that prevent you from loving freely in an empowering way. Again, once you identify these barriers, you are halfway to destroying them.

1. Fear of loving. Being the opposite of love, fear is one of the central barriers to love. When we dwell on our fear, it reinforces our illusion of littleness and displaces love from our conscious awareness. The ego part of our mind uses the pains of the past to create pain in the present and to project anticipated suffering into the future. Therefore, it makes us fear love itself.

We fear being hurt again, so we close our hearts. One man described himself as having an iron pot around his heart. We even fear showing our vulnerability, even though sharing it invites most people to be compassionate and thereby deepens intimacy. We fear losing the people we have appointed as special, and we also fear losing ourselves in a relationship.

Fear also gives rise to the emotion that is a great and common barrier to love: anger. Some schools of acting think of anger as a secondary emotion, since a more vulnerable fear or hurt usually serves as the trigger. Some psychoanalysts think of anger as a defense more than an emotion. The ego mind uses anger in an attempt to protect us from more pain, but the end result is further separation from Love—whether in ourselves or with other people. And further, our fears of love will actually cause us to not recognize bona fide expressions of Empowering Love when they do come our way.

Counterfeit "love" of the ego often confuses love with weakness and anger or hatred with strength. This is why we have so much difficulty opening ourselves to someone that we perceive as hurtful. The ego's solution is to have us hold on to resentment and anger, believing that they will protect us. It says, "Don't extend love, or you will be in danger of being hurt again." The ego voice does not tell us, however, that such a move not only separates us from others, leaving us lonely, but that it also actually makes us feel weaker, therefore bringing the perpetual hurt of being separated from love.

2. Erroneous beliefs about love. Out of our hurts and fears we draw conclusions that congeal into our beliefs about love, such as,

"Love is dangerous."

"I'll never find love."

"Closeness means I will lose myself."

"Giving is losing" or "Love is a sacrifice."

"Loving means 'I possess you.' "

"If I love, I will be abandoned."

"Love must be earned."

"Love means getting hurt."

"Love leads to loss."

"Love means being controlled."

"Love means that I will be abused."

"Love is smothering."

"If I love, I will lose control."

"Love means I will be judged."

We then live by these erroneous beliefs, making them self-confirming or self-fulfilling. Negative beliefs about love, therefore, become powerful barriers to love. As with other beliefs, you can erase these negative beliefs and replace them with loving, affirming beliefs, as you saw in Chapter Six.

3. Judging the one we love against our expectations. Have you ever expected a sweet pussycat to growl or bark like a watchdog or expected a beautifully striped zebra to run like a racehorse? Hardly! Yet we often do the equivalent with our partners. Then, when they do not live up to our expectations and are being just as they are, our ego mind judges and condemns them.

Another barrier to Love is judgment, since judgment is of the ego, not the True Self. Our minds are filled with judging thoughts about the special people in our lives. "Tom never calls me from the office." "Marge is such a mess." "Susie is always yelling. I can't stand it." "I wish George would come home when he says he will. I can't count on him." And the more we focus on what is wrong with them, the more that which we have deemed wrong seems to increase.

We want others to be different from what they are, so we judge the way they are as wrong and expend enormous effort trying to change the other person. Judgment is a form of condemnation—and how can one love someone we condemn? Yet in the midst of this judging and attempts to change the other person, we insist that we love the person—even calling our judgments expressions of love. But, like worry, judgment displaces any possibility of love because instead of relating to whoever they really are, we are trying to change them to our liking—often to fit them into the idealized image that we projected onto them early in the relationship. We become angry and blaming when they do not live up to the role that we have assigned to them. In the moments we judge, we do not love, for when we judge we forget our True Self and do not know the True Self of the other person. A strong tendency of the ego mind will be to now judge ourselves for having judged others. Instead, let us be forgiving of ourselves, for only then do we move from judging to loving.

Our judgments of ourselves and others, which are the same, is one of the greatest obstacles to peace and to the flow of love. When we say negative things about our spouse (child, parent, etc.) to another person, especially when we do it repeatedly, it only rehearses the negative and erroneous perception of the person just as much as thinking those thoughts about them. And further, saying it aloud to another often gives more credence to our negative perception, and we might reinforce the negative perception if we hear, "Yeah, that was a bad thing he or she did." As most of us know all too well, it is frequently the ego's temptation to bad-mouth one's special person to a third party. We must be very careful not to play out this temptation, for this is a powerful way the ego mind uses to block love since we are dwelling upon what is wrong about them. Because what we focus on is what we get, such a focus always serves to displace love.

Instead, we need to stop and look at ourselves! DO this first! Have you noticed how it makes you feel to dwell on the fault of another?

Notice the immediate and pervasive loss of peace and happiness that comes with each judgment, whether about others or ourselves. In fact, anytime we are not totally at peace, it is most likely that we have been judging someone else or ourselves, which is all the same. We need to go inside and notice how it makes us feel in our bellies, in our muscles, and in our hearts when we dwell on negative thoughts, fear thoughts, and judgments about another.

4. Withholding love. When we feel as if we are not receiving the love we desire often it's because we are the ones who are withholding love from someone. Donald, for example, believed that his wife and his children did not love him. They seemed busy with their own lives, and did not show any interest in being with him. He gradually came to realize that by seeking love, he had been withholding love from those he sought it from.

Conversely, those who express Empowering Love most, need to search for it the least because they are filled with what it is they give. They also discover that giving love tends to attract love as well. For example, when Donald made a conscious decision to show more loving kindness to his wife and children, he was amazed at how soon he felt filled with love—first inside himself, and then reflected back from his other family members. So, if we do not believe we are receiving love from others, the first place to look for the cause is inside ourselves: "How is it that *I* am not being loving?"

If we withhold love from ourselves, it does not matter how much love another person may give to us, we will not see it as love. George, for example, was very attentive to Laura when she talked to him. He would listen without interrupting her, and then mirror back what he had heard from her in some kind of paraphrase in order to show that he had clearly heard her words and feelings. He would often acknowledge and validate her feelings, but she continued to feel like she was not heard by him. She claimed his mirroring back to her was artificial. Whenever he claimed to understand her feelings, she would say, "You have no idea what it was like for me! You just have no idea!"

Her belief that no one could hear or understand her, beginning in her family of origin where that was largely her daily experience, colored her perception to the degree that she could not even believe in George's sincere and genuine interest in her. Therefore she constantly complained that people, especially George, did not listen to her.

5. Out of judgment and guilt comes the desire to punish those we "love" for disappointing us. We may punish a spouse emotionally for not being what we wanted them to be by withholding affection, love, kindness, listening, understanding, or sex. We may withdraw, sulk, or refuse to talk. We may scold, condemn, or punish a child, sometimes physically, even claiming that this is for their own good. But punishment comes out of fear, not love. This is not to say that children do not need guidance and discipline. Discipline, when coming from love, teaches us to consider the consequences of our behavior and develops internal self-control. Punishment says, "You are bad and deserve punishment to confirm your badness." Anytime we try to make someone feel that he or she is bad—whether it is our partner, our children, or a rude driver on the road—we are not acting from Love. We are simply driving people away, creating a bigger barrier to Love.

6. Demanding the love be earned. Similar to judgment, guilt, and the desire to punish, counterfeit "love" says that other people must earn our love first, before we will give it to them. They must be good enough and behave in the fashion we desire or please us in the ways we want. However, when we consider ourselves capable of being able to judge their worthiness, we have immediately lost touch with our loving core, as well as any awareness of another's intrinsic worth. We are judging instead of accepting. Everyone is deserving of love because at their core, everyone *is* Love—and it is only through the process of loving that everyone comes to recognize their wholeness, interconnectedness, and their core loving nature.

But the ego mind believes love and worthiness are things to be earned. We do not realize that by withholding it from another we are actually withholding it from ourselves as well. And sadly, we are also withholding the healing power of our love from the other person while waiting for them to prove their worthiness. Do we really wish to delay healing?

7. Trying to change someone. Your job is not to fix the other person, trying to make him or her into what you expect them to be. Could we ever change a turtle into a hare or a tiger into a bunny rabbit? Instead, you need to fix your distorted perception of yourself and the other person so that you can bring your wholeness and happiness into the interactions in the relationship. Paradoxically, if you fix yourself, the relationship will change in some way as well. But this is true only if your total intent is to attend to your own inner issues such as your reactions to the other. Acceptance is the only sane response. Anything else comes from the ego's voice of illusion, which is essentially insanity. When you focus on trying to change another person, it makes you feel helpless, for you have embarked on an impossible task. Therefore, you cannot but feel increased powerlessness. As such, it takes you away from the highly empowered True Self. This is why extending love always increases your sense of empowerment. It is most difficult for most of us to see that when we blame others for our hurts or deprivations, we are essentially blaming ourselves since we are indeed all One in the unified field of consciousness.

8. Hatred. One of the biggest barriers to love is hatred—both conscious and unconscious. I define hatred as anything that is not full acceptance. It includes all negative judgments, resentments, anger, demands, expectations, and attempts to control. It is hatred because it is the opposite of love, and all these experiences from our darker side perpetuate the ego's existence because the ego makes them all normal. The word "normal," however, is a statistical term that means simply "the norm." It is what most people do. But since the world is basically a world of insanity, and being the home of the ego, what else could we expect? We forget that the so-called normal world is the world of insanity, which we must transcend in order to both reach our True Selves, uncover the Love that is genuine, and thereby heal our relationships.

If you try to love while feeling hatred in your heart, it is much like having a horse hitched to opposite ends of the cart, pulling in opposite directions. But when you can acknowledge your hatred, experience it, and then choose to let it go, you clear the space for love to emerge naturally since it is what you truly are. Some people have trouble acknowledging their hatred because they find it so unacceptable to their self-image. Then they attempt to love while pushing their hatred into the closet. This process is much like putting a chocolate coating onto rotten food. The hatred can be fully released only when fully acknowledged. Once acknowledged, you can ask for help from Spirit or God to release it, especially when you have trouble releasing it yourself (we will discuss more about seeking help from God or the Spirit in Chapter Eight). To the ego, everything is about getting or trying to get. To Spirit, getting has no meaning at all. You must remember, however, that when you give with expectations, which is barter, you only feel more empty and deprived, for barter is an expression of not having. Since you always receive what you give, giving and receiving being essentially the same thing, you must totally remove the idea of sacrifice from your understanding of love. Only barter can be sacrifice, for it is what leaves you depleted since it comes out of the illusion that you do not have.

9. Addictions. All of our addictions serve as barriers to love, whether the addiction is to alcohol, drugs, work, sex, computers, food, the telephone, tobacco—even to people. Addictions cause us to focus on something or someone that we have endowed with the power to complete us, soothe us, take away our pain, or make us happy. Then we spend our energy desperately trying to get our gratification from this supposed power source. Such addictions are barriers to Love for they largely distract us from our ability to give. We are so consumed by trying to get relief from whatever we are addicted to outside of us, that we lose sight of our love, the source of healing, which exists within.

As we admit to our addictions and choose to let them go, we also let go of a major barrier to Love.

PRACTICE 6:

The Litmus Tests to Distinguish Between Counterfeit and Empowering Love

In chemistry, one uses a litmus test to determine whether a substance is acidic or alkaline. We need good litmus tests to determine whether an attitude or behavior is Empowering Love or counterfeit "love." Ask yourself the questions below to see when you might be acting from a position of counterfeit "love." Use your answers as a guide to become conscious of when and if you are experiencing barriers to love. As you become familiar with the barriers to your love, you will begin to tear down their infrastructure, making way for the installment of Empowering Love.

LITMUS TEST 1:
DO YOU FEEL HURT OR ANGRY WHEN YOU DO NOT RECEIVE ANYTHING BACK FROM YOUR GIVING?

Observe whether you expect anything back after giving love, and whether you feel disappointed or rejected when you do not get something back, even if it's just to hear them say, "I love you, too." The experience of expecting something back is an indication that the ego's illusion of separateness rules at that moment, and is the state of mind in which happiness is not possible.

What happens when we think we have given a lot of love, but just want some for ourselves in return? The ego mind has returned and is now putting forth a counterfeit form of love that is more like barter: "I'm giving to you because I want something from you in return. I feel empty and need you to fill me."

LITMUS TEST 2:

DOES YOUR GIVING MAKE YOU FEEL ENERGIZED, OR EXHAUSTED AND MORE DRAINED?

If you feel exhausted and drained, the odds are that you have been giving begrudgingly, out of duty or obligation. "Oughts" and "shoulds" have probably been a motivator. Or you may have been bargaining for love. If your love is genuinely given, you will feel fulfilled and often energized.

LITMUS TEST 3:

DOES YOUR GIVING MAKE YOU FEEL HAPPY AND JOYOUS, OR DOES IT RESULT IN YOUR FEELING DEPRIVED, UNHAPPY, OR DEPRESSED?

Love is happiness and genuine happiness is Love. If your giving leaves you deprived, unhappy, or depressed, this usually means you have given with a barter arrangement in mind, either consciously or unconsciously. Depression is characterized by feelings of helplessness, hopelessness, and despair. I have often seen in my practice that when a person begins to focus on their love and compassion for one or several people, their depression lifts quickly—sometimes immediately. It is especially true when the person focuses on more than one person whom they love. Focus on compassion can actually change the serotonin balance in the brain, thereby lifting the cause of the chemical depression.

LITMUS TEST 4:
DOES YOUR GIVING MAKE YOU STRONGER OR WEAKER? DO YOU HAVE BETTER HEALTH OR DO YOU GET SICK MORE OFTEN FROM YOUR KIND OF GIVING?

The body quickly responds to the messages from the mind through those chemical messengers, the neuropeptides. If you would like to experience the difference dramatically and kinesthetically, you can do a test of muscle strength. You will find that you are significantly stronger when thinking loving thoughts of compassion versus any negative thoughts. It is well known that loving thoughts help plants to flourish, while angry thoughts may often cause them to whither and even die.

Remember the muscle testing described in the chapter on thoughts? Have someone press down on your arm while you resist, so they can determine your normal strength. Then, focus on a situation with a person in which you thought you were being loving. While holding the image of that situation in your mind, have the other person press down on your arm while you resist. If your arm becomes stronger, you most likely have been extending Empowering Love in the situation. If your arm becomes weaker, it is most likely that you have been engaged in some form of counterfeit "love." Such "love" will clearly weaken you.

LITMUS TEST 5:
DOES YOUR FORM OF GIVING BRING FEAR AND WORRY OR PEACE AND JOY?

If you are living with fear and worry, it probably means that you have confused them with love, as the ego mind likes to get you to do. Since love brings peace and joy, fear and worry cannot be Love. Even in a most difficult situation, where a loved one is sick or injured, it is easy for any of us to fall into fear and worry because we do not want to lose that person. But this is not to be confused with Love. Instead, it is an expression of our fear of loss. This is why healers often cannot be successful with a loved one because their dispassionate love gets contaminated by their human fears.

LITMUS TEST 6:

DOES YOUR GIVING MAKE YOU FEEL EMPTY OR FULL?

If we feel full, we have given without expectations and therefore have opened ourselves to experience the fullness of genuine giving. Giving, hoping for anything in return, must bring feelings of emptiness sooner or later.

LITMUS TEST 7:

DO YOU USUALLY WORRY IN YOUR RELATIONSHIPS, OR DO YOU TRUST THEM?

If you worry about the outcome of a relationship, you are usually viewing the other person as the source of love. Loss of that person, from this perspective, would therefore be a loss of love. When you trust the outcome to be for the highest goal, then there can be no worry. Your biggest and most important trust must be in yourself—that you already have and can choose to extend Love anytime, anywhere. You can always trust Love's presence. Bodies stay for a while and then go away and die. Love, being eternal, never dies or goes away, but is always present inside of us.

LITMUS TEST 8:
DO YOU TRY TO CONTROL OR CAN YOU LET IT BE?

If you find yourself trying to control, you have identified another way in which you do not trust. But how can you control others or the universe when you cannot control your own mind? If you can trust that you are part of an infinite supply of Love, then it becomes easier to let one be and you can then let another be. The other person is then more likely to respond with Love instead of acting from their fear. Control creates fear and pushes others away. Love and trust attract, for love attracts Love to itself.

LITMUS TEST 9:
ARE YOU ATTACHED TO OUTCOMES OR CAN YOU ACCEPT THAT ALL THINGS WILL WORK TOGETHER FOR THE ULTIMATE GOOD?

Jesus and the Buddha remind us that suffering comes from our attachments. Love never brings suffering, only our fears and attachments do. When you are able to let the ego's way go, and trust that all things will work together for the highest good, then you are connected with the source of Love itself—God, the universe—however you choose to name it. All your fears will disappear, banished as all little ideas should be.

LITMUS TEST 10:

DOES YOUR FORM OF GIVING HELP YOU FEEL EMOTIONALLY STRONGER AND MORE SECURE OR DOES IT MAKE YOU FEEL MORE AT THE WHIM OF OTHERS' MOODS AND BEHAVIORS?

If you give, believing that you are devoid of love and separate from the universe, you will keep seeking Love outside of yourself. With each such quest, you will feel less and less secure, emotionally weaker and at the mercy of others. You will feel like a victim. Genuine Love without conditions of any kind can only make you feel stronger emotionally and feeling more secure, for you have then identified with your True Self, your Divine Nature.

CHOOSING EMPOWERING LOVE

In order to uncover the path to the spiritual marriage and convert our special relationship into a happy one, it is of utmost importance that we become highly adept in distinguishing between the genuine Love of the Spiritual Self, which is infinitely empowering, and the counterfeit forms of "love" of the ego, which weaken us. If we don't learn to distinguish between the two, we will remain in much unnecessary pain and suffering, wondering why our special relationships seem to bring pain and suffering instead of joy, and we will likely attribute the failure to an external cause, usually the other person. However, once we distinguish between the different forms of love, we can also begin to know our True Self's loving nature, and to know the happiness, healing, and fullness that it brings to our relationships. We will find boundless Love within us, and as we extend it to others, we will find one of the most profound truths in existence: that *we are Love*. And if we are Love, and God is Love, then we are part of God, and God is part of us. This is what it means to be "in the image and likeness of God."

In the next chapter, you will learn how to let go fully of these barriers to love and choose Empowering Love. Again, this is a conscious choice that happens at the level of thought. As in the exercises of thought monitoring, changing your core beliefs, and making a perceptual shift, you will be asked to disown your barriers to love and choose to replace them with the various forms that make up Empowering Love.

CHAPTER 8

Unblocking the Flow of Love

"Love means to love that which is unlovable, or it is no virtue at all; forgiving means to pardon that which is unpardonable, or it is no virtue at all."
—G. K. Chesterson

GENUINE LOVE

Empowering Love, the genuine form of Love, forms the essence of a spiritual marriage or happy relationship. Since this love always strengthens and brings joy, it never results in pain or diminishes anyone in any way. Empowering Love is unconditional, and expects *nothing* in return. And if we expect nothing in return, we will never be disappointed. In the Jewish teachings of the Torah, the highest form of love is giving anonymously, whether service or materially. By giving in this way, we guarantee our release from expectations of something back. In the Christian tradition, this love is called "agape." Yogananda, the author of *Autobiography of a Yogi*, expressed this same idea beautifully and practically when he said, "I never expect anything from anyone, therefore I am never disappointed." He had learned the truth that expectations are primarily setups for future resentments.

But most of our egos, by this point, are probably demanding that we have a right to expect *something* from the person we love. And what would such a love without expectations of anything in return actually look like? There is a story about two brothers who farmed the same land. Their main crop was wheat, and at harvest time they'd divide the harvest equally between them. One evening, one of the brothers began to think of his brother and his situation. "My brother," he thought, "is not getting a fair deal. He has a wife and many children to take care of, while I am unmarried and live alone. He needs much more than I do since he has so many mouths to feed." So he decided that he would take some wheat secretly each night from his barn and put it in his brother's barn.

The other brother had similar thoughts. "My brother is not getting a fair deal out of our arrangement. I have many children to take care of me in my old age, but my brother is alone. He needs more of the wheat so that he can prepare for his old age and be able to take care of himself." And with that thought, he decided to take some wheat from his own share and put it in his brother's barn each night.

This continued for a while, and each brother was puzzled as to why his supply remained the same, even though he gave some away each night. Then one moonlit night their paths crossed as they were taking wheat to the other's barn, and instantly they knew what had happened. Feeling deep love and appreciation for each other, they embraced in tears and gratitude. These brothers gave from the heart, expecting nothing in return. In this way, we can also see how their love was genuinely Empowering Love. By giving purely from our heart, we experience a sense of being filled with happiness, a happiness that is endless and unqualified.

Some people have more difficulty showing love, respect, or sympathy to strangers, while others have more difficulty showing similar feelings to family members. To be in touch with love more constantly in our lives, we need to extend it without reservation to *everyone* we encounter, withholding it from no one. There is no shortage of people who need the love we can give them, and each encounter becomes an opportunity to experience the love we innately are.

Love is not just liking someone when he or she is delightful—for that is easy. In a spiritual marriage or family, it means loving someone when they are down. In Lorraine Hansberry's play *A Raisin in the Sun*, we can see a deeply moving portrait of unconditional love in action—loving when there is nothing to receive in return, loving when someone has done something that has been harmful to us. In the play, Walter has just foolishly lost all of his family's money, and they will now lose their house. Walter's sister, Beneatha, is furious and resentful toward him and says to their mother:

> BENEATHA: *Love him? There is nothing left to love!*
>
> MAMA: *There is always something left to love. And if you ain't learned that, you ain't learned nothing. [Looking at her] Have you cried for that boy today? I don't mean for yourself and for the family 'cause we lost the money. I mean for him; what he been through and what it done to him. Child, when do you think is the time to love somebody the most; when they done good and made things easy for everybody? Well then you ain't through learning—because that ain't the time at all. It's when he's at his lowest and can't believe in hisself 'cause the world done whipped him so. When you starts measuring somebody, measure him right, child, measure him right. Make sure you done taken into account what hills and valleys he come through before he got to wherever he is.*

Loving the unloveable, loving when we do not expect anything in return—or, as the philosopher Søren Kierkegaard put it, "loving the one who harmed us"—is one of the most difficult things for most of us to accomplish. And, to the ego part of our minds, it will never make sense. But once we have consciously had even one experience of giving or receiving such love, it will be a potential in every situation, no matter how difficult it seems.

In the last chapter, we examined the different forms of counterfeit "love" and the barriers they produce. Now let us look at the characteristics of true, or empowering, Love, so that you can begin to replace your barriers with these positive, loving affirmations. Remember all creation begins with our thoughts. Therefore, when you begin thinking of love in this different way, you will see immediate changes: you will feel different within yourself and in your relationships. Indeed, by loving in an empowering way, you are connecting with your True Self.

The loving not only becomes effortless and natural, it continues to grow, moment by moment, spreading the healing through you and to your partner.

1. Love is a verb. The Love that we are is not so much a noun as it is a verb, just as we saw that our True Self identity is more of a verb than a noun. If we believe that love is a noun, then we think that it can be traded, given, withheld, sought after, possessed, and lost, leaving us at the mercy of another's whims or of life circumstances, which often generate feelings of scarcity concerning love. If, on the other hand, we know love as a verb, then giving or receiving it are ultimately the same, and love is both inexhaustible and infinite. We are in control of the love in our lives, not others. Loving is therefore a conscious act of creation and not some thing or even an emotion that controls us. Just as our identity is not fixed into any limiting form, neither is the Love that we are.

2. Love is a conscious focus of the mind. We saw earlier how our thoughts are the beginning of creation. That being so, we can choose to extend loving thoughts anytime to any person anywhere. Also, since love is not an emotion that rules us, it is not affected by our changing emotions any more than it is by the ever-changing weather. Nature teaches us this love by providing crying babies during the night to disturb our sleep. We love them and so get up to take care of them, even when we are tired.

We need, therefore, to redefine love and to see it not so much as an emotion as a conscious, willful decision that one makes in one's mind. We find it easy to love when someone is being what we want them to be, but the real test comes in difficult times—when we perceive rejection or attack—when we might ordinarily become angry or critical of the other person. When we understand the true nature of Love, we realize that we can love even when we don't feel like it.

Paul would often be attacked by his wife in outbursts of contemptuous rage. Diana had grown up in a household where her mother would be angry about almost everything. Her father, who was depressed for years, encouraged his daughter to express herself, since he was unable to. Consequently Diana not only frequently became angry (like her mother), but kept up such tirades for days since expressing her anger brought approval. In their marriage, Paul was the recipient of these rageful tirades, often feeling as if the love had been beaten out of him. He then fell into fairly negative, judging thoughts about Diana, withdrawing from her and from the relationship.

After Paul went through the exercises to break into this Vicious Cycle of Interaction, he became much more proactive: instead of quietly and passively receiving Diana's outbursts, he made perceptual shifts and focused on the frightened girl inside the body of the rageful wife. Since minds are all joined and interconnected, when Paul consciously began to monitor his judging thoughts about Diana, and began to see her appeals for love, hidden underneath her anger, not only did Paul feel more centered, but Diana's tirades began to subside as well.

Paul was then able to look more calmly at his barriers to love. With this foundation, he chose Empowering Love in a fully conscious way. Diana followed suit, persuaded by the enormous relief she found in the love that was surrounding her. They had begun to heal their relationship.

3. The main function of love is to forgive. Forgiveness and acceptance are the essential conditions of Empowering Love and though they may feel similar to falling in love, they come from a solid foundation and from conscious choice rather than hormones or our illusions about the other person or ourselves. Forgiveness becomes an ongoing state of mind, not just an occasional act, although it may begin that way. That is what Jesus meant when he told those who asked him, "How many times should I forgive my brother?" that they should forgive them, "Seventy times seven." Similarly, the Buddha taught that to let go of our suffering, we must first let go of all our attachments—including our expectations and resentments of others that poison our relationships. There can be no genuine Empowering Love without forgiveness.

When you forgive, you are basically overlooking those things that you had previously judged to be bad or in error. Forgiveness is seeing that there was no sin that was committed, only mistakes. Forgiveness sees appeals for love in the place of perceived attacks. It is no wonder that forgiveness always brings us back to happiness. Also, have you ever noticed how much more beautiful a person whom you have forgiven looks to you? And I am sure you have noticed how ugly the unforgiven person looks. But even more, have you looked at yourself in the mirror when carrying a resentment and contrasted it to the way you look when you have forgiven?

Forgiveness is the core expression of Love in the world. Forgiveness is not so much pardoning the sinner from a morally superior position for the wrongs we believe they're guilty of, for that is not Love, but a form of judgment. Instead, forgiveness is the acceptance of what is *without* judgement.

Sometimes the person we most need to forgive is ourselves. For if we judge ourselves, we judge others, too, and we end up withholding forgiveness from ourselves, as well as others. Not to forgive and hold a grievance causes you to become stuck, and lose your freedom and happiness. Forgiveness is the only way to inner peace. It is truly and literally the key to happiness, for it is the release mechanism that frees us from our self-created bondage of frustration and unhappiness and the bridge to a loving connection with the other person.

4. Love always strengthens, and never weakens. We said above that Love is empowering, while counterfeit "love" is weakening. But power is not commonly associated with love, for we often see tenderness as being foolish or a weakness or as being out of touch with reality. In fact, most people, when operating from the ego's perspective, think that love and power are opposites; i.e., if you are loving, you are not manifesting power, you are vulnerable or a softy, and can be hurt by the people you love. We know that in times of plague, the doctors and nurses who were the most exposed often escaped any illness themselves. How did Mother Teresa survive so long in the slums of Calcutta without getting one of the hundreds of illnesses she treated? How can Momaji, the hugging saint, lick the sores of a man with leprosy and escape contracting it herself?

Whenever we feel compassion for another, we fortify and strengthen ourselves. We cease being afraid and acting like a victim. When we forgive, we are healed. Such is the strength of love.

5. Love is the desire to bring only healing to any situation. Since genuine love is never harmful, it can only heal. In fact, love could be considered the basis of healing in every situation. Love's healing power never creates conflict, but teaches us how to accept those we say we love as they are, and to see them as perfectly themselves, allowing us to be perfectly ourselves as well. Love's desire is to only be truly helpful.

6. Love is the absence of fear. It says in the Bible that "Perfect love casts out all fear." In fact, Love is the only real antidote to fear in the world. Fear always comes from an illusion, for it has to do with a possible future occurrence. Since the future does not exist, but is only a figment of our imagination, fear does not exist either, it also being a figment of our imagination.

No one has ever gotten over a fear by demanding it of themselves. Such a demand only leads one to become counter-phobic, compensating for the fear that has been suppressed. Yet, when we lovingly reassure ourselves of our safety, our well being, and our ability to handle anything, we are giving love to ourselves. When we are able to give loving support to ourselves, we are much more likely to give it to others as well.

Sylvia had begun to dread the time when her husband, Jim, would return home from work. He was not just tired and grumpy, but would viciously shout and scream at her and the children. Sylvia would defend herself, which only invited greater attacks from Jim. Her fears began to mount as the months and years passed, leading her to consult with a lawyer for divorce.

The lawyer told her that it was his (very unusual) policy to begin divorce proceedings only if the person had worked on the problem with a therapist. That's how Sylvia ended up in my office. I quickly discovered that she did not really want to leave Jim because there were so many good things about the relationship. But she recognized that her growing fear of Jim was quickly diminishing her love.

Gradually, she learned that she could obliterate her fear by focusing on compassionate thoughts about Jim. Knowing that he had a difficult job, and his position was always on the line, helped her understand the nature of his fear. Further, she knew that his father had behaved very similarly. Focusing on these insights, Sylvia began to consciously choose to have compassionate thoughts about Jim every time she started to feel afraid of his coming home. She was amazed at how quickly her fear went away. By being able to genuinely care about Jim's feelings, she would reach out to comfort him as he came home. And as a result, his emotionally abusive behavior actually stopped within a few weeks. Although Jim never took any responsibility, Sylvia's intent and compassion brought healing to both of them.

7. Love is kindness. Patience is kind; impatience is not. Acceptance is kind; criticism and judgments are not. Freedom is kind; control is not. Soft words are kind; harsh words are not. Keeping your word is kind; breaking it is not. Speaking respectfully is kind; screaming and yelling is not. Asking nicely without expectations or attachments is kind; demands, whining, and expectations are not. Communication is kind; avoidance of communication is not. Generosity is kind; withholding is not.

All of us, having the ego part of our minds, find ourselves at times being unkind. We need to be patient and forgiving of ourselves, realizing that all of our unkindnesses come from some fear within us. Know that this fear can only be healed by Love. By healing our fear with love, we can then apologize for being unkind and use the apology as a return to love.

8. Love is the desire and willingness to give and to serve. The word "family" originally meant to serve. Jesus said, "He who would be great among you, let him become a servant." If we live according to Natural Law, we experience that choosing to serve rather than seeking to be served is what brings happiness.

I remember a number of years ago, when I had been heavily scheduled with a lot of speaking engagements along with my regular practice, I was feeling tired and looking forward to resting on the weekend. On my way home from my office on a Friday afternoon, I spoke to my wife on the cell phone and learned that both she and my youngest son had come down with the flu. I was compassionate with her, but inside I was disappointed. I would no longer have the weekend for desperately needed rest! Then, after a pause, I realized that this thought was just from the ego's perspective. I said to myself: "I love my wife and son, they are sick and need my love and nurturing. That is what I want to give them this weekend to help them get well." I then set about doing just that. I went to the grocery store and bought ingredients to make chicken soup. I went to the health-food store for homeopathic remedies. I took them ice water or tea as they needed it. I rented movies for them to watch and just kept them company at other times. When late Sunday afternoon rolled around, instead of feeling more exhausted, I noted that I felt very energized—probably far more than if I had rested as I had planned. My caring and loving service through the weekend gave me more strength than lying around and reading would have done.

9. Love is gratitude. It has often been said, "Where there is gratitude, love cannot be far behind." When we focus on what we are thankful for, the state of appreciation evokes loving thoughts and feelings in our minds. When we focus on what is missing, how we are being deprived, and what we are yearning for, we push aside love and falsely see ourselves as empty or incomplete. But when we experience gratitude, we focus on our fullness, which is our true nature as whole and complete, knowing we already have an endless supply of Love to give. Gratitude actually makes us aware of the reality of our fullness.

Eva began to observe that she would often get caught up in thoughts of what she disliked in her husband, Andrew. It seemed that the more she focused on these faults, the worse he became. But she also began to observe that when she focused on thoughts about what she liked and appreciated about him, their relationship always became closer and more loving. Having both awarenesses, she then began to catch the judging thoughts more quickly and apply the Five-Step Thought-Monitoring process (Practice 2) to banish the thoughts and then to consciously replace them with thoughts of appreciation. Love always followed.

10. Love is the basis of happiness. In this sense, acceptance and forgiveness, being the basis of love, are also the basis of happiness. Without forgiveness, happiness is impossible. Anytime we judge, focusing on what's wrong with ourselves or others, we immediately lose our happy state of mind. When we fight against what is, it immediately takes away our inner peace and our strength. When we hand over our power for happiness to another person by saying, "If you will change, then I will be happy," not only are we unhappy, but we either do not see or we actually repel the love that others may be offering to us. But when we accept someone just as they are, we feel genuine Love, and are happier and stronger as a result. Love, being the absence of judgment and expectations, cannot bring anything but happiness.

PRACTICE 7:

Unblocking the Flow of Love and Extending It to Others

So how do we learn to replace the characteristics of counterfeit "love" and choose to love in an empowering way? While there are diverse exercises developed in the various traditions of the world that have been used to help unblock the natural flow of love, I have made variations on a select number of them and have developed a few in addition. A central thread running through all of them, therefore, is the understanding that love is a conscious decision much more than an emotion. It is a verb, not a fixed commodity. It is not a feeling that runs us, as in infatuation, rather it is a choice to own our true identity. The philosopher Aldous Huxley stated it clearly when he said, "There isn't any formula or method. You learn to love by loving."

1. Decide to know the person. A first step is to choose to know the other person. We saw earlier that the falling-in-love experience is actually a decision *not* to know the other person. Such a decision extends to most people in our lives, just in varying degrees. Our first step, then, is to look inside ourselves, check out our own projections, and note how we are imposing our own desires of what we want that person to be. By making a conscious decision to listen to and see the other person accurately, we can more easily accept and love him. Dr. Eric Butterworth, author and Unity Fellowship minister, draws thousands to hear him speak at Lincoln Center in New York City each Sunday. He likes to say to himself: "If I knew you and you knew me, we would love one another—regardless of who I am and who you are."

We may often fear that if others get to know us, we will not be liked. We fear they will discover horrible things about us or see our belief in littleness, and then they will judge us, criticize us, and ultimately will reject us. I led numerous psychotherapy groups each week for many years, and most people entering the groups had such fears. However, contrary to most people's expectations, an amazing thing happened. As people got to know one another at a deep and intimate level, they got past those fears, dropped their defenses, and a depth of caring and love flowed in a beautiful way that they never could have imagined. It verified for us all the idea that to know is to love. If we knew the fears behind others' rejections and angers, we would feel compassion instead of going into a defense mode. If we know their deepest hurts instead of just their surface personas, it is hard for us not to care—love tends to become unblocked. Why is this so?

2. Focus on and appreciate the person you intend to Love. If the truism "what we focus on is what we will get" is valid, then when we are having trouble loving someone, if we focus on things we appreciate about them, it can help to unblock love's flow. Begin by focusing your thoughts on things you appreciate about the person. Some people find it helpful to make a written list. Others find it rewarding to express their gratitude to the other person directly. Still others find it helpful just to focus on their sense of gratitude, replacing their thoughts of what they do not like about the person.

How can we be grateful for the person who has been angry with us, or who has been self-centered, preoccupied, unaffectionate, or cold? How can we be grateful for the person who has been critical of us or unkind in another way? Perhaps we have been able to learn how to stay centered in the face of anger or criticism. Maybe it forced us to meditate, monitor our thoughts, or make a perceptual shift. Sometimes the only thing we might think of to be grateful for is the challenge that person has been to us, and how he or she has been our spiritual teacher by helping us face ourselves and use our spiritual practices to deal with him or her creatively. We can be grateful, therefore, not just for the things that are nice, wonderful, and joyous, but actually stretch our gratitude to another level. We are then grateful for the spiritual growth and the increased awareness of our True Self, which has come from the challenges presented by this person.

3. Stop asking for Love as a commodity, and you will begin to discover the true nature of Love. The more we seek "love," the more it eludes us. When we cease trying to earn it, manipulate it, or even demand it, it will come naturally, springing from us—because we are already Love. And when we give up our attachment to the outcome of our loving, then real Love can flow. The more we consciously choose to extend Love, the more Love we have. To Love is a conscious decision we can make moment by moment.

4. Unblock Love when someone is criticizing or yelling at you. Start by taking several slow deep breaths into your diaphragm. It will supply needed oxygen to your brain, and by focusing on your breath, it will be easier to avoid becoming hooked into their criticism or anger. Instead, you can more easily hear them without becoming defensive or counterattacking.

It also helps to keep your body in a grounded posture. We know from schools of acting that the posture we assume supports the emotion we want to feel in a certain situation. To be grounded, if standing, place your feet about shoulder width apart. Unlock your knees, tuck in your buttocks, let your chest rise a little higher, and focus on your solar plexus as you take your deep breaths. If you are seated, sit erect, place both feet flat on the floor, lift up your chest, and then begin to breathe slowly and deeply into the diaphragm. Now you have a foundation to deal with the person differently in your mind—a way that will promote the flow of love.

Listen very carefully to what the other person is saying, but at the same time, say to the other person *silently* inside yourself, "You are part of God; I am part of God. We will resolve this peacefully." Or you might say *silently*, "You have lost your peace. I wish you peace now. I wish you peace and love." Or you might pray for strength and compassion in dealing with this person in this situation.

My experience is that the amount and intensity of the anger or judgment seems to diminish significantly when we practice these intentions. And as a result, we do not feel like victims when the other person is angry or judgmental.

5. Remember and focus in your mind on the good memories and happy times you have had with the person. Since what we focus on is what will surely increase, and since one mind reaches forth to all other minds, then to increase happy times, focus on those memories. Remember when you have been joyous together, recall loving interactions you have had, or moments of closeness and sharing. You might pause and make a list of a number of those things. You might even decide to share some of them with that person, telling him or her what the joyous or loving moments meant to you. Or you might recall the memories throughout the day as you walk down the hall at work, when you are driving the car, stop by the store, or pause to make a phone call. As you do this, you will very often find you are rejuvenating the flow of love.

6. Embrace your hatred in order to unblock Love. When we deny our annoyance or anger or minimize them because we find them unacceptable, we inevitably block the flow of our love.

We need to recognize that all of our grievance, annoyance, and anger come from our deep hatred and that our hatred could not exist if we did not adhere to the illusion of separation.

How can we embrace hatred when it brings so much destruction? We cannot successfully treat a cancer by covering it with a bandage. Nor can we deal adequately with the ego's hatred by denying or suppressing it. So anytime we feel upset with someone else, especially when they do not live up to the role we expected them to play, say, "Right now I feel such hatred for ______! I feel it so deeply and so strongly." Then note where and how you feel it in your body. Notice the bile or knot in your stomach, the rigidity of your muscles, and how disturbed your peace is. Then, after fully recognizing and feeling it, you are usually ready to be free of it. Then you might say, "I now release all my hatred from every part of my being to make way for love!" You will now feel the hatred flow away, out of your body.

7. Pray for the person who has offended you. Even if you are finding it difficult to love someone, you can pray for him or her. Prayer, being "the deepest intent of the heart," as physician Larry Dossey defines it, can transcend the chatter of the mind that may be holding on to defensiveness or attack thoughts of judgment. We are not so much suggesting that you are pleading with a God out there somewhere, but instead, by focusing on our deepest wishes for the person's well being or happiness, we are being our god self and sending forth loving power, which we are. Some people who are visually oriented may find it helpful to picture that person in the state of love, feeling happy, feeling joyous, having love work for them in a more satisfying way, feeling safe, or having their emotional wounds heal. Visualization can be helpful in focusing our intent.

If you feel resentment toward someone, praying for him or her can be one of the best cures. If we pray for someone daily for a few weeks, the resentment tends to evaporate. Once resentment fades, then love can flow. Perhaps this is why we find admonition in the Bible to "love your enemies."

8. Forgiveness is the direct road to Love. When we forgive, we have relieved ourselves from the pain of hurt and resentment. Further, we have ceased to judge the other person or ourselves. When we cease judging, which is forgiveness, we have immediately opened ourselves to the flow of love in our lives.

The central ingredient in the practice of forgiveness is the *willingness* to forgive, and this requires a decision. Once you have decided to forgive the one you think of as the offender, the largest piece of the work has already been accomplished.

To practice forgiveness, hold the person in your mind toward whom you hold a grievance. Note where and how you feel that grievance in your body. Notice how it affects your inner peace and sense of well being. Then, say to yourself, "Holding on to the grievance only hurts me. To keep it makes me suffer. Therefore, I forgive ________ (name of person) as a gift to myself." Sometimes you may need to add, "Forgiveness does not mean that I am condoning their behavior. It means that I accept what is, or what has happened, without placing a judgment on it, for judging it merely makes me suffer." Some people find it very helpful to use the posture in the Tapas Accupressure Technique while making the above statements.

If you still have trouble forgiving, pray for help: "I pray for help to forgive ________ (name of person). I want to be at peace, therefore I want to be able to forgive. I need help." Such an expression of your desire and willingness while opening yourself to the help of your divine source, can often make the difference.

9. A meditation to expand the circle of Love. Our love is often blocked by reserving it for special people and special relationships. Instead of restricting it, we need to expand the circle of love to all other human beings, or the flow of love will get stuck. As many have done before me, I have adapted the following meditation that originally came from both the ancient Jewish mystical tradition and the Buddhists:

The Meditation:

- Sit in a relaxed place and begin to focus on your breath. Watch it go in and out, slowly and deeply. Then, deep within yourself, allow yourself to feel your heart's deepest desire to experience your interconnectedness with all people and all living things. Ask your Higher Self or God, or whatever name resonates most with you, for help in experiencing your connectedness with the All That Is.

- Next, imagine yourself sitting in a large circle. You are in the center with your parents, siblings, children, other relatives, and friends seated all around you. Take time to identify each one of them, and then acknowledge all the qualities you like as well as the ones you dislike in each of them. Try to do this without any judgment or shame, particularly as you see how each has affected you in any way. Take time to experience the full richness of their personalities, positive and negative. Then say to each of them, silently inside yourself, "Let me recognize my oneness in love with you."

- Now, allow yourself to enlarge that circle. Include acquaintances, people with whom you work, colleagues, as well as old classmates and friends you have not seen for years. See each one as you have known them, with their desirable qualities as well as their negative traits. Once again, say quietly inside yourself: "We are One in Love—only that which is not Love separates us. Let us be One in Love."

- Now allow your circle to widen, to include neighbors, service people you see occasionally, political leaders, drivers and passengers in other cars, people you pass walking down the street, including all colors, nationalities, ethnic and economic groups. See the faces, both known and unknown, and then say, "Let us be One in Love together."

- Let your circle widen farther, this time to include all the people in your town or city, even in your county or state, and say, "Let us be One in Love." Now expand the circle even more, this time including all the people in your country, and once again say, "We are One in Love."

- Now open your heart to embrace anyone or any group or nation you consider to be an enemy, and then say, "We are One in Love."

- Now open your heart to embrace all those who are in pain and suffering anywhere in the world. Then include everyone living on the planet, all the animals, and every lifeform, and say, "We are One in Love."

- The next step is a very important one. Gently remove yourself from the center of the circle and take a place of your choosing in the circle. And then place the Divine or God in the center of the circle using whatever image is meaningful to you as that which connects us together with all others and all living things.

- Use music, poetry, or a quotation to remind yourself that Love is an active state of giving. Just as you go away singing the songs from a great Broadway musical, you might use the same medium to reinforce a desired perspective.

  A line I have found helpful to recite to myself as a reminder is taken from *A Course in Miracles:*

  God is but love,
  and therefore so am I.

  Jews and Christians might find it helpful to recite a line from the the Old Testament:

  Love God . . .
  And love your neighbor as your Self.

  Or Christians may find it helpful to recite Jesus' admonition:

  Love one another as I have loved you.

  (That is, love without expectations of anything back in return, knowing that the reward is in extending love.)

  So, find a song, a quotation, or a poem of your choosing that reflects the true nature of love with a perspective you wish to integrate into your being, and say, sing, or chant it to yourself repeatedly throughout the day. The repetition helps to assimilate it into your subconscious mind as well as holding it in your consciousness, replacing the erroneous and deceptive ideas of counterfeit "love" so prevalent about us in the world.

Love is our essential nature, not something to be learned. Our task, therefore, is not to learn to love, but rather to release the love that we are. Taking the time to get to know a person, living in gratitude, practicing forgiveness, living love instead of seeking it, practicing empathy and compassion, using selective remembering, praying for one who offended or hurt us, chanting or singing reminders of love's true nature, or meditating on expanding our circle of love, all help to unblock the flow of love within us. But mostly remember, Love is a choice, not something we have to feel first!

CHAPTER 9

Learning to Trust in the True Self

The Power of Surrender

"Anyone who follows an insane guide must be insane himself."
—A Course in Miracles

IF A PROBLEM FEELS TOO BIG

Despite our power to choose Love over fear and create a spiritual marriage, problems will always arise in all our relationships, just as problems are inevitable in the world. Since the beginning of time, the great masters have recognized the reality of suffering prevalent in the world. The Buddha, recognizing suffering all about him, admonished, "Be at peace, even in the midst of those in conflict." Jesus stated the situation poignantly when he said, "In the world you *will* have tribulation" (stress is mine). But he added, "Be of good cheer, for I have overcome the world." He is saying that just as did he, we also can transcend the world's perspective on problems and remain at peace inside ourselves.

Both Jesus and the Buddha recognized that we do not have to be victims; nor do we need to experience ourselves as such. And yet, some of the problems we face in our relationships are seemingly insurmountable conflicts and may be too big for us to handle alone. We have tried thought monitoring, but the ego mind relentlessly overwhelms us. We want to see the other person differently and try to extend love, but our fears or resentments are so strong, we just cannot seem to let go of them. Even attempts at meditation or prayer seem useless.

In such circumstances, when we have difficulty extending love and cannot seem to forgive in a way that opens the path to healing, we may need help transcending from the ego level. Specifically, we need help from our Higher Self, Higher Power, True Self, or God—whatever name you prefer to use to refer to that higher dimension of Self. We need to say sincerely, "I, my little ego self, cannot solve this problem. I'm having difficulty in loving my mate or my mother or boss. I need help and am open to receiving it now!" Or it might be, "I am having difficulty solving the problem in my relationship and I feel so estranged. I need help to solve these problems!"

I have found in my experience and in the experience of many clients that when we do so, our helplessness vanishes, problems are frequently solved effortlessly, and miraculous results often occur for we have aligned our mind with the universal mind. This is especially true for our most special relationships, for they seem to be more complicated and deeply layered. For example, I have observed times when my wife and I have had a conflict that did not get resolved from talking it out. The next time we interacted, I would find her to be still angry, so that whatever we started to talk about would end up in a conflict. But after practicing surrender and opening myself to help in solving the conflict, our next interaction would invariably be peaceful, as though there had never been a conflict. Each time it seemed like a miracle, since there had been no "tangible" problem solving between us. The change began in me.

We need multiple ways of healing to use at different times. Sometimes we can use thought monitoring or make the perceptual shift. Other times we might be able to release ego thinking through meditation, which I will describe in the next chapter. Other times we may need something more dramatic, a specific ritual for letting go of our reliance on ego thinking. Sometimes we must come to a more desperate position in our lives in which we cannot mastermind a crisis situation, and this is when surrendering is most applicable.

Molly tells of a most dramatically moving experience of surrender she learned to use in the midst of an overwhelming crisis. When her mother died, she called her daughter in the same town to tell her of grandmother's death, and that they would travel to the funeral in the Midwest the next day. The daughter, Susan, was recovering from a cocaine and crack addiction, and had been straight for almost a year. The next day, however, when it was time to leave for the airport, Susan had not arrived at her mother's house. There was no answer at her apartment phone. Molly, in desperation, called Susan's next door neighbor, who could get no answer at the door, and then told Molly that she thought that she had not been home at all last night, for she had been trying to reach her for another reason until late in the evening, and again early in the morning. She knew that she had been seen with her old boyfriend, who had also been addicted to the same drugs.

Molly knew deep inside her what had happened. Using the crisis of her grandmother's death, Susan must have found an excuse to go out and get drugs again. Molly also knew that when a crack addict goes back out again after having been clean for a while, it is not at all uncommon for her to overdose. She felt a weakness in her legs that almost overcame her ability to go on. Yet, she knew that she must travel to her mother's funeral. Now she had to go, but with the fear that her only daughter could be dead as well.

She managed to get to the airport, and flew with her husband to Chicago, where she had to change planes. While awaiting her connecting flight, she tried again to reach Susan, but to no avail. Finally, she reached Susan's boyfriend and found out that indeed they had been together, and that Susan had been using cocaine. They had gone to a crack house together, but she refused to leave when he knew he had to leave in order not to overdose himself. He had not heard from Susan since that time.

Hearing his news, Molly was in even more terror, knowing that it was very probable that Susan had unwittingly overdosed. Returning to her husband, she sobbed with grief in the airport. Her terror still remained, however, and the thought that her daughter could be dead along with her mother was just more than she could bear. She wondered if she might be about to go over the edge herself. Then, she remembered another way to handle it. She told her husband that she was going to the side of the waiting room to meditate a few minutes. While there, she was able to surrender the outcome of the situation totally to God (as she thought of it). She said, "God, I just cannot handle this. I am at the end of my rope. I do not know what to do. It is totally in your hands." And with that, she ended her meditation, and returned to her husband. He noted the remarkable change in her face and demeanor, and she told him what had happened. Molly said that she, following the act of surrender, felt a wave of peace come over her like none she had ever known. She could not understand it, but she knew that she would be OK, whatever the outcome, and that she now had a source of strength she could count on.

Molly had not heard from her daughter by the day of mother's funeral, yet her peace remained. She had been able to make decisions about the funeral arrangements and talk with relatives and friends in an amazingly centered way. When she returned to the hotel after the funeral, there was a call from her daughter. Molly had left the hotel phone number several times on Susan's answering machine. Susan had almost overdosed, but had miraculously survived, and requested that she go into a good rehabilitation center. Of course, Molly felt relief, but her greatest relief had already come much earlier—at that moment of surrender of putting it all in God's hands. Molly said that after that time, it became quite easy for her to ask for help about all sorts of little things as she had never been able to do before. Her trust and her happiness multiplied as a result of this major surrender in time of desperate need.

Molly faced the fact that she could not control or mastermind a solution to Susan's addiction problem. She wanted to help, but had tried every way she knew. She had to face the possible loss of her daughter and had to give up her attachment to helping. Only through surrender of the ego did she discover peace. She also found release from feelings of powerlessness and the pain of loss. When Molly became free of her attachment to helping Susan, she became freer to just love her daughter for her fear could no longer interfere.

This is the power and promise of surrender. But before I show you how surrendering to the omniscient, omnipresent, omnipotent power of the True Self can bring healing and renewal, I want to spend a little time discussing the idea of surrendering itself.

REDEFINING SURRENDER

I used to think of surrender as something that was almost always undesirable; it was weakening and frightening, and therefore something to be avoided. I conceded that maybe the only good time for surrender would be in a war when an army commander realized that not to do so would bring the needless death of a multitude of his soldiers with no advantage gained.

In the kind of psychotherapy I used to practice, I would work hard to help people analyze and mastermind their problems, all the while thinking that I was helping them to feel empowered. I did not know that sometimes I was helping to empower the wrong source—the ego.

I had often heard spiritually minded people talk about surrender, saying, "I turned it over to God." People in twelve-step programs often speak of "turning something over to my Higher Power." Such statements used to make me cringe inside, for I viewed such turning over as a giving up of self and a shirking of responsibility—an act that was very frightening. Since I had grown up in a moderately authoritarian culture, the idea of surrendering to anyone else did not carry any appeal whatsoever. I also thought that such surrender would be a loss of personal empowerment, one which would result in feeling significantly weaker than when I started out.

Surrender, as I have grown through experience to understand it, does include all the frightening characteristics that I listed above. There is one difference, however, and a major one at that. The only self I am surrendering is not a self at all—just the ego or counterfeit "self." When I surrender the ego, I am allowing myself to experience my unity with the All That Is—with God, my True Self. In surrender, I rise up from the ego state of mind to reclaim my True Self identity. It seems that I must lose my "self" to find my Self. As I surrender the ego, I let the God within and without, of which I am a part, take charge instead of my little ego. It is not an outside force controlling me, but it is God that is in all and through all, and is the one mind of the unified field of intelligence of the universe, not the distant, medieval, flat-earth sky god. In this sense, God's mind is also my mind—only the ego mind is different.

Surrender, therefore, is not a surrender to someone outside me, which I previously believed. And it is not giving over to God, who is separate and apart from me. Rather it is allowing the True Self to take over and trusting in that connection with the Divine in the universe. Indeed, the mind to which I surrender is my own, for my mind is part of All That Is. In our relationships, this is especially important when we reach roadblocks that seem insurmountable. Maybe you and your partner have committed to the path of a spiritual marriage, consciously practice the various exercises for breaking the vicious cycle and extending love, but you still find yourselves feeling powerless over your conflicts. This could be a time for surrender.

Similar to Molly's experience with her daughter, a couple, Sue and Tom, had been engaged in spiritual marriage "training" for over a year when Tom lost his job. Unfortunately, Sue was pregnant with their second child and not working. To make matters even more desperate, they had accumulated very little savings, putting an enormous financial burden on the family.

This outside force was so strong that it shattered the calm the two of them had been enjoying. They struggled to remain centered, but alas, they fell back into a previous pattern of withdrawal. However, unlike what they had done in the past, they questioned their withdrawal from each other. This is when I suggested that they open themselves to the power of surrender. With this leap of faith and reaching out to God (in their case, they were members of a Unitarian church in their community) through prayer, they were able to find each other again. Once united again by their love, they were able to address their changed circumstances with much less fear and much more hope that all would turn out well. And it did. Armored with a positive attitude, Tom was able to find a new position in two months.

LEARNING TO SURRENDER

Many years ago, when I visited the grounds of Sathya Sai Baba's ashram in Puttaparte, India, I encountered a large statue of Ganesha, the representation of god with the elephant trunk who is the remover of obstacles. Gradually, I learned that the Hindus were not really polytheistic as my professors of world religions had implied. Rather, they just had anthropomorphic symbols for the 120 or so faces or manifestations of God that they had identified.

I will never forget the first time I saw a native Indian woman go up to the Ganesha statue, break a coconut open, prostrate herself before it, walk around the statue, and then prostrate herself again before it. I cringed even more deeply, if that was possible, when I saw a man prostrate himself before the statue as well, and to continue through the same ritual. I suppose I identified myself more with him and therefore it was more disturbing. Harsh critical judgments arose in my mind about "these primitive people" who were bowing down to idols! It made me feel nauseous inside, and I had to walk away.

I had long ago learned that when I have a strong emotional charge on something, it is worth taking a look inside to understand what it is about. Usually, I had learned, such a strong charge is a signal that I have not worked through an important issue and warrants some thoughtful reflection. In particular, if I strongly dislike something or have a harsh judgment about it, it makes sense for me to search within for the same behavior or trait I am judging. Perhaps I have not owned it as one of mine, and by rejecting it in another, I am further disowning it in myself. This time, however, I had absolutely no desire to do so, feeling totally justified in my self-righteous judgments about these people's bowing to idols.

I could hardly wait to find some other Americans toward whom I could vent my judgments about these idol worshipers. When I did so, however, the American listened patiently and kindly, and when I had finished spewing my venom, she asked sweetly, "Would you like to know what the people are doing with this ritual?" "Sure," I replied, confident that I would find only further evidence to support my judgments.

She told me first that "Ganesha was the face of God known as the remover of obstacles, and that when a person broke the coconut, it symbolized the breaking of the pride and arrogance of the ego." And she added, "When they prostrate their bodies, it further means the humbling down of the prideful ego and body 'self,' which had not accomplished any solutions to the problem anyway. Next, while prostrating they recite three times their request concerning the obstacle they want to be removed in their life. Then they stand up and begin to circle the statue three times, all the while reciting their request over and over in order to implant it deeply in their minds. Finally, they return to the original spot, and while prostrating their bodies again, they give thanks for its already being done."

When I heard this explanation, I thought, "How brilliant!" Then I felt deeply ashamed inside that I had been so judging and contemptuous of such a profoundly valuable ritual that I now deeply appreciated. It reminded me once again of the problems of judging something that I am observing and know nothing about—indeed judging anything or anyone at all! My own judging ego had once again been humbled down to its nothingness.

I bought a tiny two-inch statue of Ganesha to take home with me in remembrance of this important learning, thinking it would also be a nice table or shelf decoration. One day, a few months after I had returned home, I was struggling and agonizing over possible solutions to a relationship problem in my life that was disturbing me deeply. As usual, I was getting nowhere in this approach. In fact, I was quite capable of persisting unproductively for days and even weeks trying to mastermind problems. However, it is probably no coincidence that out of the corner of my eye, I spotted the tiny statue of Ganesha on the shelf nearby and remembered the significance of the ritual as it had been explained to me. "Dare I take this statue and engage in such a ritual now?" I queried myself. When I squarely faced that I had not been successful in my customary approach, I decided I would do it. What could I lose? It would be safe here in the privacy of my own home. And since no one else was home, no one would see me and think I had gone mad, so I decided to do the ritual.

I fetched it from the shelf and placed it onto the floor in front of me. How strange it was, a 6' 3" man towering over such a tiny statue of Ganesha, the remover of obstacles. Perhaps it was better for me that the statue was so tiny. It took me quite awhile to be able to prostrate myself before this little brass figure with the elephant trunk. In fact, as I began to bow down, I felt the strangest sensation inside my body. It was as though something was tearing inside me with each inch I bowed. I soon realized that, since the body is equated with the ego, my body ego was literally having to open new neural pathways to process such a different behavior from what I was more accustomed to, for I held my head high. Even though no one could see me, I still felt embarrassed that a big, capable, independent man like me was prostrated on the floor in front of a two-inch statue, about to ask for the removal of obstacles. What would my colleagues or my patients say if they could see me now?

I had to remind myself that I was not praying to an inert statue. I focused on the statue of Ganesha as a symbol of the face of God that was capable of removing obstacles. I reasoned that since I am part of God, then Ganesha represents a higher part of my True Self. With such reassurance I was able to proceed.

I carefully phrased my request concerning the obstacle I was experiencing in my life. Now I was truly ready, for I had not been able to solve it in my little ego self. Then I stood up and recited my request repeatedly as I circled the little figure, alternating between feeling foolish and genuinely stating the request that I knew I wanted resolved. And finally, I prostrated myself again, this time much more easily, and expressed my thanks for the problem already being resolved.

Strangely, I felt an unusual and complete peace when I arose. Somehow, I trusted that the problem was solved and I was excited to wait and see exactly how that would be. I could hardly believe the peacefulness I felt, for I had never felt such peace when in the midst of trying to solve problems on my own—my separate little false self. It certainly came from no rational solution. I knew for the first time what the phrase in the Bible meant when it refers to "the peace which passes all understanding." Up until now, it has been some kind of esoteric, but empty, phrase.

The next few times I felt overwhelmed by a problem to be solved, I turned to my little Ganesha ritual, and found the same peace each time. And the resolutions were usually far more effective than any my little ego could have masterminded. And certainly I was far more peaceful and trusting. One day, when about to use my little statue of Ganesha, I had a deeper realization that it was only a symbol, and that I could humble down my arrogant ego inside without necessarily having to prostrate my body, although it was now all right to do so. I did the process only in my mind, and found the same kind of peace. Now I understand more completely the mantra that I had learned when in India: "Om ne-mah shi-va-yah," which means, "I (my ego) bow down to the God within which is my Self."

Gradually, I learned to apply this process to almost any situation that brought any stress at all. If there was a problem with any of my children, I "turned it over," with solutions following that always worked out for the good of all. If there was a problem with my wife, or I did not know how to resolve a conflict between us, I surrendered it, and results often came in ways that seemed miraculous. If we had a big argument, we used to feel tense, if not estranged, for several days. Now, when I turned it over, out next interaction would most often be peaceful and normal, as if nothing negative had occurred—which I now know really had not—it was just the nightmare my ego mind had helped to create, and by practicing surrender I had freed myself from it. By *my* letting go of it, my wife often did not seem to need to keep it going either. As we have seen, when one mind is healed of its erroneous thinking, others around may often be healed in their minds as well.

Surrender can be used by itself or in conjunction with the other exercises. Ultimately, all the exercises are asking you to do the same thing: reach out to, connect with, and trust in your True Self.

PRACTICE 8:

The Power of Surrender

It is most difficult for us to feel empowered in our True Self as long as we try to be in control. And do we not try, from the ego level, to control everything we are attached to? Observe how it feels to you to make the following statements:

> "Spirit (or God), my life is in your hands. I cease struggling."
>
> "Spirit (or God), my relationship with ________ is in your hands. I trust that I can and will receive the guidance I need to bring peace. I pray and trust for the outcome, whatever it may be, to be for the highest good of all."
>
> "I trust that this job is in your hands, and that whether I stay or leave or am asked to leave, it will be for the highest good."
>
> "I trust that the outcome of ________________ will be for the highest good of all."
>
> "I trust that all the guidance and strength I need to be the parent my child needs will be given me."

Do you find you feel fear or peace when you make these statements? If it's fear, we know that it is the ego trying to "hang on to the limb." If we feel peace, we know we have fully surrendered the ego—for now. We may have to do it again in a few minutes or in a few hours, but we now know we have a choice. Perhaps it is in this kind of surrender that we discover "the peace which passes all our understanding."

In every situation, our ultimate surrender of the ego and deepest trust is in the synchronistic flow of the universe. It is expressed in the only real prayer we can pray—"that the outcome of whatever it is will be for the highest good of all." Only then will our own energy support such an outcome. Not to surrender the ego and trust in this way only means that we contribute our negative energy to the outcome instead.

The act of surrender is the main way in which we gain all the help and strength we ever need to deal with any problem.

SURRENDERING IN EVERYDAY LIFE

A phrase from the Bible often rings in my ears, especially when I, from the ego state of mind, fear surrendering something to the God or spirit of truth within: "God only wants good gifts for his children." I realized that anything I had experienced and feared that I would experience as punishment or deprivation from God, was not of God. Rather, it was my own little ego creating the judgment, the punishment, or the deprivation that I experienced. It had nothing to do with God. Later, after starting to study *A Course in Miracles,* I found a similar statement, "God's will for you is perfect happiness." If this is true, how could it ever be frightening to surrender to the God within, of which I am a part, for it is only my Self that I had disowned. And it only wants perfect happiness for me. What could be frightening about that? For it could only be my ego that could be frightened of it, for its life is therefore threatened with the potential peace of surrender. And, true to form, the ego always gives an upside-down view of what will work. It tells me that in surrender, I will be lost, powerless, and lose myself, which would be catastrophic. It does not tell me that I will find my True Self as the result of losing my false self.

Even when I might experience writer's block, all I need do is quiet down my mind, and surrender my ego mind to inner guidance as to what to write and how to write it, and the block just goes away. When I am about to see a client for a psychotherapy session, I ask for inner guidance, realizing that my little ego self cannot ever be an effective therapist. Only my Spiritual Self, part of the All That Is, can ever heal. Often the ego will want to take credit, or will try to mastermind the healing based on previously learned knowledge from my years of training. But it is not that which heals. If I am in a session and find that I cannot understand what is going on or what I can do to be of help, I find that "i" have been engaged in trying. At such time, I just say silently inside, "I need help. I do not know what would be of most help for this person right now. I am open to guidance, for 'i' am not the therapist." I always find that when I do this genuinely and sincerely, something always shifts in the interaction. Something may just pop out of my mouth, which "i" never would have masterminded. Or it may come out of the patient's mouth. But, inevitably, the shift is profound and something of true importance to healing seems to happen that I cannot explain, for the same things do not happen in ordinary psychotherapy work when I do not open myself to inner guidance from Spirit.

I have seen this same kind of mysterious transformation in my clients as well. Cindy had always been in a contentious relationship with her mother. Each time they would speak, her mother would invariably find several things to criticize Cindy for, which would usually lead to a screaming match or one of them hanging up on the other. Cindy would visit her only about once a year and only then out of obligation. When Cindy decided that she could no longer tolerate these painful interactions with her mother, she gave up the struggle and decided to surrender and ask for help.

As do most people, Cindy felt an immediate sense of peace just from letting go of the struggle. She was amazed at the difference in the next conversation with her mother. In the entire half-hour conversation, her mother made only one critical comment, and it was a very little one. And further, Cindy had no need to react as she usually did. So the conversation not only ended peacefully, but each acknowledged that they had enjoyed the talk. Cindy described this change as "nothing short of a miracle!"

Remember, the ego mind knows nothing, but acts as if it knows all. The ego has no answers of any value to solve any problems, but always purports to have great answers. Since its solutions always bring more of the problem which it promises to solve, it discredits itself as a reliable guide. It has no knowledge and no power aside from that which we give it by listening to it. Yet, it is the voice most of us listen to most of the time. We must be insane to follow a clearly insane guide. It is no wonder that we suffer from anxiety, depression, guilt, and struggle needlessly. If we can say, as in the words of an old gospel song, "I surrender all," and if we can say it moment by moment, then our suffering vanishes. For when we surrender the ego, stop listening to it as if it is a trustworthy guide, then we can listen to the inner Guide which knows the answer to all our relationship problems, now or in the future.

When we cease following the "insane guide" we return to our sanity of peace and joy in every relationship.

One form of surrender takes place in the shamanistic journey. Here, one may take an herbal concoction that the shaman provides, which takes the person through a hallucinogenic journey of the mind, often quite frightening. Essentially, one goes through the experience of losing his or her attachments to everything that was important to them in this world. They may experience the loss of loved ones, of health, of beliefs, of things, become a tiger or a serpent, and even experience the death of their own body. Out of this experience comes a new life with a new perspective, one not based on the previous ego attachments so common to us all.

Most of us do not seek out a shaman in order to have the shamanistic journey of awakening; it would be too terrifying to most of us. Sometimes we go through such a journey, one event at a time, in our actual life experience, much like Molly did. We may lose a spouse through divorce or death. We may lose a child, if not by death, by the child's turning out to be someone or something different from what we had wanted to choose for her or him. We might miss the opportunity of marriage and family, even though we always yearned for it. Our careers may not turn out as planned. Our philosophies do not hold up in all situations. Our health may fail just as we decide to retire to begin enjoying life. The philosopher Aldous Huxley, when his house filled with all his memorabilia was burning in one of the California forest fires, is said to have commented to his neighbor standing next to him, "As I watch my house go up in smoke, I feel the strangest sense of freedom." As a result of life's disillusionments and losses, we may finally come to the place of recognition that there is nothing of value in any of our attachments.

The story of Job in the Bible is another case in point. Job went through the loss of all his crops to locusts, lost his cattle and sheep to plagues, his wives, children, house, and barns to tornadoes, and finally his health. At this point he said with great wisdom, "That which I feared most has come upon me," where he recognized the magnetic pull of our fears, often making them self-fulfilling prophesies. The story of Job goes further, however. After he has suffered all these losses, he shows his trust in God (not the ego), and he is given even more wives and children, houses, cattle, and barns. The moral of the story is that once he surrendered his attachments, which made him afraid of losing and thereby resulted in loss, he could finally fully enjoy abundance. We, too, can know true abundance in our relationships once we have surrendered our attachments to any preconceived outcome.

IT'S ABOUT TRUSTING

When there is surrender of the ego, there can be complete trust. Those who do not trust must be relying upon the ego's insane guidance, and deep within know that it cannot be trustworthy. Often such people project the ego onto a god who would want punishment or bad things for them, so surrender would be terrifying. On the other hand, if we habitually follow the True Guide within, and through our experience come to know that it's solutions are always sane and bring peace and joy, we are naturally trusting and happy. We know that peace is then inevitable when we trust a trustworthy Guide. If we are not feeling at peace, is that not an indication that we must have been surrendering to the wrong voice and putting our trust in what is not trustworthy?

To relinquish ego thinking is not always so easy for most of us because we tenaciously hold on to the ego's solutions. Surrender of the ego is usually done in a halfhearted way. The Danish philosopher, Søren Kierkegaard, when writing about the need to "take the leap of faith," observed that most of us tend to leap off the precipice while holding on to a limb at the same time.

A few years ago, after reading Neale Donald Walsh's *Conversations with God*, I was struck by the fact that he said that most of us talk to God, but that we rarely listen. He said that there was nothing special about his conversation, just that he took the time to listen to God's answers. He then encouraged us to do the same. I took his challenge and decided to sit down with my pen and pad, and see what would come from my own conversation with God about this topic of surrender. This is what followed:

> H. G.: "*God, what is in your hands?*"
>
> GOD: "*Nothing.*" *And he opened his hands revealingly—much like a parent to a child.*
>
> H. G.: "*But what about all those things people place in your hands?*"
>
> GOD: "*The 'nothing' in my hands represents the space where you can use your creative power, which you have like mine, to create your own individual wish. Just as I create out of nothing, so do you, since you are part of me.*
>
> *You cannot build a skyscraper on top of an old building in your world. First, you clear out the old building, prepare a deep foundation, and then you design and build a magnificent structure.*
>
> *The ego thoughts in your mind are much like the old building. They need to be cleared out so you will create like me—out of nothing. Otherwise, your creations will be contaminated.*
>
> *Since my Mind and the Mind of your True Self are the same, when you surrender to me, you are surrendering your 'self' to your Self. Our minds are One; only your ego thoughts are separate. This means that your true will is the same as mine.*"
>
> H. G.: "*What does this have to do with surrender?*"
>
> GOD: "*All you surrender is something that is not real anyway—only an illusion, your false self. When the ego is out of your way, we create as One, with the same power and out of the same Will.*

As you will see in the next chapter, surrender takes us immediately into a connection with our True Self as Spirit. This act of transcendence is the goal of a spiritual life, the result of extending love in a spiritual marriage. Yet is always valuable to remind ourselves that the surrender we do is not something passive or weak. Instead, it is a conscious act of pure intention that we use to surrender the ego mind, knowing it is really nothing of value. It is a conscious intent to surrender to our True Self, which enables us to fully embrace our partner in a relationship, allowing for healing as well as magnificent joy, love, and peace.

CHAPTER 10

A Deeper Knowledge of the Spirit Through Quieting the Mind

DIAPHRAGMATIC BREATHING EXERCISES
MEDITATION EXERCISES

THE TRUE SELF DIAGRAM

In the last few chapters you have been on a tremendous journey in which you have begun to examine, heal, and ultimately transform your relationship. If you've been practicing thought monitoring, erasing your core beliefs and traumas, and making perceptual shifts in order to remove the barriers to love that interfere with your relationships, then you have begun to unblock your flow of love. As I'm sure you see by now, this work you've been doing not only helps lift the stress and conflicts out of your relationship, it also—and necessarily—begins to heal the self at the same time! Each time that you recognize, question, and thereby choose to counteract the ego (your counterfeit self), you are acting in the True Self and accessing your divine creative power within. With consciousness, commitment, and practice (of the exercises), we become increasingly able to observe the deceptions of the ego's voice and begin to change our behavior, thus giving us new experiences that teach us how to build new habits of behavior. When we begin to see how the promises of the ego are untrustworthy and unworkable, and that they actually cause many of our problems, we begin to break out of its illusion and enter into the realm of the True Self.

And once you live from this place, you are living in a spiritual way, and your relationships are increasingly transformed from ego-based to spiritual.

Remember the diagram of the self that you encountered in Chapter Two (the upside-down triangle), in which you saw how the ego, though making up a small part of who we are, is also the place where most of us live? Remember how the upper reaches of that diagram represent the magnificent possibility and potentiality of who we truly are? Though the True Self is whole and cannot be divided, it's easier to conceive of it as dimensional, in order to help us understand the different functions more clearly. Take a look at the Dimensions of Self diagram again, which shows the True Self divided into three levels. These levels represent the path of gradual ascendance to higher levels, where feelings of wholeness and interconnectedness become progressively more available.

Level 1: The Transcendent (or Higher) Self. The Transcendent Self is the part of the mind that can engage in self-reflection, see through the ego's disguises, and engage in practices that help us to awaken to our True Self as Spirit. From a transcendent place, we can see the illusions of the ego part of our mind that are the cause of pain and suffering. At this transcendent level of mind, we are able to see that our behaviors, words, and especially our thoughts affect both ourselves and others, and therefore the nature and quality of our relationships.

Level 2: The Spiritual Self. The core of True Self is what I call the Spiritual Self, since it is neither the ego nor the body, but is our essence, which is Spirit. Who and what we are is so magnificent that it far exceeds our wildest imaginations and dreams. We are at our core individual aspects of Spirit expressed through a body. And if we conclude this to be true, then our True Self, being Spirit, contains all those qualities that we have typically disowned, and have projected outward onto a theistic up-in-the-sky god, separate and apart from us: omnipotent (all powerful), omniscient (all knowing), and omnipresent (present everywhere). When we experience this God as love itself, we are glimpsing our own essence reflected back at us.

Level 3: The Universal Self as Omnipresence. The universal self can be understood as the more universal experience of the True Self as Spirit. It is the full awareness that we are part of the All That Is. If God is everywhere, and we are part of God, then we, at this level, are also everywhere. When others suffer, we feel their pain. When we experience joy, it radiates out into the universe.

While this experience can never be fully and accurately put into words, it has been written about by poets, frequently experienced by mystics in all religions, and probably by each of us at occasional moments or peak experiences. The recognition of the difficulty in describing such experiences is reflected in ancient Hebrew thought, where one could not speak the name of God, for even to speak it is to limit it. Such a practice has resulted in the carryover into Judaism today of spelling it G-d. Similarly, in China, the Tao is that which is indescribable.

Perhaps we have been sitting by the ocean or on a mountaintop and for a moment or two we experience a sense of oneness with the ocean or the earth. At moments like these, we come to realize that destruction of any part of the eco-balance of the world affects the entire earth and people everywhere. Aboriginal cultures who have lived close to the earth are known for respecting this balance deeply and for trying to leave the earth as they found it. In this way, those who were once called savages—including *everyone's* ancestors—were far more advanced in their understanding of how we individually, as Spirit, could best live in harmony with the world. For example, the Australian Aborigines live in a very wasted and barren land. Yet they know where they will find water underground by sticking a reed through the sand, even when skilled geologists and scientific testing cannot see anything on the surface that suggests the presence of water.

Some people in meditation, once the chatter of the mind has quieted down, have had the direct experience of feeling a oneness with the All

That Is. Others may have felt a sense of transcendence and oneness when listening to great music. For others it might happen while viewing a film that inspires compassion. An artist may experience a moment of creative inspiration that moves him to ecstasy. Some might feel this during a particularly deeply loving sexual experience in which their sense of separateness from their lover disappears. Parents often experience moments of total and unconditional love for their children. In each of these moments—and many more—we directly experience being a part of the All That Is.

This omnipresence was described by Michael Talbot in *The Holographic Universe:* "Just as every portion of a hologram enfolds the whole, every portion of the universe enfolds the whole. This means that if we knew how to access it we could find the Andromeda galaxy in the thumbnail of our left hand."

This is why, in the universal self perspective, we feel a deep connection with everyone and with all of life. It goes without saying that it is not the reality of the body of which I am speaking, but rather our greater Self that transcends the body, which is not born and does not die with the body, and is not limited to the knowledge and experience of the body. Such a perspective of universality and Oneness has been understood by various poets, especially Walt Whitman:

I celebrate myself, and sing myself,
And what I assume you shall assume,
For every atom belonging to me as good belongs to you . . .

Swiftly arose and spread around me the peace and knowledge
that pass all the argument of the earth,
And I know that the hand of God is the promise of my own,
And I know that the spirit of God is the brother of my own,
And that all the men ever born are also my brothers, and the
women my sisters and lovers,
And that a kelson of the creation is love. . . .

("Song of Myself,")

Likewise, when the poet William Blake looked at the world, he saw that everything was enfolded inside every piece of it, and wrote, in his poem "Eternity":

To see the world in a grain of sand
And a heaven in a wildflower,
Hold infinity in the palm of your hand,
And eternity in an hour.

It is this universal self or omnipresence that tells a mother that her son has been in an accident three thousand miles away. It is what told Edgar Cayce (and many more medical intuitives) the diagnosis of difficult illnesses in patients that he had never seen, people who often lived thousands of miles away from him, and in situations where even their local physicians could not discover what was wrong with them. It is a dimension in which the mind is obviously much larger and inclusive than the body and is not restricted to its physical limits.

THE METAPHOR OF AWAKENING

Conceiving and experiencing yourself as Spirit may seem quite esoteric, even otherworldly. However, it's not only a natural phenomenon, it's been described for ages in stories based around the metaphor of awakening. Many different cultures and religions have created stories to explain how it is part of the human condition to lose touch with our innermost being, and it is also part of the human condition to search for and hopefully find the True Self.

Many ancient peoples knew intuitively that we never lose our innermost being, we simply lose sight of it. These people possessed an inherent knowledge that when we (as humans) lose our way or become disconnected from our essence (True Self), we need to awaken to what we always have been, much like waking up from a dream or nightmare. When in a nightmare, the frightening and ominous images seem very real to us, but upon awakening and turning on the light, we see that these characters do not exist, but were just part of our dream, and this experience is echoed in many traditions.

For example, in the ancient Vedic science of India, they believe that we live in a dream state unless we awaken our divine essence. They call the dream state *maya*, or illusion. In this tradition, the people use yoga, (the ancient word meaning to "yoke" or "join together") as the practice wherein one in a bodily form becomes aware of his divine essence.

A similar reference to life on Earth as being a sort of sleep state exists in the Jewish tradition. In the Jewish creation story, Adam (the Hebrew word for "man") falls into a deep sleep. Nowhere does it say that he ever woke up. Later, the prophet Ezekiel grieves over the valley of dry bones, (his metaphor for the walking dead). He is mourning for all those who are living without an awareness of who they really are; he implies that they are not really living at all.

In the New Testament, the Apostle Paul admonishes: "Awake thou that sleepest! Arise from the dead!" He, too, recognized that people were living a life akin to death—certainly not living with the full spirit of joyfulness—and he wanted to shake them awake!

Chuang Tzu, the Chinese mystic of the third century B.C., who set out the beginning ideas of the Taoist school, stated this idea with humor, insight, and poignancy:

> *He who dreams of drinking wine may weep when morning comes; he who dreams of weeping may in the morning go out to hunt. While he is dreaming he does not know it is a dream, and in his dream, he may even try to interpret the dream. Only after he wakes does he know it was a dream. And some day there will be a great awakening when we know that this is all a great dream. Yet the stupid believe they are awake, busily and brightly assuming they understand things, claiming this man ruler, that one herdsman—how dense! Confucious and you are both dreaming! And when I say you are dreaming, I am dreaming, too. Words like these will be labeled the 'Supreme Swindle.'"*

Maharishi Mahesh Yogi, the founder of Transcendental Meditation (TM) calls this awakened state "heaven on earth." In our awakened state, we see clearly the suffering of others and, since we are free from our own suffering, spontaneously feel complete compassion for others. In the Buddha's words:

Live in joy, in love,
Even among those who hate.

Live in joy, in health,
Even among the afflicted.

Live in joy, in peace,
Even among the troubled.

The winner sows hatred because the loser suffers.
Let go of winning and losing, and find joy.

With this awakening we experience what the Apostle Paul in the Bible refers to as getting past seeing "through a glass darkly" or as "the peace which passes all understanding."

In contemporary literature, we also find the metaphor of awakening from a dream into another state of being. Edgar Allen Poe saw life as "a dream within a dream within a dream." And D. H. Lawrence compared mankind's existence to Ezekiel's in that "Mankind has gone mad in his sleeping, and cannot seem to wake up." And further, in his short story "Know Deeply, Know Thyself More Deeply," Lawrence gave instructions for how this might be accomplished: "Let us lose sight of ourselves, and break the mirrors. For the fierce curve of our lives is moving again to the depths out of sight, in the deep living heart."

Awakening to our True Self is merely becoming aware of who we really are, in our spiritual essence. In *The Critique of Pure Reason*, the philosopher Immanuel Kant recognized that "[i]f we could see ourselves and other objects as they really are, we should see ourselves in a world of spiritual natures, our community which neither began at our birth nor will end with the death of the body."

Indeed, all these stories of awakening from the dream state of life are expressions of our desire to reconnect with our True Self in order to transcend the ego and live a full, spiritual life in which our relationships are filled with indisturbable joy—which is the basis of a spiritual marriage. And just as this is a natural process, so there is a natural and simple tool to help enhance this experience: meditation. Once again, a simple practice has the power to transform your life—and your relationships.

THE POWER OF MEDITATION

Some might wonder why a description of breathing and meditation exercises would be included in a book on healing relationships. First, we saw earlier that thought monitoring is an essential aspect of transforming our relationships since creation begins at the thought level. Yet we all know how much our minds are filled with thousands of judging thoughts, fear thoughts, and other thoughts that not only disturb our inner peace, but also seriously undermine loving relationships. Therefore we need a tool to help us be more effective in our thought monitoring and meditation is such a tool, for it is essentially a practice session on being objective witness to our thoughts and then consciously and gently returning our minds to focus on a place of our choosing, such as a mantra or breath. Since we get better at anything with practice, having one or two regular practice sessions of meditation on a daily basis prepares us to be significantly more effective in our thought monitoring.

Second, stress sets us on edge and not only contributes to ill health, which seriously impacts our ability to be present in a relationship, but also sets us up to be more irritable, impatient, angry, and critical. In such a state, most people find it very difficult to be loving and close. Diaphragmatic breathing and meditation are highly effective ways to reduce all stress.

Third, most of us find it difficult to stay centered when our partner begins to rant and rave or nitpick or complain. It's also difficult to stay centered when our teenager decides it's time to rebel, our ten-year-old is defiant, or our parent is critical. We also often feel defensive when a partner confronts us with something that feels like an attack or blame. Breathing and meditation benefit us enormously, helping us to stay centered in difficult situations.

Fourth, meditation helps us to develop the habit of going within for the causes and solutions to our relationship problems. Typically, the ego mind's activity is to look outside ourselves for both cause and solution. But when we look inside, and get into this habit of looking inward, we open ourselves to our True Self.

Why does the regular practice of something so simple as diaphragmatic breathing or meditation help so much to heal relationships? In almost twenty years of practicing and teaching meditation, I have yet to see one situation in which relationships were not significantly improved when the person started a regular meditation practice. When both members of a couple practice meditation regularly, I see fights, arguments, and conflicts diminish along with greatly reduced anger and yelling at each other and their children. More loving kindness seems to increase naturally. But even one person meditating can have profound effects on one's self, as well as changing the nature of interactions.

In short, these exercises provide you with a concrete method of accessing your True Self in an immediate, physical way, as well as a tangible experience of how we are all connected in the universe. Meditation and breathing provide the vehicle through which we can actually feel the truth of what the physicists have been telling us all along—that we are all part of a unified force field of energy matter.

Yet, the ego mind might respond by saying: "It's sounds too good to be true." "I'm too busy." "My mind is too active. I could never do that," or "I could never sit still long enough." We must remember that such responses are just typical of the ego voice, as we have seen, and will inevitably come up to oppose anything that could bring more peace, joy, or empowerment in our relationships. Quieting and training our minds is one of the more helpful things we can do to unveil more of our essential divine nature, our god self, while healing and enriching all our relationships at the same time. Such practices work because they are the means by which we disempower the ego thinking in our minds, making it possible for us to experience the purity of consciousness of our True Self.

We live in a culture that places great emphasis on doing in order to accomplish. Hence, in order to improve our relationships, we have tended to focus largely on learning better communication skills, more and varied sexual techniques, management of anger, and ways to deal with differences. No doubt all of these can be helpful, but we all know how easy it is to forget to use such skills in moments of frustration, stress, or tiredness. As if we have a polluted river, we do not clean it up by installing a purification plant at its mouth, for that would be a daunting task. Instead, we must stop all the sources of pollution upstream—the factories, farms, and towns with all their wastes. Similarly, we need to stop the pollution in our minds upstream as well, or else our other learned skills will not sustain us for peaceful and joyful relationships. We need to learn the more powerful "work without doing" that the Chinese philosopher Lao-Tzu spoke of. This is the beauty of meditation.

One does not have to be religious to meditate, for meditation is essentially a form of mind training; practice in concentration. In meditation, one learns to be the objective nonjudging observer of one's thoughts instead of being ruled by those thoughts, as with most of the world. Nor do you have to practice a certain religion in order to practice meditation. There have always been contemplative strains in the esoteric practices of all religions, which is the practice of going within in order to influence the without. On the other hand, exoteric or external religious practices, which are largely the external forms, rituals, beliefs, and doctrine, have not typically included such practices. And now, meditation is taught in numerous hospitals around the country as a way to promote healing and maintain health.

I found meditation and breathing most helpful at the time of the World Trade Center disaster on September 11, 2001. After feeling and acknowledging my shock, fear, terror, anger, and rage over something like this happening to our nation and in my backyard, I recognized that to hold on to the feelings would work like a magnetic force field and attract more negativity into my life as well as our collective lives. I chose to have a long meditation—about 45–50 minutes—preceded by a few minutes of deep breathing since no other patients could get to my office and all public transportation was shut down in Manhattan. Given the strength of my fear and anger about what had happened, it took a much longer time than usual to quiet down my severely troubled mind. However, the depth of peace that followed, especially given the horrendous circumstances, is one that would be hard to explain, especially since it was an even deeper peace than I had known for some time. It is hard for most of us to believe that one can reach such a state of peacefulness in the midst of such a deep crisis.

Out of the meditation, I had a highly focused clarity about what I wanted to do to be of help. First, I called everyone I knew to whom I could get through and who practiced any form of meditation or prayer, asking them to join me in such practice to bring our minds to peace. I was reminded of Ghandi's admonition: "If you would change the world, first be that change in the world." Perhaps we, and the others we would invite to join us, could reach a critical mass of consciousness and help to bring healing to our minds, to the perpetrators' minds, and to our leaders' minds, that they would have the intelligence and wisdom to lead us out of the crisis with the least loss of life and faith. We could pray that out of this tragedy could come a greater awareness of the Divine through love, caring, forgiveness, service, and thoughts of peace instead of fear and hatred.

As I made such calls, people often thanked me enthusiastically, sometimes through tears, saying, "Even though I usually meditate or pray, I was frozen in fear in front of the television. Thanks so much for the reminder. I'm going to turn off the TV and meditate now." Following the calls, I felt inspired to walk over to Roosevelt-St. Luke's Hospital which is near my Manhattan office, and offer my services to work with traumatized victims or families. Meditation took me out of my fear and hatred and gave me the awareness of how I could serve instead. Needless to say, I clearly preferred the latter over the former.

I was able to do this practice during this crisis, no doubt, because I had been doing it for over fifteen years in response to all other crises, big and little. I was deeply grateful that it had become a habit to deal with difficult situations in this way. I had been practicing going within by meditating in response to every difficult situation or conflict I faced in my marriage, parenting, and in any other relationship. Each time, it gave me peace and clarity.

PRACTICE 9:

Diaphragmatic Breathing Exercises

Most of us are significantly oxygen deprived. First, the amount of oxygen in the atmosphere has become depleted over the last century, as we have destroyed forests that manufacture oxygen while we have increased the human population that uses up the oxygen. Second, as air pollution has increased, particularly around our cities, we have even less oxygen to breathe. And third, in our fast-paced lifestyles, we hardly "have time to breathe," which is literal, not just metaphorical. When we race about, we tend to breathe shallowly and quickly, barely taking in any oxygen, just what we barely need. And further, with greater activity we burn more oxygen, therefore needing more.

Without enough oxygen, we experience a weakening of our immune systems, become anxious, have anxiety attacks, become depressed, or suffer from a loss of energy. In fact, the more anxious or depressed we become, the less we tend to breathe, thereby further worsening the condition. We are muddled in our thinking, and decisions become more difficult. We find it hard to remain centered in trying situations or to arrive at creative solutions to problems. We are literally starved of our life's breath. Is it not easy to see that all of these problems have a tremendous effect on the quality of our relationships? All of us have noticed how we are more irritable, less patient, or less engaged when we have not had enough sleep. Similar results may come from a lack of oxygen.

If we truly want to be a helper, healer, and friend in our relationships, we need to continually restore ourselves in order to give. We need to take care of what is in this little "bodysuit" we have put on for our time on earth in order to keep it energized, that we may use it as a means of communicating love to others. WHAT CAN WE DO?

DIAPHRAGMATIC BREATHING—EXERCISE 1

First we must become conscious of our breathing.
Start to observe your breath right now. (pause)
Notice how shallow or deep your breath is.
Notice how fast or slow it is. (pause)
Do not judge yourself or your breath—just observe its rate and depth to become conscious. (pause)
Notice any changes in your breathing that occurred just because you were observing it, not even trying to change it. (pause)

Next, with each breath, allow your breath to be a little slower and a little deeper, ... a little slower and a little deeper. (long pause)
Now, concentrate on exhaling fully. Push out all the stale air before taking in any fresh air.
When you think you have exhaled completely, push out a little more air in order to retrain your muscles in your diaphragm to exhale completely. It is important to empty your lungs of the residues of carbon dioxide in order to make room for more oxygen. If, for example, you have a jar three-quarters' full of muddy water, you do not get a clear jar of water by filling the last fourth with fresh water.
First, you must empty the mud, then fill the jar with fresh water. So it is with our lungs.

Most people, when they think to breathe, attempt to inhale without emptying the stale air first. Therefore, they not only remain deprived of oxygen, but also become more anxious that they cannot breathe in enough oxygen. That is why *we must first exhale completely before breathing.*

Finally, be sure that your breath is going into the diaphragm first, not so much into the chest. Breathing into the chest often makes some people more anxious as well. In order to make sure you are breathing into your diaphragm, you might place one hand on your chest and the other just below the rib cage. As you breathe, imagine your lungs as being like two big balloons that expand as you inhale, pushing away the hand that is below the rib cage. The hand on your chest should remain relatively still—at least until the lower diaphragm is filled first. This ensures that you will get a large supply of oxygen as you breathe.

In Summary:

1. Exhale completely—and then exhale a little more!
2. Let your body decide when to start inhaling, but do it slowly through the nostrils.
3. Fill your diaphragm (belly) first and
4. Only after your diaphragm is full, allow your chest to expand with a little more air.
5. Hold your breath for a count or two, perhaps to three if you are comfortable,
6. And then slowly, very, very slowly exhale, chest first, and then the diaphragm. Your exhalation may be through your nose or through your pursed lips, in order to slow down the exhalation.

Repeat as long as necessary to become relaxed and calm. Try not to stop until you feel calm.

If you find that your mind is active with disturbing thoughts as you breath, you might do the following variation on the exercise.

THE SERIES OF SEVENS—EXERCISE 2

If you remain disturbed as you breathe, consider adding counting along with your breathing. This will help distract your mind from focusing on the disturbing thoughts that upset you in the first place.

Step 1: After exhaling fully, inhale through the nostrils to a slow count of seven:
one . . . . two . . . . three . . . . four . . . .
five . . . . six . . . . seven . . . .

Step 2: Hold for two or three counts.

Step 3: Exhale slowly to a slow count of seven through the nostrils or through pursed lips:
one . . . . two . . . . three . . . . four . . . .
five . . . . six . . . . seven . . . .

Step 4: Hold for two or three counts.

Repeat seven times.

After doing the entire process seven times, breathe normally for a minute or two and then repeat the series of sevens another time or two. If the count of seven is not comfortable for you, reduce the number to four, five, or six. It is most important to use the number that is comfortable to you and to do so slowly. With practice, you may work up to seven. It is also important to say the numbers to yourself very slowly—not at a quick pace—in order to get the desired benefit.

When flying on an airplane, the flight attendants instruct you at the beginning of flights that in the event of an emergency, if traveling with small children, you are to place the oxygen mask over your face first, and only then place one on the child's face. This ensures that you will be able to function to take care of your children. The same is true when you start to be disturbed in any way—especially in dealing with another person in a relationship. If you breathe first, then you will be better able to take care of yourself and the other person. You will be better able to use one or more of the other practices described here.

THE 4-8-16 BREATHING—EXERCISE 3

This breathing exercise is especially helpful to people whose minds are overly active. It requires a little more concentration to carry it out, which helps increase your focus. Further, by filling the lungs more quickly, and emptying them more strongly, you get a prolonged use of the oxygen you have taken in. For many, the slower pace of exhalation or the counting in-between serves to deepen the relaxation.

1. Inhale through the nostrils moderately fast to a count of four.
2. Hold your breath for eight equal counts.
3. Exhale through the nostrils or pursed lips to a slow count of sixteen.
4. Hold your breath for four counts.

Repeat as many times as is comfortable.

Practicing breathing exercises regularly, at least once or twice daily for four or five minutes each time, will ensure that you will be better able to use your breath effectively when in the beginning of a relationship crisis or other problem. Further, the increased oxygenization of your brain will increase your mental clarity to deal more effectively with whatever is happening. If you are in the midst of an ongoing crisis, you will find it helpful to repeat the breathing exercise numerous times throughout the day. Any skill that is practiced will be easier to use effectively when in the midst of a crisis. But remember, we also need to practice breathing deeply and slowly every day so that we are not oxygen deprived.

THE MANY USES OF BREATHING EXERCISES

Paul was referred to me by his physician because the problems in his marriage were so out of control that they were becoming physically debilitating, including high blood pressure, anxiety attacks, and depression. The medications that his physician had prescribed for Paul's depression and anxiety were of minimal help, and his continual obsessions with his physical symptoms were exacerbating the turmoil in his marriage. Paul explained that his wife was no longer able to tolerate his outbursts of anger and rage at her and the children.

A wealthy young man, making massive amounts of money from his electronics manufacturing company each year, Paul was able to buy multiple luxury cars, boats, and houses, but increasingly felt miserable physically, emotionally, and spiritually. Mostly, he was terrified that he would lose his family.

I noticed in his first sessions that as we spoke, he was barely breathing. His breaths were very shallow and quick, and when I asked him if he was aware that he was hardly breathing, he had said "no." I then taught him the above breathing exercises. Since he was feeling desperate, he was willing to practice them diligently. He used the breathing in a somewhat meditative way. As he would breathe, he would notice his mind wandering to disturbing thoughts, he would observe them, gently let them go, and return his focus to his breathing and counting.

Next, we became aware of the plethora of negative thoughts that were occupying his mind incessantly. He noticed negative thoughts about himself, his wife, and about people at work—all of which were very harsh and sometimes cruel. He learned the Five-Step Thought-Monitoring Process, as described in the last chapter. He began to practice monitoring his thoughts throughout each day and when he would wake up at night. His anxiety and depression began to abate—in only a few weeks. Gradually his physical symptoms faded away as well. Paul had been aware that he was 35–40 pounds overweight. But even though we had not been focusing on his weight, as he quieted his mind it reduced the anxiety and depression that drove him to the refrigerator. He came in one day observing, "Henry, since I have been practicing this breathing and thought monitoring, my pants are about to fall off. I think I have lost 25–30 pounds, and I haven't even been trying."

As Paul quieted his mind through breathing and counting, and monitored his thoughts, his outbursts of anger diminished to occasional annoyances in his relationship. He and his wife began to renew their affection and actually spent time enjoying talking together. For the first time, he began to enjoy spending time playing with his two small children. And then he noticed that his excessive spending and his compulsive need to acquire so many luxuries just wasn't there anymore. These two practices alone helped him begin to fill his deep spiritual void as he discovered more of his godlike essence with its empowerment.

Breathing exercises can be helpful in many situations where you are prone to feeling stress, excitement, or need to focus particularly well. Consider the situations below:

- If someone attacks or criticizes you, begin to do slow deep breathing, and you will feel more centered, helping you to monitor an ego reaction to the criticism.
- If you need to assert yourself with someone, spend a little time breathing and what you say will be more effective.
- Before you answer the phone, breathe two or three times first; then you are prepared to receive your caller more fully.
- Breathe when you are making love. Sexual energy will flow more easily and fully. You will connect with your partner more deeply. Orgasms will be experienced more easily by women and better controlled by men.
- Breathe when you are listening to someone talk. You will be better able to listen completely and will be less likely to interrupt.
- Check in with yourself hourly and notice the rate and depth of your breathing. Then take a few very slow, deep breaths. This will increase your overall state of calm and ability to focus.

THE POWER OF MEDITATION

Hundreds of studies and multitudes of self reports confirm that meditation helps one to reduce stress. Eppley, Abrams, and Shea presented a metaanalysis of ninety-nine independent studies at the American Psychological Association that showed that Transcendental Meditation (TM) was twice as effective as other forms of relaxation techniques in reducing anxiety. Since giving is central to creating happy relationships, one who is burdened with and distracted by anxiety and stress has little to give.

When people practice meditation fifteen or twenty minutes twice a day, not only is their stress reduced significantly, they are also more available for loving relationships with their partner and in their family. They are more attentive, patient, kind, and therefore less critical and edgy. When we are more loving, giving, and accepting, which are essential qualities of our True Self spiritual essence, we strengthen our true identity while at the same time nurture happy relationships. Such qualities are necessary for any successful relationship. It is especially true in family relationships, in which bitterness and estrangement occurs when certain family members are withholding. Even in business, it takes one giving of his time to train, supervise, inspire, and communicate with business associates. Without giving, any relationship begins to deteriorate.

R. J. Monahan reported in the *International Journal of Addictions* as early as 1977 that meditators show significant reduction in use of caffeine, tobacco, alcohol, marijuana, and prescription drugs. Such studies suggest that meditators would then have a greatly reduced tendency to look outside of themselves for satisfaction. Such a shift from addictions to external things to quieting the mind and looking inside begins to take a person back to his or her True Self, which is love. Therefore, meditation cannot help but impact our relationships in highly significant ways.

How does this work practically?

One example is Kenneth, the president of his own manufacturing company in a New Jersey suburb of New York City. He manages over two hundred employees, and spends hours dealing with quality concerns in manufacturing, shipping commitments, negotiating and signing new contracts, and dealing with payments to and problems with subcontractors. When he outgrows his space, he has to find another and carry out a move without disruption to his production schedule. It's enough to stress out most of us. But he seems to be able to handle all this with more ease than most, and has created an outstandingly positive working environment for his employees. Most important, before he starts the workday, he arrives early, closes his office door, sits down comfortably with his phone off the hook, and meditates for twenty minutes. Also, at the end of the day before he faces the rush hour traffic home, he once again closes his door, loosens his tie, and meditates.

How does all this affect his family relationships? He is now at peace as he drives home—whether or not there is traffic. He is refreshed as he greets his wife and children for dinner. And instead of being agitated, stressed out, and exhausted, he is present, full of energy for conversation or play, and communicates lovingly. He now has energy to give to his family and their needs, whereas little of this was so before he began to meditate. Instead, he would arrive home exhausted, was irritable with his wife and children, there would often be fights over dinner, and he would go to bed estranged from his family, only to have a fitful sleep.

How can we learn to meditate—put ourselves in touch with our True Self identity, and experience the manifold benefits in our relationships and in our lives? Since there are multiple techniques for meditation, there are multitudes of books describing the philosophies and techniques that can be purchased in most bookstores, as well as audio tapes with guided instructions. Our purpose here will not be to describe all the different forms, but rather to describe one of the more common meditation practices used in the West so that, if you are not already a meditator, you will have a way to begin. If you already know how to meditate, perhaps this chapter will inspire you to practice it with greater diligence and dedication, remembering the enormous benefits personally and for your relationships.

PRACTICE 10:

Meditation Exercises

PREPARATION FOR MEDITATION

It is helpful to have a regular place to meditate, especially when beginning. While some people are comfortable sitting in a lotus position on the floor or on a cushion, many Westerners who did not grow up sitting that way find it uncomfortable. Therefore, many may use a chair. Make sure that it is a comfortable chair, but one that is straight enough to keep your spine aligned to enhance energy flow in the body. If it is a chair you use for other purposes, many find it helpful to turn the chair in a different direction for meditation. The context which is associated with meditation helps us get into a meditative state more easily.

Just as a policeman feels different in uniform than out of one, or an Orthodox Jew feels different when he puts on his prayer shawl, or we feel different in a cathedral than a football stadium, so we have associations to various environments or clothing, which help or detract from quieting our minds.

THE MANTRA MEDITATION

The word "mantra" has often been translated to mean "mind clearing tone." In a culture such as ours, filled with so many active pursuits and excitations, many find it helpful to have a slightly more active technique than others. Some people might like to use the universal sound of creation, "ohm" or "ahm." Others might be more comfortable with the word "One." While sitting comfortably with eyes closed, you simply say the word slowly and thoughtfully to yourself, silently or aloud in a prolonged tone. If your thoughts wander, which they will inevitably do, just observe what they are without judging yourself or your thoughts, and gently return your focus to your mantra. Each time you become aware that your mind strays off its focal point, just observe the thoughts and gently return your focus. Continue this for as long as comfortable, and then add a minute or two. You need not go over twenty minutes, which is considered by many to be an optimal time.

Others may prefer to use a meaningful phrase as their focal point instead of a tone or word. Phrases such as "I rest in God" or "God is but love, and therefore so am I," taken from *A Course in Miracles*, are ones some spiritually minded people like. Others may like to chant words like "peace and calm" slowly and thoughtfully to themselves.

What the word, tone, or phrase is, is far less important than that we practice regularly. Research shows that the optimal time is fifteen to twenty minutes twice daily. Two times a day seems to produce much more than double the benefit over one time daily, and quickly reinforces the practice. But do not let this deter you. If you are unable or unwilling to start meditating the optimal two times a day, try beginning with the time you are willing to do. I began with a short time and quickly expanded it because I liked the results of feeling more peaceful and centered. The most important thing is to practice each day. On the other hand, if you can begin with two times daily, you will experience more of the benefits more quickly, which will be highly reinforcing.

Few people are successful in keeping a regular ongoing practice of meditation unless it is scheduled into their day as much as any other appointment. Otherwise the ego part of our minds will find countless ways to get us distracted by other things so that we will never get to it. The ego will be threatened by our meditation practice, for it takes away its power and puts us in touch with more of our intrinsic god power within.

BRINGING IT ALL TOGETHER

I have found meditation to be a wonderful way to build on the relationship benefits of thought monitoring, erasing core beliefs, making a perceptual shift, and extending love. The consistent and diligent practice of all will enable you to carry out each of the other eight practices more effectively. I have yet to see anyone who began to meditate who did not experience a significant improvement in their relationships. Being more centered, they are able to identify and monitor their thoughts more effectively, as well as make the perceptual shift into love with more ease. And further, they find it easier to stop and reflect on themselves—thoughts, feelings, and behaviors—instead of being stuck on projections onto others.

However, I have found that meditation works at a higher, or deeper level, for it works more mysteriously within the self. In this way, it truly offers a tangible experience of our interconnectedness, and gives us a vital sense of the spiritual dimensions of the True Self.

The result of awakening is often called "enlightenment." Enlightenment is not a long journey, but a moment-by-moment awakening from our illusions into the true reality. In one story of the Buddha, it is said that after enlightenment he was walking down a road when he came upon a man sitting under a banyan tree. The man noticed something unusual about this stranger and called out to him, "Who are you? Are you a special God or something?" The Buddha said that he wasn't. "Well, are you a sorcerer?" No, he was not a sorcerer either. "Then, are you a special saint of some kind?" No, he was not a saint either. Finally the man asked, "Well, who are you then?" The Buddha replied, "*I am just awake.*"

I believe that this awakened state that the Buddha reached is possible for each of us for all that it entails is getting in touch with our essence, the source of authentic Love, which is the True Self. It is in such a state, moment-by-moment, in which each of our special relationships transforms into a spiritual relationship, one that sees the Divine Nature in everyone. If you could see the Divine in your partner, in your parents, and in your children, would not all these relationships be healed from conflict? The answer is yes.

CHAPTER 11

The Spiritual Divorce Versus the Ego-Based Divorce

"The spiritual relationship is 'a common state of mind, where both give errors gladly to correction, that both may happily be healed as one.'"
—A Course in Miracles

For the spiritual marriage to be truly joyful in joining as One, both partners need to have as their goal the healing of their sense of separateness from each other, from all others, and from God. Both need to have as their goal to transcend the ego mind at every possible moment, and the desire to awaken to the True Self identity, in which acceptance and forgiveness are the characteristic ways of being together and being in the world. Essentially, this is the central purpose of all relationships. When we focus on healing the sense of separateness that comes from living in the ego's mind, we cease projecting and blaming our partners. We also allow for love's steady presence. And we trust in the spiritual dimensions of the True Self. These are the core factors that make up a spiritual marriage.

As we've seen without a conscious awareness on these factors, most marriages are designed to fail. Like buildings built on sand, they are built upon the foundation of slippery illusions. In particular, most marriages or special relationships play out from the premise that we as individuals are separate and powerless. In this situation, people will continue to seek love outside of the self, and will find it nearly impossible to Love unconditionally. It is actually a wonder, given the ego mind's relentlessness, that any marriages or partnerships are happy and actually stay together! And yet there is not one of us on the Earth who has not suffered from this perpetual search for love and happiness, or who does not tend to blame someone else for the lack of this love and happiness. And even when we become aware and conscious of desiring a spiritual relationship, we must remain vigilant to catch the ego's voice of illusion, tempting us almost every moment of our relationship.

IS DIVORCE EVER JUSTIFIED?

Although you have the power to heal and change the unhealthy or negative dynamics of your relationship using the practices presented in this book, sometimes a relationship can remain stuck in a cycle of negative interaction. In such cases, when despite one or both people's best intentions, the negative interaction cycle is so deeply entrenched between the two people that there appears to be little chance for healing short of a miracle. Usually this means that one or both people have not been willing to commit fully to awakening their True Selves and the goals of the spiritual marriage. Or one or both do not do the practices diligently and sincerely. If we clear out the effects of our early traumas and the negative beliefs that grew out of them, and change the thoughts we think about our partners, we will see our partners as appealing for love instead of attacking or rejecting. In particular, we will see the other person as a mirror of our own insides, and the relationship will necessarily change for the better. In recalcitrant relationships in which couples cannot break out of the negative patterns, even by devoted practice of the exercises, some may decide to separate or divorce rather than stay engaged in an ego-driven cycle that even the power of surrender is unable to help.

Often, in marriages that do not continue, one of the partners has no desire or commitment to live by the spiritual principles discussed in this book or to do these or similar exercises in order to live by principles greater than the ego provides. Yet, in spite of this, there are numerous times when one partner has been successful in totally transforming the relationship just by making the changes himself or herself, and miracles do result. There are other times when this does not happen, no matter how much one partner does the practices. In this case, the participating person will grow spiritually from doing the practices and discovering more and more of his or her True Self, in spite of great difficulties with the other partner. The participant is like a skier who must always challenge himself by skiing only double, black-diamond, advanced, expert trails, rarely having the opportunity to relax and enjoy a nice rhythm on a beautiful intermediate bowl. Such people may learn an enormous number of lessons from the challenges of their relationship, which brings great satisfaction, but after years of such challenges and learning, he or she may opt to rest. In this case, that individual may decide to separate in order to move on to a different school of learning in another relationship, wishing to apply all that he or she has learned with a person who is committed to the same goals. They decide to separate not because they expect that a new relationship will make them happy. But instead, they now know that there will be a new set of lessons to be learned—perhaps a deeper level of communication or communion, a deeper level of intimacy, a deeper level of shared unconditional Love, and a joined quest for the True Self. Both people will have this as their common goal.

This is not a chapter to tell anyone whether or when to divorce! Not only am I not capable of determining such a decision for someone else, it would also be greatly inappropriate to do so. Studies have shown that many couples who are unhappy and on the edge of divorce, but who stay together, report after five years that they are now happy. On the other hand, there are those who stay together for a quarter or half a century, but are continually miserable. Therefore, the decision to stay together or to divorce is not the most basic issue. Most important is the need to find our True Selves and see the other's True Self, whether staying together or divorcing. Essentially, the same principles that apply to a spiritual marriage are what makes for a spiritual divorce:

- Recognizing the ego voice.
- Using effective practices to transcend the illusions of the ego.
- Uncovering the True Self.
- Accepting Empowering Love and extending it to yourself and your partner without expectations in return.
- Forgiving the unforgivable.

Again, since the purpose of any relationship is to uncover our Divine Nature, we act on the same spiritual premise when we decide to separate or divorce. The basic goal for each of us should be the same: reaching out toward your partner in loving kindness, in acceptance and forgiveness—not blame, guilt, anger, or disappointment.

In the case of a spiritual marriage, these actions require examining who you really are by breaking into your Vicious Cycle of Interaction in order to discard the illusions of the ego, which are being played out in your relationship. Each moment you break into your vicious cycle, you begin to heal your relationship by reuniting with your True Self. At these moments, the path to the spiritual marriage becomes effortless and joyous, for all you are is Love. Continual consciousness and constant vigilance are needed in an ongoing manner, however, for the ego mind will emerge at every turn.

But when either or both of you are stuck in a Vicious Cycle of Interaction, which is anything but loving, unable to break out of it even with the practices presented here or with professional help, then divorce is often chosen. This is especially true in emotionally or physically abusive relationships. Contrary to some common beliefs, it is not God's will that we suffer, but that we be joyful. Jesus expressed it thus: "I have come that your joy might be full!" or "That you might have life and have it more abundantly!" The Buddha advised, "Live in joy, in love, even among those who hate." We do not need to devalue ourselves by subjecting ourselves to continual abuse. Some people continue to do this, while continuing to hope that they can make it better. They actually get attached to the suffering. They confuse struggle and hoping with love, and stay in the painful relationship continually trying and trying to remake the other person. Such a relationship is not love, but the ego's repeating the struggles of a painful childhood over and over again as an adult, in order to destroy the joy of the now moments. Such codependency cannot be a happy or spiritual marriage. If we become aware that we are staying in an abusive relationship, trying to remake the other person, much like trying to fix a parent so that then they can love us, we can let go of such a struggle.

Most people can be difficult at times—or at least we see them that way. But in general, if you or your partner has extremely persistent difficult behaviors and is not willing to look at herself or himself, taking responsibility for his or her anger, hatred, negativity, emotional or physical abuse, it may become impossible to serve your goals of a spiritual marriage. When the interaction cycle is so one-sided, steeped in the negative, then it may make sense to you and your partner to decide that it is better to end the marriage. Taking responsibility for such thoughts, emotions, and behaviors is a choice, just as extending love or forgiving is a choice. It is a conscious decision that carries with it its own set of results, for not to take responsibility may carry serious consequences for the relationship.

Again, we might let go by simply seeing what we are doing, and begin to practice changing our thoughts, our perceptions, and our beliefs. After doing this, some may choose to stay, others may separate. It is important to recognize, however, that we can never really separate, since all separation is an illusion anyway. This is why we need to deal with all the same issues whether, in the world's terms, we remain together or divorce. For even when divorced, we are together. The feelings and thoughts you have about each other continue to affect not only yourself, but also invite thoughts and feelings back about us. If you send forth the negative, you attract back the negative, whether you are with the other person in body or not. In essence, you never escape, even by divorcing, the cycle of "what goes around comes around."

LEARNING TO LET GO

If you accept the premise that you are creators because you are "in the image and likeness of God," you must also see that you do not create alone. Therefore in relationships, you act more as cocreators. It's true that when you heal your own mind, it spills over to those about you and you can help heal others in this way. As we have seen, our own thoughts, perceptions, and choices may make considerable differences. However, you cannot create a spiritual marriage on your own. Sometimes others will heal enough to join with us in a joyous act of creation for an ongoing loving relationship. Other times, even if you heal the illusory thinking in your own mind, another may not join with you, or even strongly oppose or thwart your efforts. He or she may have such a fear of love and closeness, making it too great a barrier to allow joining. If you want to be in a spiritually based marriage, acting in love and not from ego-based thinking, then your goal is not to get involved in a power struggle, trying to get the other person to join you in your quest. Rather, it's necessary that both of you want the same goal equally. Otherwise, the marriage will not become a spiritual marriage—a relationship of wholeness and oneness.

For example, Victor enjoyed a close spiritual connection with his wife, Elaine, in the beginning of their relationship. This was a large basis of their getting together initially. They practiced yoga and meditation together, attended church services together, and read spiritual and inspirational books together and discussed them with interest and enthusiasm. But after a few years of marriage, Elaine became increasingly involved in her career. She became desperate to earn more and more money, and worked ungodly long hours. Any free time she had, she seemed to want to spend it researching for her job rather than being with Victor or their daughters. The more she worked, the more and more stressed Elaine became, often becoming angry and critical of those around her, especially her family.

Understandably, Victor felt increasingly distant from Elaine. But, believing in the tenets of the spiritual marriage, he tried to take responsibility for his share of issues. It was at this point that Victor began his therapy with me. He learned to monitor his thoughts about Elaine, especially his judgments. He dealt with his yearnings to have her back by letting go of his attachment to having her be a certain way with him. He worked diligently on coming to see her differently. While these practices were not without their difficulties, Victor knew he must not let his love for her die. He made conscious decisions to accept Elaine and to extend loving thoughts to her, which caused things to be much more peaceful between them more of the time. However, there was still very little joining and they were unable to close the gap of their disparate goals. Elaine held on to every hurt and grievance through the years. No matter how hard Victor tried to persuade her to choose love, Elaine was unable or unwilling to forgive; she was tied to her interaction cycle. She finally concluded that she could not be happy with Victor, and she suggested they get a divorce.

Does this mean that Victor had failed? Hardly; for years he did the best he could to be a loving presence. He knew and accepted that their relationship was the product of their cocreation. Elaine could not or would not work on the marriage. Even when they would go for marriage counseling, which they did on several occasions, Elaine would use it to thrash out her litany of grievances and could never get beyond her continual blame of Victor for her unhappiness.

Victor saw that it would do him no good to try to hold on to Elaine, for that would be control, not love. He must love her enough to let her go. As Victor did this, they began to prepare for a more spiritual divorce, although tempted repeatedly to engage in the anger, blame, and guilt of an ego-based divorce. Even though it was largely Victor who did not let their desire for a spiritual divorce go off track, they were cocreators in this outcome. By catching their angry and blowing thoughts, and making a conscious decision to keep the process peaceful, they were able to solve the practical problems, not just out of selfish interest, but also based on what would be fair to the other. Now, they could part as friends.

ONCE YOU HAVE DECIDED TO DIVORCE

Remember, I cannot tell anyone when to divorce or when one has stayed long enough to work on healing one's self and the relationship. That is a personal decision only you as an individual or couple can make. I am simply suggesting that if you have come to the decision to separate or divorce, that you choose to do so in a spiritual way. If you have made a decision to divorce, please consider the following before taking an action in order to make certain you have learned all the lessons you need to learn, or you will be likely to repeat the same issues and problems in future relationships:

1. *Do not divorce when running to another person or in search of another ideal mate who will give you happiness.*
2. *Do not divorce when you are feeling vindictive.*
3. *Do not divorce while condemning your partner, making him or her wrong.*
4. *Do not divorce while feeling deprived.*
5. *Do not divorce when at war. Remember, it takes two to fight a war. You need to look at your part at stopping the war first.*
6. *Do not divorce while not accepting your differences without judgment.*

Sometimes when you have dealt with each of the above issues, you may no longer feel like divorcing. On the other hand, if it is still your choice, you will proceed in a more centered, peaceful, and mutually respectful way, making it a more spiritual divorce. Perhaps you can be good friends.

IF YOU HAVE DECIDED TO DIVORCE, WHEN IS IT TIME TO MOVE AHEAD?

1. ***When there is physical abuse that the other person cannot or will not stop.*** In such a situation, it is often wise to move ahead quickly and find other living arrangements. Once you are in a safe physical situation, you might begin to reflect on ways in which you might have helped to attract such behaviors toward you. I am not recommending that anyone engage in self-condemnation. Instead, it is a genuine reflection, since all interactions carry effects from each person. If you do not identify the role you played, or the beliefs that may be getting confirmed, you might be likely to replay a negative script in some form, though not necessarily with physical abuse.

2. ***When there is emotional abuse,* but only *after using the ten practices presented here.*** By using the practices in this book you will discover the ways in which you have contributed to this abuse, which sometimes may change the relationship in dramatic ways. You may move out of feeling like a victim and therefore cease sending forth that which would attract abuse to you. On the other hand, your practices may make you more centered, and you may even have compassion for your emotionally abusive partner seeing his or her behaviors as an appeal for love, but your partner remains with the same emotionally abusive behavior. In such a situation, you may still choose to part ways, but in peace, not in blame. The Buddha advised, "Do not look for bad company or live with men who do not care. Find friends who love the truth." Jesus instructed his disciples similarly when they asked him what to do when others did not receive the gospel message. His reply was to shake the dust off his sandals and move on to the next place. In essence, do not get involved in a perpetual struggle or battle of any kind. Leave the struggle or battle, one way or another, and choose to live in peace and love.

3. ***When partners need to be apart in order to heal their old wounds and to grow.*** If the destructive patterns are too entrenched, and despite all the use of the practices, you are pushing against a heavy river that

threatens to sweep you away, perhaps you may need to do your growing in a less difficult situation—one that promotes and supports healing rather than aggravation of the old wounds. A temporary or indefinite separation can sometimes be of help, if used in this way, to gain a better perspective, and to take back one's own power to have an effect. When feeling empowered, some may choose to move back together to try to work things out in a more productive way. Others choose to continue their learning in a new relationship.

4. ***When you have completed the lessons and learnings that this relationship brought you.*** In relationships, we always come together for a purpose, whether it is for a lifetime or for a momentary encounter. All marriages may not be intended to last for a lifetime. We always come together for a time of learning, but when it seems that all the learning has been completed, we may choose to move apart. This decision is tricky, however, and should not be impulsive. The ego can often have us think we have completed our learning when we have not. The ego would have us leave in order not to keep learning the lessons. We might have given up making this partner special, but still have the inclination to make someone else special, so the problems would continue. We must spend much time in meditation, reflection, and in consultation with a psychological or spiritual guide to help identify any ego issues, and continually open ourselves to guidance from within about what to do.

5. ***When there is no more need to change, criticize, blame, or condemn your partner.*** If we have not been able to free ourselves from criticizing and blaming our partners, we now have another wonderful opportunity to do so when divorcing. Remember, our basic goal is to find our True Self, our Divine Nature; it is not to stay in or leave a relationship. We cannot find our Self when in a state of judging and condemning. Perhaps in the context of thinking about leaving, you can finally let go of your judgments and find the peace that follows. When full acceptance of what is without judgment has been accomplished, then we can part with love and forgiveness. Or, we may change our minds and stay. But, most important, we have then ceased splitting our

minds into the good and the bad, and projecting the bad part onto the other person. In this way, we can part in friendship, which certainly saves many thousands of dollars in legal fees, and the children, if any, are much less likely to be as wounded. When divorced parents can coparent as friends, everyone benefits. But if everyone does not benefit, ultimately no one benefits.

6. ***When we know we are whole and can continue to be whole, whether with our partner or apart from him or her.*** As long as we are not feeling our wholeness (holiness), we cannot make an intelligent and sane decision. It will be motivated by the ego part of our minds and will be out of separation and neediness. When we come to acknowledge our wholeness, we are not divorcing out of desperation, but out of a choice that makes sense to us.

7. ***When we have looked fully at our own issues, not at our partner's.*** We need to identify our negative core beliefs and clear them out along with the traumas that brought them about. We need to monitor our negative thoughts diligently about ourselves, our partners, and our relationship. We need to be able to see our partner's appeals for love expressed in perhaps many unproductive ways, to be able to respond in our minds with compassion. Are we replaying scripts from our original family? Are our behaviors like ones that we hated in our parents?

MAKING A DIVORCE SPIRITUAL: A CASE STUDY

Terry was going through a contentious and difficult divorce. She and Noah were not only fighting over how to divide up the assets, and how much alimony was to be paid, but over the custody of the two boys and one girl. Noah wanted to have the children with him, even though he did a reverse daily commute from New York to New Jersey that took over 1½ hours each way. Terry was hurt and angry that Noah was giving her a hard time about each of the issues, suddenly becoming very angry and contemptuous toward her. She had hoped for a peaceful resolution, and at first, could not understand why Noah was treating her so badly.

When I asked Terry to review the events leading up to her decision to divorce, she began to connect the affair she had while still in the marriage. When I asked her why she thought she had had the affair, she explained that she had felt so deprived emotionally from Noah's physical and emotional absence, that she sought out comfort, companionship, and sex with someone who was willing to respond to her and be attentive to her.

Terry had decided, after much consideration, to go ahead with the affair because she had now found someone who would listen to her, talk to her, treat her with respect, and who was very considerate of her while having sex. When she reflected on the fact that it was she who had started to move out of the marriage first, she could see how Noah was probably feeling very hurt and rejected. And she also saw that since he could not show more vulnerable emotions, he played them out in anger—against her.

I asked Terry to go farther upstream and see if her behavior in her marriage had any similarities to other past relationships. Upon reflection on her childhood, we found that both her parents were neglectful. Her father was rarely present, and when he was, he was either cold and distant, or if he were drinking, he would become more present, but angry and emotionally abusive. Terry's mother was depressed, self-involved, and emotionally absent throughout her growing up years. By tracing her family tree in such a way, Terry realized that she had chosen a partner in Noah who was quite familiar to her, and who would reflect what she believed she deserved.

These realizations made Terry intent on clearing out all the causes of such unhealthy choices. So, after using a variety of energy psychology and EMDR processes (see Chapter Six) to clear out the traumas of deprivation and abuse from her childhood, and then to clear out the beliefs about not deserving love, she felt a renewed sense of peace about her decision to divorce. She accepted that Noah, for all his love of her, was unwilling or unable to commit to opening himself to empowering love and his overall spiritual growth. Now Terry was able to drop her hurt and resentments toward Noah, for she saw that it was she who had unconsciously chosen him to play the roles he did, precisely in order to confirm her beliefs about herself and about family.

As Terry worked through her own issues, she shifted her attitude toward Noah, and was utterly amazed at the change in interactions with him throughout the remainder of the divorce proceedings. She was able to hold him in her mind with thoughts of compassion, wishing him joy and happiness. Consequently, he was no longer antagonistic toward her, and they became cooperative in their negotiating a fair financial settlement and in the coparenting of their daughter and two sons.

Terry and Noah are not different from most of us who have gone through the process of a divorce. Most often a decision to divorce is inspired by feelings of hurt, deprivation, blame, and anger, for we mostly experience the world through the ego's eyes. And though it is most important that we acknowledge these feelings, we must then move away from seeing the other person as the cause of such feelings. So much of our pain comes from seeing the world now through the eyes of the past. When we move from blaming our partners for our feelings, to looking inside with genuine honesty and reflection, we usually find old, deep wounds that have colored the way we see our partners. Or we may notice that we have been behaving just like a parent did—especially in ways that we did not like!

We saw earlier that our old hurts even colored the choices of partners we made. If we notice the behaviors and attitudes of our partners that produce a strong emotional charge in us, we have most likely identified an old hurt as well. Use this awareness to go back and reflect on where you felt similar feelings as a child. Toward which parent did you feel these feelings? When we look inside at our own past pains and the beliefs that grew out of them, and take responsibility for our choice and our perceptions of the one we chose, we begin to take back our power. Then, if we are not able to use that power to heal the current relationship, we can at least use this new knowledge and power to make a choice of a partner next time. Our next choice of a partner will then not be dictated by the pains of our past; we will be able to select one who may wish to join with us to create a spiritual marriage.

Note: If you are still feeling hurt and angry, you have not completed your own internal issues that have been brought up in the mirror of your partner, nor have you moved to the stage of forgiveness, which is necessary for your own inner peace and which is the hallmark of a spiritual divorce.

BE LOVING

Remember, all we have to forgive are our own illusions about what we wanted our mate to be. He or she was just busy being who or what they are. It is our lack of forgiveness that binds us to suffering and to their so-called faults, reinforcing our attachment in a negative way. To forgive is to release ourselves from the pain of the illusions that we are still harboring about our partner.

When deciding whether to separate or divorce, remember that the ego part of your mind does not know how to make a decision that would be in your best interest or the best interest of anyone else. If, for example, you "can't wait to leave" or "can't wait for him to get out," chances are that you have some unfinished business inside to attend to. From the ego mind, we tend to want to run away from dealing with our own barriers to love, and the strong impetus to separate is most likely a red flag going up, signaling us to take the time to identify our barrier to love that is at work.

When trying to make such a big decision, it is especially important to surrender the ego fully and ask for guidance from Spirit, from God, your True Self, about what to do or not do and what would be for the highest good of all. Trust that answers will come in diverse, multiple, and sometimes in subtle and unexpected ways. And the true answers will bring a sense of inner peace and calm assurance instead of fear or conflict in whatever the decision is.

Review the following list frequently while going through a divorce in order to keep spiritually focused. Use it to help you move out of the ego's mind of war and defense and toward your True Self's mind of peace and confidence:

- Recognize that we can never be truly separate because we are interconnected.
- Decide to be a full presence of divine love in all your divorce dealings: be your Self!
- Be.nonattached to outcomes.
- Be respectful of your partner's fears and "needs."
- Be nonattached to things, for they are ephemeral. It is your loving inner nature that is eternal.
- Continue to practice surrender and stay open to inner guidance.
- Pray for your partner's happiness and well being.
- Show loving kindness in all negotiations.
- Pray for the outcome to be for the highest good of all.

Remember that it is just as much your goal to be aware of your Divine Nature in divorce as it is in the marriage. It is when we forget this truth that we become contentious and attached to our anger, hurt, and pain.

THERE IS NO SUCH THING AS DIVORCE

Only the divorce of bodies can occur, for minds are eternally joined. Therefore, we can never really divorce ourselves from anyone, and it is only an illusion that we think we can. This is why we not only need to look at marriage differently, but also need to look at divorce differently. Since mind is interconnected in the unified field of consciousness, we are constantly affecting each other at profound levels. Therefore, we need to take responsibility for how these emotions and behaviors affect others whether together or apart.

Jesus was quoted as saying to his disciples, "I am with you always." The same is true of all of us. We are all with each other always. Our minds are always joined in one universal mind. When we return to our awareness of this truth, we will abide in peace in all our relationships, whether or not we are together as bodies.

Epilogue

GETTING PAST THE SPECIAL RELATIONSHIP

Probably one of the most destructive aspects of marriage, as well as other relationships, has been specialness—the tendency to appoint someone to the position to give and receive a special and exclusive form of love. Since this counterfeit "love" insidiously takes us further and further away from Empowering Love, we need to get past specialness and learn to extend our love to all persons and beings. Otherwise, we place undue demands and expectations on those we call special, and change the love relationship into a hate relationship.

On the surface the special relationship may appear to be grounded in love, but when the other person fails to meet our expectations, we move from love into hate—and all our anger and hatred comes not from what the other person is doing, but from our own unhealed past, our own ego thinking.

And yet special relationships can also be wonderful because they often are so meaningful and important to us that they stimulate a motivation for us to change in order to get out of the pain that the relationships seems to be causing. We can tolerate only so much pain, and then we look for a better way. It's at this point that many of us begin to look inside the relationship, only to find our True Self, which is Love.

If we remember our most basic task, stated clearly in the words of the Lion King as he admonishes his grown cub, "Remember Who You Are!" then we can bring healing and peace not only to ourselves, but to our special relationships as well.

An Invitation

WOULD YOU LIKE TO HELP OTHERS BY SHARING YOUR LOVE STORIES?

Have you had success in using any of the practices presented in this book, whether you learned them here or not?

- Thought monitoring
- Making a shift in perception—choosing to see someone differently
- Practicing surrender (surrendering the ego)
- Seeing others as a mirror
- Seeing problems as lessons not previously learned
- Erasing traumas or changing core beliefs
- Quieting the mind through breathing, meditation, or prayer
- Consciously choosing to extend unconditional love—without any expectations
- Practicing the principles of a spiritual marriage

- Practicing the principles of a spiritual divorce
- The practice of conscious intentionality

We would like to share stories like yours in a book which would inspire others to use these practices in their lives. For every story we accept for publication, *we will pay you* $150. Plus, we will send you a copy of Dr. Grayson's six-tape audio series from Sounds True, *The New Physics of Love: The Power of Mind and Spirit in Relationships*, which retails for $69.95. Most of all you will have the joy and satisfaction of knowing that you helped multitudes of others with your story.

Please send a hard copy of your story to: Love Stories, 606 Post Road East, Suite 618, Westport, CT 06880.

www.MindfulLoving.com

Bibliography

A Course in Miracles. Mill Valley: Foundation for Inner Peace, 1996.

Bach, Richard. *Illusions*. New York: Dell, 1971.

Barnett, L. *The Universe and Dr. Einstein*. New York: Harper and Row, 1948.

Bohm, David. *Causality and Chance in Modern Physics*. Philadelphia: University of Philadelphia Press, 1957.

Bohm. *Wholeness and the Implicate Order*. London: Routledge, 1980.

Borg, M. *Jesus and the Buddha: Parallel Sayings*. Berkeley: Seastone, 1999.

Calder, Negil. *Einstein's Universe*. New York: Greenwich House, 1979.

Capra, Frijof. *The Tao of Physics*. Berkeley, Shambala, 1975.

Capro, Frijak. *The Hidden Connections*. New York: Doubleday, 2002.

Chopra, Deepak. *Quantum Healing*. New York: Bantam, 1989.

Clark, R. *Einstein: The Life and Times*. New York: The World Publishing, 1947.

Cooper, David. *God Is a Verb*. New York: Riverhead Books, 1997.

Davies, Paul. *God and the New Physics*. New York: Simon and Schuster, 1983.

Dhammapada: The Sayings of the Buddha. Boston, Shambhala, 1993.

Dossey, Larry. *Healing Words*. San Francisco: HarperSanFrancisco, 1993.

Eliade, Mircea. *The Sacred and the Profane*. New York: Harper Torchbooks, 1957.

Einstein, A. and L. Infield. *The Evolution of Physics*. New York: Simon and Schuster, 1961.

Frankl, V. *The Doctor and the Soul*. New York: Alfred Knopf, 1960.

———. *Man's Search for Meaning*. New York: The World Publishing Co., 1969.

———. *The Will to Meaning*. Boston: Beacon Press. 1959.

Gallo, F. *Energy Psychology*. New York: CRC Press, 1999.

Gallo, F. and H. Vincenzi. *Energy Tapping*. Oakland: New Harbinger Pub., 2000.

Goswami, A. *The Self-Aware Universe*. New York: G. P. Putnam, 1993.

Green, Brian. *The Elegant Universe*. New York: Norton, 1999.

Heisenberg, W. *Physics and Beyond*. New York: Harper and Row, 1971.

———. *Physics and Philosophy*. New York: Harper and Row, 1958.

Jacobson, N. and A. Christensen. *Acceptance and Change in Couple Therapy*. New York: Norton, 1996.

Jampolsky, J. *Forgiveness: The Greatest Healer of All*. Hillsboro: 1999.

Jung, C. G. *Collected Works*. vol. 9, Princeton: Princeton University Press, 1969.

Jung, C. and W. Pauli. *The Interpretation of Nature and the Psyche*. Princeton: Princeton University Press, 1955.

Kasl, C. *If the Buddha Dated*. New York: Penguin Putnam, 1999.

Krishnamurti, J. *The Urgency of Change*. New York: Harper and Row, 1970.

———. *You Are the World*. New York: Harper and Row, 1972.

Levy, Joel. *The Fine Arts of Relaxation, Concentration, and Meditation*, London: Wisdom Publications, 1987.

Luskin, F. *Forgive for Good*. San Francisco: HarperSanFrancisco, 2002.

Maharishi Mahesh Yogi. *Life Supported by Natural Law*. Fairfield, Maharishi International University Press, 1988.

Mishlove, J. *The PK Man*. Charlottesville: Hampton Roads, 2000.

Pearce, J. C. *The Crack in the Cosmic Egg*. New York: Pocket Books, 1971.

Robers, Bernadette. *The Experience of No-Self*. Boston: Shambhala, 1984.

Roth, R. *TM: Transcendental Meditation*. New York: Donald Fine, 1987.

Russell, Peter. *The Global Brain*. Los Angeles: J. P. Tarcher, 1983.

Salzberg, Sharon. *Loving Kindness*. Boston: Shambhala, 1997.

Sandweiss, Samuel. *Sai Baba: The Holy Man and the Psychiatrist*. New Delhi: Singh and Sons, 1975.

Schrödinger, Erwin. *What is Life?* Cambridge University Press, 2000.

Schwartz, G. and Linda Russeck. *The Living Energy Universe*. Charlottesville, N. Car., Hampton Roads 1999.

Shah, Idries. *The Way of the Sufi*. New York: E. P. Dutton, 1966.

Shapiro, F. *Eye Movement Desensitization and Reprocessing: Basic Principles, Protocols and Procedures*. New York: Guilford Press, 1995.

Suzuki, S. *Zen Mind, Beginner's Mind*. New York: Weatherhill, 1973.

Templeton, J. *Agape Love: A Tradition Found in Eight World Religions*. Radnor: Templeton Foundation Press, 1999.

Tillich, Paul. *The Shaking of the Foundations*. London: SCM Press, 1949.

———. *Systematic Theology*. Chicago: University of Chicago Press, 1951.

Trungpa, Chogyam. *Cutting Through Spiritual Materialism*. Boulder: Shambhala, 1973.

Walker, Evan H. *The Physics of Consciousness: The Quantum Mind and the Meaning of Life*. Cambridge: Perseus Publishing, 2000.

Watts, Alan. *The Wisdom of Insecurity*. New York: Vintage, 1951.

———. *The Book: The Taboo Against Knowing Who You Are*. New York: Vintage, 1989.

Willis, Harmon. *Global Mind Change*. San Francisco: Institute of Noetic Sciences Press, 1998.

Wheeler, J., et. al. *Gravitation*. San Francisco: Freeman, 1973.

Williamson, Marianne. *A Return to Love*. New York: Harper Collins, 1992.

Wolf, F. A. *Taking the Quantum Leap*. New York: Harper and Row, 1981.

Yogananda, Paramahansa. *Autobiography of a Yogi*. Los Angeles: Self-Realization Fellowship, 1971.

Zukav, Gary. *The Dancing Wu Li Masters*. New York: Bantam Books, 1979.

If you're interested in hearing more from Henry Grayson, his six cassette audio tapes, *The New Physics of Love,* are available from Sounds True and can be ordered from www.soundstrue.com or 1-800-333-9185.